# GLOBALISATION, COMPETITIVENESS AND HUMAN SECURITY

## OF RELATED INTEREST

ETHNICITY, GENDER AND THE SUBVERSION OF NATIONALISM
*edited by Fiona Wilson and Bodil Folke Frederiksen*

ADJUSTMENT AND SOCIAL SECTOR RESTRUCTURING
*edited by Jessica Vivian*

AGUING DEVELOPMENT POLICY:
Frames and Discouses
*edited by Raymond Apthorpe and Des Gasper*

CULTURAL PERSPECTIVES ON DEVELOPMENT
*edited by Vincent Tucker*

INTERNATIONAL COMPETITIVENESS IN LATIN AMERICA AND EAST ASIA
*by Klaus Esser, Wolfgang Hillebrand, Dirk Messner and Jörg Meyer-Stamer*
(GDI Book Series No.1)

SHAPING COMPETITIVE ADVANTAGES:
Conceptual Framework and the Korean Approach
*by Wolfgang Hillebrand* (GDI Book Series No.6)

SYSTEMIC COMPETITIVENESS:
New Governance Patterns for Industrial Development
*by Klaus Esser, Wolfgang Hillebrand, Dirk Messner and Jörg Meyer-Stamer*
(GDI Book Series No.7)

# Globalisation, Competitiveness and Human Security

edited by

CRISTÓBAL KAY

Routledge
Taylor & Francis Group
LONDON AND NEW YORK

*First published 1997 by*
FRANK CASS AND COMPANY LIMITED

Published 2005 by Routledge
2 Park Square, Milton Park, Abingdon, Oxon OX14 4RN
711 Third Avenue, New York, NY 10017, USA

First issued in hardback 2017

*Routledge is an imprint of the Taylor & Francis Group, an informa business*



British Library Cataloguing in Publication Data

A catalogue record for this book is available
from the British Library

ISBN 13: 978-1-138-41911-7 (hbk)
ISBN 13: 978-0-7146-4392-2 (pbk)

Library of Congress Cataloging-in-Publication Data

A catalog record for this book is available
from the Library of Congress

This group of studies first appeared in a Special Issue on
'Globalisation, Competitiveness and Human Security' of *The European Journal of Development Research*, Vol.9, No.1, June 1997
published by Taylor and Francis.

# Contents

# Introduction: Globalisation, Competitiveness and Human Security

CRISTÓBAL KAY

This is the fourth time that the journal of the European Association of Development Research and Training Institutes (EADI) has devoted an entire issue to papers from the Association's General Conference. This has now become a well-established tradition of the *European Journal of Development Research* (*EJDR*) which next year celebrates its tenth anniversary; the Association having celebrated its twentieth anniversary in 1995. The first conference papers to be published in the *EJDR* came from the Sixth EADI General Conference held in Oslo in 1990. A selection of the papers on the first theme of 'Changes in Europe: Implications for Development Studies' were published in Vol.2, No.2, 1990. Another set of papers on the second conference theme of 'Sustainable Development', whose star performer was Gro Harlem Brundtland, were published in Vol.3, No.1, 1991. The theme of the Seventh General Conference, held in Berlin in 1993, was 'Transformation and Development: Eastern Europe and the South', and this also formed the title of Vol.6, No.1, 1994.

Over 250 papers were presented at the Berlin conference in 1993, probably the largest number ever recorded for an EADI General Conference. At the 1996 Vienna conference the crop was less abundant but still ample as almost 200 papers were discussed during the three day proceedings. In addition to the papers selected for publication in this issue, a few more will find their way into the journal in subsequent issues. Judging from past experience, more conference papers will be published after further rewriting. Some may appear in future issues of this journal, as chapters in the EADI Book Series, also published by Frank Cass, or in other journals and publications of various kinds.

Given the space limitations of the journal it is only possible to publish eight to ten articles in each issue. As Editor of the journal, I had some tough choices to make as many good publishable papers were available. The main selection criteria I used were relevance to the conference theme and quality. I also had to ensure that the papers selected collectively covered the most important aspects of the conference theme and had a degree of coherence and complementarity. Thus I also strove for overall balance. I made an initial selection of about 30 papers on the basis of a preliminary reading of all papers

Cristóbal Kay, Associate Professor, Institute of Social Studies, The Hague, The Netherlands. E-mail: Kay@iss.nl and on advice I sought or received from conference participants. These papers were then sent to three and sometimes four external referees; almost all referees contacted agreed to read and review the papers. Some took more time than others to write the report, and some wrote more extensive comments than others. However, all the hundred or so anonymous peer reviewers, most of whom had not attended the conference or were not even EADI members, took considerable time off from their busy working schedules to support this enterprise. I never cease to be amazed at the solidarity and collegiality of members of the development community whose efforts in this respect remain anonymous and who receive no tangible reward. On the basis of these reports and using my own judgement I was able to select the papers presented in this and subsequent issues. All papers were revised on the basis of referees' comments as well as those received from participants during discussions at the conference and, in some instances, from colleagues and friends elsewhere. This issue is therefore a truly collective enterprise. I am most grateful to the authors for submitting themselves to the refereeing process and revising their papers accordingly, and to the referees for so selflessly contributing their time and ideas to this co-operative venture. Without their support this issue would not have been possible.

Helen O'Neill's contribution provides a most useful introduction to the theme of this conference issue by examining the different meanings given to the three central concepts of globalisation, competitiveness and human security and discussing their mutual linkages. A particular concern of O'Neill is to explore the implications of globalisation and competitiveness for human security. How does the process of globalisation and drive to increasing competitiveness affect people's lives? She notes that development institutions and researchers are beginning to explore this question. She highlights the UNDP's *Human Development Reports* with their evolving human development index (HDI) and calls for the construction of a 'human security index'. A key question raised in O'Neill's introduction is to what extent, if at all, are globalisation, competitiveness and human security a positive-sum process. If, on the contrary, globalisation and competitiveness are leading to further human insecurity and inequalities is it possible to design development policies and bring about institutional changes which can revert such a state of affairs? To answer these questions is indeed the main challenge facing development studies and policy today. In my view these questions remain unanswered and far more research needs to be undertaken on the victims of globalisation, that is on those regions, countries, localities, social groups and individuals who are the losers of globalisation and competitiveness.

The article by Sandro Sideri is a comprehensive and thorough review of the literature on globalisation and the formation of regional economic blocs. This is a worthy and tricky exercise, given the burgeoning scale of the literature, that is carried out in a clear, balanced and fair manner. He attempts to assess the relevance and connections between the processes of globalisation and regional integration by examining the experiences of major integration groupings. A key issue explored is whether the rise of regionalism complements processes of trade liberalisation, thereby fostering globalisation, or whether it leads to fragmentation of the world economy in trading blocs which hinder further globalisation. Sideri is clearly of the view that markets are embedded in society and as such have to be regulated by the state, in contrast to the position of extreme neo-liberals, and contrary to the efforts of powerful financial groups and multinational corporations to free themselves even further from controls by civil society. However, Sideri is not against globalisation but argues that this process should be mitigated by regionalism, devolution, and the development of a social market economy in which small and medium-sized enterprises play a significant role and where vulnerable groups are protected.

The issue of regionalism is explored further in the contribution by Björn Hettne. Hettne applies in an original manner the ideas of Karl Polanyi, who wrote his major book during the Second World War, to the recent developments in the world economy and polity. He thinks that we are experiencing a Second Great Transformation (echoing Polanyi's [First] Great Transformation) that is characterised by a double-movement; on the one hand continuing market expansion with globalisation which, on the other hand, provokes a reactive force with the rise of regionalism. The question of whether regionalism is a stepping-stone towards globalisation and at the same time a safety net, a point also raised by Sideri, is discussed further in this study. Globalisation, in Hettne's view, leads to marginalisation, social exclusion, subordination and peripheralisation, thereby threatening human security, weakening civil society and producing instability and disorder. The market has been given too much freedom and needs to be reigned in by political means.

This 'Second Great Transformation' is a challenge to development theory and policy. On this point, Hettne develops a theme which he raised in a previous issue of this journal (see the Special Issue of which he was the Guest Editor – *EJDR*, Vol.7, No.2, 1995). He makes a plea for the merger of development theory with international political economy. While development theory is hampered by its nation-state centrism it has the advantage of tackling normative issues such as equity. International political economy can contribute its world approach to development theory while benefiting from the latter's normative concerns. In his earlier article Hettne called for the creation of an 'international political economy of development'. Here he makes a plea for 'development regionalism' as a counterpoint to globalisation. Development regionalism would be a mechanism for enhancing the security and developmental prospect of the periphery while at the same time challenging the globalist hegemony of the core.

In the following contribution, Zuhair Dibaja raises a provocative voice against globalisation which he interprets as a project of Western cultural domination. He performs an important task by tracing the links between modernisation and globalisation. Dibaja gives vent to views from the periphery (in both the South and the North) and his fire is directed principally at modernisation and globalisation theorists, and Robertson in particular. His polemical critique is also a challenge to development theory and he invites us to reject the capitalist globalisation project and to embrace people-centred development approaches that favour cultural interdependence rather than domination.

Jan Nederveen Pieterse is less concerned with globalisation and more with human security. His reflections on an old theme are timely as globalisation and growth have manifestly failed to achieve greater equity. In order to examine the relationship between equity and growth he starts by reviewing the ideas of those who reject growth altogether for ecological, equity and anti- or post-development reasons. He then examines the various approaches in favour of equity and growth from redistribution with growth to human development and finds them all wanting. Some eyebrows will be raised (though not necessarily mine, I hasten to add) by his statement that the human development perspective follows the mainstream neo-classical economic paradigm and fails to challenge neo-liberalism. Nederveen Pieterse draws relevant lessons from the experiences of the East Asian NICs and the Western Welfare States and argues that the equity and growth debate has to go beyond the confines of the nation-state and be placed within the global context. He dismisses those views of social development that see it merely as a damage limitation exercise; instead he sees it as a means of creating a new social contract by investing in social networking which he refers to as a 'social capital or participatory civic society' approach to social development. Such an approach might yield a fertile avenue in development studies but needs, in my view, to be explored further to become a credible alternative.

Many of us think of decentralisation as something to be welcomed, but after reading the essay by Frans Schuurman many of us may think again. In Schuurman's view structural adjustment programmes (SAPs) opened the way for the decentralisation discourse as it neatly complemented the call for rolling back the activities of the state. Thus decentralisation initiatives are a counterpart to globalisation. The restructuring thrust of globalisation provokes local responses, a double movement which some authors refer to as 'glocalisation'. Schuurman studies the emancipatory potential of decentralisation and concludes that under present conditions it further disempowers the poor and erodes the state. Indeed the decentralisation discourse has become a globalised phenomena as it suits the neoliberal forces who are behind the globalisation project. However, Schuurman is not against decentralisation as such, but for it to empower the victims of globalisation a 'global social contract' is required. How such a global social contract would look like, let alone how to achieve it, is an issue which requires further investigation.

In the final four contributions some of these issues are explored by means of case studies taken from Asia, Africa and Latin America. The relationship between the global and the local, analysed by Schuurman, is taken up in the article by Erhard Berner who contributes to an emerging field of research concerned with transnationality from below or grassroots globalisation. He views globalisation as a contradictory process and this is exemplified by his analysis of Manila. The mushrooming local informal settlements are the underside of the globalisation that engulfs Manila. These settlements are spawned by the globalised corporate sectors in the city that need the urban poor, but at the same time compete with them for land. In the ensuing struggle for land, and in their search for human security squatter and illegal settlements have shown an ability to build local organisations and establish alliances that have empowered them through collective action. Localities have thus been able to defend themselves from the depredations of globalisation as well as taking advantage of the opportunities it affords.

In Lars Engberg-Pedersen's article on a rural area of Burkina Faso, the view from below is also at the forefront of the analysis. Lars Engberg-Pedersen uses both actor-oriented and rational choice approaches to emphasise the symbolic aspects of institutional contradictions which can arise between rural producers and project officials. He finds that significant contradictions can arise between the local power structure and the new organisation created by the development intervention which in this case involved natural resource management. This study is yet another illustration of interactions and possible conflicts between the global, in this case the outside development project, and the local, which is the village community. In view of the potential tyranny of globalism it is inspiring to read that local actors do matter. Engberg-Pedersen finds that outside intervention is unlikely to succeed if it does not gain the support of at least the most influential group within the locality. He thus proposes that state intervention agencies would be well advised to support and develop local organisational forms instead of constructing new ones that are likely to result in failure.

The next case study concerns another African country, Zaire, and transfers the discussion from a rural to an urban setting. Tom de Herdt and Stefaan Marysse, who survey the dramatic collapse of the Zairian economy, were intrigued to discover that the inhabitants of Kinshasa have been able to cushion the blow through a variety of informal economic and social networks that have allowed them some degree of security. The ingenuity of these survival strategies and the strength of informal social security networks is indeed remarkable, especially in view of the country's alarming economic regress and collapse of the state. This study is a useful contribution to the little researched area of regress, and it also illuminates aspects of human security that are not often considered in the development literature.

The background to the next contribution is more heartening. From a remote and marginal area of the Peruvian highlands, Fiona Wilson brings a note of reconciliation, reconstruction and recuperation. The area in question had been devastated by the violence unleashed by *Sendero Luminoso* (Shining Path). Many villagers had fled the area in search of security and some villages had been abandoned. Wilson, who courageously took part in one of the first visits by outsiders to a conflict-torn area, acutely observes and recounts an act of recuperation by the displaced people. This recuperation is not only territorial and spatial but also social, cultural and symbolic. However, the recuperation as yet is only partial and might never be completed, since the violence has changed the lives of peasant community members for good. New leaders and new relationships are emerging in the multiple acts of rebuilding the fractured and damaged livelihoods of the Andean peasantry. This is a vivid and poignant illustration of the importance of human security in people's lives and development research should direct far more attention and resources to this field of study than hitherto.

This collection does not cover all aspects related to the theme of globalisation, competitiveness and human security, and the question of competitiveness is relatively neglected. Neither does it do justice to the subtitle of the Vienna EADI Conference which was 'challenges for development policy and institutional change'. This is partly a reflection of the lack of conference papers which explored the manifold dimensions and interconnections of the issues raised by the conference theme. To what extent is this indicative of what is going on in the wider development community? I certainly think that the conference theme was well chosen, being central to development theory and policy, but there is still much more work to be done before we are able to respond to the challenge that the conference so clearly exposed. However, the contributions here are a good starting point for further reflection and action.

Finally, I wish to thank Jolanda Kaloh from the Institute of Social Studies for her efficient administrative efforts and Diana Kay for her valuable editorial support. The EADI Secretariat in Geneva ensured that I received all conference papers and were generally most helpful. The Institute of Social Studies provided crucial material backing for which I am most grateful.

# Globalisation, Competitiveness and Human Security: Challenges for Development Policy and Institutional Change

HELEN O'NEILL

*This contribution discusses the consequences for human security of the interlinked processes of globalisation and competitiveness among nations. It begins by defining and examining each of the three concepts in turn. It queries whether the internationalisation of the global economy today, widely described as globalisation, represents a fundamentally new process. It goes on to consider the costs and benefits of globalisation and competitiveness in terms of human security. It concludes that, while the impacts are uneven, with winners and losers from both processes, there are particular risks for the least-developed countries that still find it difficult to open up their economies to global competitive forces and for already-marginalised groups within industrialised countries. The contribution also discusses some implications for research, development policy and institutional change.*

Whether true or not, there is a widespread perception among people in all walks of life and in all parts of the world, that the pace of change today is very fast, and in many ways unexpected and beyond their control. Much of the blame for the sense of unease and insecurity is being put on processes and changes occurring at 'global' level. The ability to influence, let alone control, such changes is perceived to be beyond the capability of the individual person or community – and even, in many cases, the individual nation state. What kinds of processes and changes are causing such feelings of insecurity – within rich countries as well as poor ones?

Was not the ending of the cold war supposed to have been an example of positive change and to have reduced people's fears by ridding the world of the ultimate threat to peace and security – that of global military conflict? It is true

Helen O'Neill, Director of the Centre for Development Studies, University College Dublin and President of EADI. The author would like to thank the three anonymous referees for their comments on an earlier draft. The usual disclaimer applies.

that the repercussions for Europe and the rest of the world from the events of 1989 and the ending of the cold war have been largely positive. Much needed reforms, both political and economic, have been launched inside developing countries and transitional economies and they are perceived to have brought widespread benefits to many people. At the global level, a greater sense of security from the threat of nuclear war has taken root. And yet, and also to a large extent perceived to originate at the global level, new types of uncertainties and insecurities are gaining ground. Which specific threats to human security are now causing so many people to fear for their lives and livelihoods? Many of these threats have international or global dimensions in the sense that their root causes can be traced to events and processes occurring outside their own territories. Two such processes are globalisation and competitiveness. And the key question being addressed in this contribution is: what are the implications for human beings in their everyday lives of what is being described as the 'globalisation' of much activity in the world today, and the relentless competition among globalising actors? To put it more colloquially: how are things 'out there' affecting people 'in here'? This gives rise to other questions: what are the implications for development research? and what challenges then arise for development policy and for institutional change?

## HUMAN SECURITY AND HUMAN INSECURITY

Our understanding of development has itself developed over the past few decades in terms of both approach and substance. The process is universally seen as a multidimensional one and the most useful approach to understanding it is acknowledged to be multidisciplinary. However, while there is still a necessary concern with the determinants of economic growth and of social and political change at the national level, the implications for people, as beneficiaries more than as labour 'inputs', is increasingly becoming the main concern. There has been a shift in focus from places to people – from growth as an outcome to growth as an input; and from people and their capabilities as development inputs, to the enhancement of human choices and capabilities as the outcome.

Our approach to measuring development has also changed. As far back as 1976, Galtung was advising us that while conventional indicators such as GNP per capita and related measures served the purpose as long as development was identified with economic growth, once it was generally seen as a complex multidimensional process, not one but rather a *set* of indicators, showing aspects of satisfaction of human needs, with a concentration on outputs rather than inputs, is the appropriate approach to measuring development. Galtung included in his dimensions of human development, not just satisfaction of basic needs such as food, shelter, health and education, but also work, freedom of impression and expression, freedom of movement, political participation, greater equality and social justice, self-reliance (the capability of self-sufficiency in a crisis), and sustainability. He eschewed averages, claiming that they obscured one of the most important indicators of human development (namely the degree of equality and social justice achieved by a population). He suggested instead that the indicators should seek to measure levels and distributions of need-satisfaction, that is, the percentages above agreed-upon social minima and the percentages between agreed-upon social minimum and maximum levels under the various need headings [*Galtung, 1976: 261–5*].

The UNDP defines human development as the process of expanding the range of people's choices – and, more recently, of their capabilities as well. In its 1994 Human Development Report, the UNDP introduced the new – distinct but related – concept of human security. It has two aspects, first, safety from such chronic threats as hunger, disease and repression and, second, protection from sudden and hurtful disruptions in the patterns of daily life. It is, of course, related to human development in the sense that human security means that people can exercise their expanded choices (and develop their capabilities) safely and freely and can be relatively confident that the opportunities they have today are not totally lost tomorrow [*UNDP, 1994: 23*].

The components of human security fall under two main headings, freedom from fear and freedom from want (two key principles underlying the UN Charter). The UNDP list delineates aspects of human security and the various threats that can be identified under each heading.

*Economic security* (the threats to which include unemployment, insecure jobs, income inequalities, poverty, homelessness);

*Food security* (inadequacies in terms of food availabilities and food entitlements);

*Health security* (infectious and parasitic diseases, new viruses including HIV, respiratory infections from polluted air);

*Environmental security* (degradation of air, water, soil and forests);

*Personal security* (conflicts, poverty- and drugs-related crime, violence against women and children, terrorism);

*Community security* (ethnic clashes);

*Political security* (violation of human rights).

Since the publication of the first Human Development Report (HDR) in 1990, the UNDP has continually introduced new concepts relating to human development and, in all cases except that of human security, has developed indicators for them. Thus, over the past six years, it has provided us with the human development index (HDI), human freedom index (later dropped because of its political sensitivity), gender-related development index, gender empowerment measure, and, in 1996, even a 'capability poverty index'. Owing to the widespread concern today with various aspects of human security, it would be appropriate for the UNDP to return to this concept and, although it would be difficult to do so, it should attempt to provide some measurable indicators relating to it. These might then be amalgamated into a single 'human security index' which could be incorporated into the wider (evolving) set of development-related indicators.

Human security is a universal concern. There are many threats that are common to all people, rich and poor alike, but their intensity may differ from one part of the world to another [*UNDP, 1994: 22*]. The UNDP claims that, in seeking security, people in rich countries tend to focus on the threat of crime and drug wars in their streets, the spread of deadly diseases like HIV/AIDS, soil degradation, rising levels of pollution and the fear of losing their jobs. The results of a 1995 EuroBarometer Survey tend to confirm this view. It showed that the top three concerns of European citizens in order of importance were: fighting unemployment; protecting nature and fighting pollution; and fighting terrorism. People in poor countries have similar concerns but they also demand liberation from the continuing threats of hunger, disease, and poverty [*European Commission, 1996*].

In fact, if we differentiate between rich and poor *people,* rather than rich and poor *countries,* we find that the human insecurities world-wide may look more alike. Food security, for example, has become an intense issue in Europe as manifested in fears, not about the availability of food, but rather its safety from the effects of animal diseases, pesticides on fruit and vegetables, and milk and water contamination, to mention but some of the perceived threats. There is universal agreement that the spread of the BSE virus can be explained by the unrestrained deregulation of the animal-feed industry in the mid-1980s by the government of one European state intent on promoting the global competitiveness of its food industry. Thus a measure of food security could include not just quantitative indicators (food availability and entitlement) but also a qualitative one (food safety).

As regards economic security, the concerns of rich and poor people, although differing in intensity, include many similar elements. Unemployment is concentrated most among the unskilled in both poor and rich countries. The EU Commission suggests that a 'two-speed labour market' is emerging in Europe; on the demand side, a high-speed market is driven by new technology and competition between enterprises in global as well as domestic markets while, on the supply side, the speed is slower because education and training cannot meet the demand for new skills [*Financial Times, 1996a*]. Within labour markets in both rich and poor countries, it is not just unemployment (no job) that is seen as a threat to economic security, but also job insecurity, manifested by an increasing tendency toward contract and casual jobs (what competitive global actors tend to praise as 'labour flexibility'). This concept of economic insecurity might be captured by an indicator showing the average duration of jobs.

Widening income inequalities constitute another threat to economic security. While life expectancy and some other social indicators have shown general improvements over the years, income inequalities between rich and poor countries, as well as among developing countries, tended to widen during the 1980s compared with the period between 1965 and 1980 [*Griffin and Khan, 1992: 2*]. Current data suggest that these inequalities are also rising within many developing countries – and some industrialised countries [*UNDP, 1996: 13–17*]. The 1996 OECD *Employment Outlook* provides evidence of widening earnings inequalities in OECD countries which, it claims, will lead to 'more marginalisation of people (social exclusion) – and increased pressure on welfare budgets' [*Financial Times, 1996b*]. The OECD blames substantial labour and product market reforms for the increase in social exclusion in the US and the UK. It also suggests that countries with generous welfare benefits and widespread unionisation of workers have a less unequal distribution of earnings than those that do not. Although widely criticised by the more aggressive globalising corporations and their advisors, these benefits, which are important contributors to economic security, probably enhance labour productivity – considered to be one of the key factors in the competitiveness of nations.

## COMPETITIVENESS: DO NATIONS REALLY COMPETE?

Having first considered the concept of human security, including its components and possible indicators, it is now appropriate to examine the other two concepts in the title of this contribution. We could begin with either one of them, since they are closely related. Indeed, as both processes appear to gather pace, it is often difficult to disentangle them. Thus, although ideally the two concepts should first be considered separately and sequentially, and then in combination, this neat approach is not always possible and inevitably there are overlaps in those parts of the presentation that are intended to consider competitiveness and globalisation separately.

Everyone would agree that individuals compete with each other and also that enterprises compete. But, do nations compete? Michael Porter, despite having written a very influential book, whose title, *The Competitive Advantage of Nations*, might suggest that he believes they do, nevertheless states quite firmly that they do not. 'Firms, not nations, compete in international markets' [*Porter, 1990: 33*]. Still, if he does not accept that nations compete with each other, and claims that the notion of a competitive nation is unclear, nonetheless his book is an exploration into the determinants of 'national competitiveness' and the 'competitive advantage of nations' – which he defines as 'the decisive characteristic of a nation that allows its companies to create and sustain competitive advantage in particular fields' [*ibid.: 84–5*].

There is no theory, Porter states, to explain national competitiveness – which he describes as 'one of the central preoccupations of government and industry in every nation'. He considers the aspects that are often associated with it: bountiful natural resources, cheap and abundant labour, superior management capabilities, government policy (macroeconomic, industrial, and trade), but concludes that, on their own, none of these provide a satisfactory explanation. 'A broader, more complex set of forces seems to be at work.' Ultimately he equates national competitiveness with productivity; the productivity with which a nation's labour and capital are employed. This must be continually improved and such improvement demands continual improvement at the national level.

> Sustained productivity growth requires that an economy continually *upgrade itself.* A nation's companies must *relentlessly* improve productivity … They must develop the necessary capabilities to compete in more and more sophisticated industry segments, where productivity is generally high … No nation can be competitive in everything … We are particularly concerned with the determinants of international success in technology- and skill-intensive segments and industries, which underpin high and rising productivity [*ibid.: 84–5*].

While Porter claims that no nation can be competitive in everything, it could also be added that the same applies in the case of large enterprises. No enterprise, no matter how profitable, can be competitive in the production of all products – even though their penchant for mergers and take-overs might suggest that they believe that they might be. The recent trend toward 'downsizing' in many large enterprises, especially those that are competing in global markets, suggests that once they come to this conclusion, they can be totally ruthless in shedding those parts of their operations that are not considered profitable enough to justify maintaining them – or the workers whose livelihoods depend on them.

The United Nations Conference on Trade and Development (UNCTAD) argues that the term competitiveness refers to both firms and countries. It suggests that the competitiveness of firms can be considered from a number of angles. It can be described as the ability of individual firms to maintain or increase market share on a sustained basis; or the ability of firms either to lower costs or to offer products of superior quality at a premium price; or, normally, competitiveness may be derived from profitability and hence from the interplay of costs and prices [*UNCTAD 1995: 3*]. At the national level, UNCTAD suggests that competitiveness is a more complicated concept. It considers the arguments of those who claim that, since it is firms rather than countries that are involved in international business, the term competitiveness at the country level may be a misnomer. It wonders if it may be more useful to think in terms of national welfare rather than national competitiveness. However, it then suggests that national competitiveness (now equated with national welfare) is not simply a linear aggregation of the competitiveness of individual firms. Thus, analysing it 'requires a much broader consideration of a wider set of issues which could include factors such as productivity, technological innovation, investments, export and import prices, trade and capital balances, working conditions, taxes, political stability etc.' [*ibid.: 4*]. As will be seen later, this list begins to sound rather like the list of factors used by the World Economic Forum and the International Institute for Management Development when they set about measuring the levels of competitiveness of various countries around the world.

Krugman completely dismisses the notion of national competitiveness, claiming that the analogy of a nation competing in the same way that firms do is nonsense. He too focuses on productivity, stating that a country in which productivity grows more slowly than others will experience slower overall economic growth – and thus will become relatively less well-off. Firms can go out of business, nations do not. He implies that competition between firms is a negative-sum game while he is sure that in international trade, both countries gain. *The Economist*, while agreeing with Krugman that the basis of competitiveness is improving productivity, nonetheless claims that productivity (presumably it has in mind some concept of 'national' productivity), can be influenced by government policy. 'Nations compete', it states, 'in that they choose policies to promote higher living standards'. Moreover, it claims that measures of competitiveness 'are not complete nonsense' as Krugman implies [*The Economist, 1996: 84*].

So, do nations compete or not? The publication of annual league tables entitled 'Global Competitiveness Report' produced by the World Economic Forum (WEF) and 'The World Competitiveness Yearbook' produced by the International Institute for Management Development (IMD) both rank countries on the basis of their competitiveness, suggesting that a number of influential actors at national and international levels believe that they do and that Porter is correct when he claims that it is a major preoccupation of governments and industry today. These publications get widespread coverage in the international press and relevant government ministries and national confederations of industry peruse them for lessons to be learned. They are certainly widely studied within the European Union where competitiveness is seen to apply, not just at the national level, but also at that of the region. The Union of Industrial and Employers' Confederations of Europe (UNICE) produced a report in 1993 explaining 'the extent of the decline in the competitiveness of Europe and its causes' and in 1994, followed it up with an 'Action Programme for decision-shapers and decision-makers throughout Europe' which was designed 'to reverse the declining competitiveness of Europe, to create additional growth, and to generate new jobs' [*UNICE, 1994*].

As far back as 1983, a European Parliament working paper, which compared the performance of the European economy with that of the US and Japan, established 'successful global competition' as the primary goal of European integration. Ten years later, the Commission of the European Communities produced a white paper entitled 'Growth, Competitiveness and Employment' which was drawn up in collaboration with the member states and after consultation with the social partners. Moreover, within the Commission's Directorate-General XII (Science, Research, Development), the main emphasis to date has been on research on technological development to promote the competitiveness of European industry (the global market focus).

Sandholtz and Zysman [*1989*] were arguing in 1989 that the project of economic and political unification in Europe was instigated by 'a complex web of intergovernmental bargains and accommodations among the various national business elites' whose terms were set in the main by core European governments and business elites (cited in O'Hearn [*1993: 175*]). But, as already pointed out above, inspiring people to participate more productively in an economic project can best be assured if the initiator (employer, or government) provides inputs in the form of economic security. O'Hearn relates this notion to the 'European project'. He states that the history of European social democracy has created powerful interests in the welfare state, and the legitimacy of a new Europe would be challenged if there were significant erosion of social welfare programmes. He suggests that peripheral members increasingly view 'cohesion' as a strong basis for their participation in the project. He also cites Bornschier [*1992*] who described the tension or contradiction between the requirements of competition through 'lean production' and the 'lean state' on the one hand, and the demands of non-business social forces, on the other.

In this regard, it might also be added that there are some signs that the exclusive focus in DG XII on economic competitiveness within its research programme is about to be relaxed. In the discussions on the design of the Fifth Framework Programme (FP5), which will cover the years 1999 to 2003, one of the key actors involved in the process has already suggested that EU science and technology research should be 'visible to the man in the street' and that it should also address the 'needs of society' (the global village focus). If this happens, it suggests that a more integrated human development approach might be incorporated into FP5 and that the global market approach and the global village approach might be thus better integrated with each other.

Up until 1996, WEF and IMD jointly produced an annual world competitiveness report in which they ranked 40–50 (mainly industrialised) countries according to a wide range of factors. In 1996, they split up and each produced its own report. Inevitably, their approaches have much in common. However, there are some interesting differences between them. The IMD survey covers 46 countries (24 industrialised countries including all member states of the EU; 12 Asian and Latin American new-industrialised countries (NICs); four middle-income developing countries (MICs); India and China; Russia and three central/east European countries). The WEF [*1996*] survey covers 49 countries, very similar to the IMD list but with the addition of a few more MICs. The vast bulk of developing countries, and all least-developed countries, are omitted from both lists. The only African country included in the lists is South Africa.

WEF and IMD both use eight principal 'factors' to compile their indices of competitiveness but these factors in turn are divided into a very long list of sub-factors or 'criteria', bringing the total number of variables to over 300 in the case of WEF and to 224 in the case of IMD. Each tries to weight their inputs: in the case of WEF, weights are assigned to the factors; in the case of IMD to their sub-factors. Both of them use a combination of 'hard' data (published statistics) and 'soft' data (survey data compiled from executive opinion surveys) in compiling their sub-factors. While the eight principal factor headings used by them differ somewhat from one another in terms of names, and while the number of sub-factors under each heading, and the ways in which they are distributed under factor headings also show some variations, overall the two lists tend to cover the same general issues.

The factors are: internationalisation or openness of the economy; the domestic economy and government involvement and policies (including the legal and regulatory environment and institutions of civil society); financial institutions, including their size and transparency; physical infrastructure, environment and energy; management skills; science and technology capability and facilities; and people, including skills and access to education, unemployment levels, working hours, welfare and social services, equality of opportunity, quality of life and attitudes to work. Aspects of a number (although by no means the majority) of the elements that go to make up the concept of human security are to be found among the vast array of sub-factors in these two competitiveness reports.

Both WEF and IMD stress that their definitions are undergoing continual review and each would claim that their index of competitiveness needs further refinement. This would seem to be confirmed by the differences in their league tables. (For comparisons, see Appendix 1, which also includes the 1996 rankings of the same countries according to the HDI. As already stated, there is, as yet, no satisfactory indicator for human security).

Had the territorial coverage of the reports been universal, instead of being confined to fewer than 50 countries, it would have been interesting to compare the conclusions of WEF and IMD in relation to the contribution of the common sub-factors to national competitiveness and the conclusions of the UNDP regarding their importance for human security. It goes without saying that, in a number of instances, what the UNDP might consider as a positive contribution to human security, the WEF and IMD might consider as a threat to national competitiveness. To take a few examples: job security, guaranteed old age pensions, and a comprehensive welfare programme would all contribute positively to human security. In contrast, WEF and IMD associates them with 'inflexibility' of labour markets and 'social costs' – both of which constitute threats to national competitiveness. On the other hand, improvements in skills and better access to education and training at all levels would be perceived by both sides as positive contributors to both human security (by improving capabilities) and national competitiveness (by improving productivity).

WEF and IMD define national competitiveness differently. For the former, it is 'the ability of a national economy to achieve sustained high rates of economic growth (as measured by the annual change in GDP per capita)'. IMD's definition is more complex. It rejects the narrower approach of WEF (and of Porter and Krugman), claiming that competitiveness cannot be reduced 'to the mere notions of GDP and productivity. Firms need also to cope with the political, economic, socio-cultural human and educational dimension of a country' [*IMD, 1996: 42*]. Thus, in defining competitiveness as 'the ability of a country to create added value and thus increase national wealth by managing assets and processes, attractiveness and aggressiveness, globality and proximity, and by integrating these relationships into an economic and social model', IMD implicitly makes a strong case for the application of the concept of competitiveness to the nation state. It also provides an altogether more thoughtful exploration of the concept of competitiveness than does the WEF and, were its coverage to be extended to include a more representative sample of countries, and especially more poor countries, it could offer interesting possibilities for the exploration of linkages between globalisation, competitiveness and human security.

To deny that nations compete with each other is to ignore the evidence presented by the competing incentives packages (grants, tax breaks, 'a pool of young computer-literate workers' and so on) offered by (especially contiguous) nations and regions which compete with each other to attract foreign direct investment (FDI). IMD would describe such packages as part of the attempt of countries to become 'attractive' to foreign investors. It states that 'nations approach the process of internationalisation by being "attractive and/or aggressive"' (p.6). Some nations focus on attractiveness by creating a domestic environment that is conducive to FDI being made *inside* their country (it points to the example of Ireland) while others aggressively strive to enter international markets by making direct investments *outside* their countries and through exports (for example Japan). IMD claims that only the US seems to manage both approaches equally – and it is well ahead of all others in its competitiveness league table. Attractiveness has the significant advantage of creating jobs in the domestic economy, but IMD recommends a blend of both.

According to IMD, nations manage two types of economies: one that is close at hand (proximity, or what economists call the non-tradables sector) and one that is far-reaching (globality, or the tradables sector). The first adds value close to the end user while globality assumes that the factors related to production need not necessarily be actually near the end user. There are risks in pursuing the latter option – and many of them have consequences for human security. As IMD puts it, 'it affects decisions regarding the degree of exposure, regulation and, eventually, social volatility of the economy' (p.7). We could repeat the question posed at the beginning of this contribution: how are things 'out there' affecting people 'in here'? IMD believes that the friction between globality and proximity will be at the centre of the economic debate in the coming years. 'In many ways' it states, 'the public now perceives the economy of globality as one which destroys jobs at home, does not guarantee revenues (incomes), remains unpredictable and, ultimately, is not loyal to the nation' (p.14).

National competitiveness may stem from assets (large populations, natural resources, old universities) or from processes (a nation's present ability to create value added). IMD is critical of GDP or GNP as a measure of value added 'since they only account for the monetary aspect of the economy. Progress in education, science and technology, and social harmonisation are not taken into consideration' [*ibid.*]. National wealth, composed of inherited assets (such as natural resources) and created assets (an excellent educational system – and, it could be added, one that is universally accessible), is the end result of competitiveness according to IMD. It adds that the wealth of the present generation in rich countries is the fruit of the competitiveness of past generations. Put another way, it can be said that countries will be wealthy in the future if they invest today, especially in their people, since, as IMD puts it, 'nations do not compete with products and services alone, but also with education and value systems' (p.15).

Value systems, according to IMD, continually evolve. It identifies four stages – hard work, wealth, social participation, and self achievement – 'which describe the key motivating forces in a society' [*ibid.*]. It puts Korea and China at the first stage; Singapore at the wealth stage; Japan at the third stage; and Europe and the US at the stage where, according to IMD, 'individual values, especially self achievement, have replaced collective values' [*ibid.*]. It states that one of the key responsibilities of a modern society is to be able to manage the transition from one stage to another 'and to make choices' [*ibid.*].

The World Competitiveness Report of 1990 described three types of society: (1) the South European Model which is characterised by weak infrastructure, business regulation and social protection, a parallel economy, and low labour costs; (2) the North European Model characterised by a strong emphasis on stability, social consensus and regulations; and (3) the Anglo-Saxon Model characterised by deregulation, privatisation, labour flexibility, and a higher acceptance of risk. Over the past decade, it claims, a shift has occurred from the North European model to the Anglo-Saxon one, 'triggered perhaps by the Reagan and Thatcher years' [*ibid.*].

But, if there are tensions between what IMD calls the economy of proximity and the economy of globality inside nations, tensions can also arise between competing nations and regions – or, as IMD might have put it, between the South-European model and the other ones. A 1996 study for the Federation of Swedish Industries (FSI) claims that East Asian economies (especially China, Malaysia, and Indonesia) are 'competing unfairly' in world markets by erecting barriers to foreign exporters such as governmental administrative guidelines for industry, legal uncertainty, denial of trading rights to foreign companies, import quotas, discriminatory technical standards, and preferential government procurement. Although it concedes that these are often permissible under world trade rules, 'they circumvent their spirit' thus 'distorting local economies and world trade' [*Federation of Swedish Industries, 1996: 6*].

FSI identifies a concept that it calls 'natural competitive advantage' which, it implies, should be the basis of international trade. Instead of being so based, it complains that many exports from newly-industrializing countries are based on what it calls 'artificial competitive advantages in the form of subsidies and tariff and non-tariff protection to enhance export-oriented production based on a protected domestic market' [*ibid.*]. It calls for further global trade liberalisation and 'the full integration of industrialising Asian nations into the world economic regulatory framework for trade and investment' and even suggests that the European single market could serve as 'a useful point of reference' (p.2).

Thus, threats to human security are perceived as arising, not just within countries (from tensions between the economy of globality to the economy of proximity), but also between countries and regions – and the direction of causation is not always perceived as coming from relatively rich to relatively poor, as the Swedish example shows. The so-called 'giants' of Fortune magazine's 'Global 500' are praised for having 'pushed across borders to seize fresh markets and swallow up local competitors' during 1995 [*Fortune, 5 August 1996*] while the CEOs of many global enterprises listed in Business Week's 'Global 1000' describe their sector of industry as having become 'brutally competitive' causing them to 'come to work every day on the razor's edge of a competitive battle' [*Business Week, 1996: 49*]. Both magazines conclude that the only way for these enterprises to remain competitive is 'to go global' and begin investing overseas (thus fulfilling IMD's 'aggressiveness' characteristic). If developing countries are to benefit from such investments, UNCTAD suggests in its 1995 World Investment Report that they need to have 'an investment climate characterised by growing markets and increasingly favourable regulatory frameworks coupled with the general trend for firms from all countries to invest abroad in order to remain competitive internationally' [*UNCTAD, 1995: 114*].

## GLOBALISATION

Globalisation is one of the most widely used – and misused – words in the field of international relations today. It appears to have many meanings. In business circles and in the media, it is employed in a rather loose sense to describe increased internationalisation of economic activities or (less often) political negotiations or even cultural trends. Academics tend to interpret it more narrowly and to attach the word only to specific forms of internationalisation – ones that involve the 'deepening' rather than just the 'widening' of international linkages.

Because of the many interpretations attaching to the word, there are wide differences of opinion regarding its implications for the world economy, its constituent parts, and for human security. Some would argue that globalisation is spreading so fast that it spells the end of the national economy and the role of national governments in policy-making. Others would argue that the type of globalisation that would lead to that outcome is simply not happening – indeed that the internationalisation of the world economy today differs only quantitatively, and not qualitatively, from the one that operated during the *pax Britannica* period prior to the First World War.

In any debate, it is important to have clarity regarding concepts. In other words, if participants in the debate do not agree on definitions then, at the very least, each should understand how the others are interpreting the key concepts. Unfortunately, many of those involved in the globalisation debate fail to define what they mean and fail to enquire what others mean by the term globalisation.

As a result, widely different conclusions are drawn by different actors regarding its status and pervasiveness, its consequences for developing countries and North–South convergence, and its implications for human security.

The key issues to be explored are: Is globalisation happening? Is the world economy becoming internationalised in an entirely new way? If it is, has it positive or negative consequences – and for whom? Does globalisation threaten the human security of the weak? Who are the key actors involved in the process? Does it reduce significantly the capability of national governments – and, through them, inter-governmental and international organisations – to intervene in ways that can ensure positive outcomes for human security? Or, is the trend toward globalisation greatly exaggerated? – the world still has borders; nation-states, not transnational corporations, are still the most influential actors in international relations; and they (or perhaps the more powerful among them, or partnerships of them?) can still exercise a decisive influence on the global political economy and its consequences for human security. As in all such explorations, it is appropriate to begin by examining the various definitions.

### *What is Globalisation – and Is It a Reality?*

In defining globalisation, academic economists have tended to begin by stressing that it is a micro-economic process – in contrast to regionalisation, which links countries, and is therefore described as macroeconomic. Globalisation is thus defined as the process by which enterprises (related or unrelated) become interdependent and interlinked globally through strategic alliances and international networks. Alliances may be for individual projects or more long term. It is seen as relating to production rather than to trade – although increasing trade links are part of the process since the splitting up of production processes and their location in often widely-dispersed plants (car engines in one country, bodies in another, and so on) induces more trade during the course of production.

Regionalisation, whilst a distinct concept, is none the less related to globalisation. Regionalisation can be either 'market-led' (characterised by increasing economic linkages among a group of contiguous countries but without any accompanying institutional or policy framework) or 'policy-led' (where the process is initiated through an international agreement to establish a regional integration scheme designed to promote trade among a group of contiguous countries). Regional integration schemes lead to increased intra-regional trade (described as shallow integration) but, in order to get a foothold in the expanded markets of other regional groupings, enterprises in one region will tend to begin investing in other regions. Often these foreign branches compete with domestic enterprises for local resources and markets but, more recently, there is an increasing tendency for FDI to become involved in strategic alliances with domestic firms. The result is 'deep' integration, or integration at the level of production, facilitated through 'investment creation' across regions [*O'Neill, 1993*]. In this way, the processes of regionalisation and globalisation become intertwined.

Increasingly, as tariffs have become less important as impediments to international trade flows, the focus of liberalising efforts has shifted to non-tariff barriers and especially to differences between countries (or regions) in trade and investment policies, as well as differences in standards, regulatory environments, and government involvement in the economy. Thus, deregulation and privatisation are seen as promoting international trade and investment, or internationalisation – or, in the language of some, 'globalisation'.

Technological progress, not only in production, but more especially in communications (transportation and information technology) is also perceived as an engine of globalisation, facilitating wider and faster linkages between people and places. The integration of financial markets is perhaps the most remarkable manifestation of the role of the new IT in the globalisation process.

Thomas Friedman [*1996*], a columnist with the *New York Times*, includes many of these elements when he defines globalisation as 'that loose combination of free-trade agreements, the Internet and the integration of financial markets that is erasing borders and uniting the world into a single, lucrative, but brutally competitive marketplace'. Day and Reibstein [*1996*] define globalisation rather similarly but also perceive it as the driving force of new forms of competitiveness. According to them: 'Globalisation and technological change are spawning new sources of competition, deregulation is changing the rules of competition in many industries, markets are becoming more complex and unpredictable and information flows in a tightly wired world permit companies to sense and react to competitors at a faster rate' (p.2). McGrew [*1992*] also describes globalisation rather broadly as 'the forging of a multiplicity of linkages and interconnections between the states and societies which make up the modern world system. The processes by which events, decisions and activities in one part of the world can come to have significant consequences for individuals and communities in quite distant parts of the globe' [*ibid.: 262*].

Globalisation is also described as a multidimensional process. This broader interpretation of the process is to be found most frequently in the publications of some of the United Nations institutions and agencies. Buendia [*1995*], in a study for UNU/WIDER, describes it as having three main trends, namely, the globalisation of markets, the globalisation of culture, and the globalisation of security – the first being 'the more comprehensive, more solidly grounded, and more advanced of the three'. In his preface to Buendia, Simai describes its political dimension as a long historical process, characterised by intense competition between the main global centres of power, and its economic dimension as the integration of states into a structure, approximating a single, unified international economic system or as the intensification of economic ties, interactions and interdependence of states. On the level of firms, he describes it as the building of integrated multi-tier networks [*Simai, 1995: v–vi*]. In a 1995 study entitled 'States of Disarray: The Social Effects of Globalisation', the United Nations Research Institute for Social Development (UNRISD) lists 'six key trends' of globalisation as being: the spread of liberal democracy; the dominance of market forces; the integration of the global economy; the transformation of production systems and labour markets; the speed of technological change; and the media revolution and consumerism [*UNRISD, 1995: 22*].

Oman [*1994*] of the OECD Development Centre perceives globalisation as extending to 'a broad range of issues that bring together the politics and economics of change today on a global scale'. These include

> the viability of the world trading system, the growing need for 'deep' international policy integration, and the apparent decline of national economic policy autonomy. They include the impact of the technological 'revolution', the sources of long-term economic and productive growth, the importance of change in systems of corporate management and industrial organisation, and the bases of competitive strength of countries as well as firms. They include the implications of the emergence of a tri-polar world, rapidly changing North/South relations, growing diversity among the developing countries, poverty and the threat of expulsion for a large proportion of the world's population and, in the leading economies, severe problems of unemployment and growing wage and income disparities. And they include the role of government and the nature of state-market relations ... as well as the emergence of competition between different social systems or types of 'capitalism' [*Oman, 1994: 1*].

In a rather similar vein, participants at a 1991 UNCTAD 'encounter' stressed that globalisation was only one dimension of a wider process touching every aspect of the human condition. The other dimensions include demography, employment, education, poverty, endemic diseases, and environmental degradation. According to those at the meeting, these issues need to be addressed globally and thus fall within the realm of global governance.

However, not all international organisations, even not all of those within the UN family, take a multidimensional approach in defining globalisation. In general, those concerned with economic issues tend to focus on the economic aspects of the process. Michel Camdessus, Managing Director of the IMF, associates globalisation with more open liberalised trade policy; privatisation; foreign exchange and financial liberalisation; deregulation; increased access to international markets; a reduced role for government in the economy; less import substitution industrialisation and more emphasis on export-led growth; and comprehensive adjustment and reform programmes [*IMF, 1996: 214*].

UNCTAD [*1991*] perceives globalisation as the third of three layers of internationalisation. Historically, the first layer was the expansion of international trade. The 1970s witnessed the rapid emergence of a second layer, labelled financial integration, whereby international investment flows outpaced trade flows. Then, starting in the 1980s, a third layer (globalisation) was superimposed on the first two, by placing technology, and especially IT at the forefront of competition. Strategic alliances between firms and the widespread use of IT networks 'are spearheading a reshuffling of comparative advantages, in which continuous innovation and flexible organisation become crucial sources of profitability'. Therefore UNCTAD suggests that the analysis of interdependence today requires putting more focus, in addition to trade and finance, on technology and the global strategies of private firms. It is also mindful of the complexities and the 'contradictions' associated with globalisation 'whereby trends towards global integration (for example, of financial markets) co-exist with growing regionalisation as well as with tendencies towards fragmentation, in particular through the establishment of incompatible and competing standards and procedures in sectors dominated by proprietary networks' [*ibid.: 1–2*].

Indeed, in the vast and expanding literature on globalisation, the majority of the contributors tend to focus on the economic dimensions of globalisation. Of course, this is especially so in the case of economists, including development economists. Indeed, Simai, in a paper entitled 'Globalisation, Multilateral Cooperation and the Development Process', takes a conventional (if extremely broad) economic approach when he defines globalisation as

> the entirety of such universal processes as technological transformation, interdependence caused by mass communications, trade and capital flows, homogenisation and standardisation of production and consumption, the predominance of the world market in trade, investment and other corporate transactions, spatial and institutional integration of markets, and growing identity or similarity of economic regulations, institutions and policies [*Simai, 1996: 7*].

Cook and Kirkpatrick [*1996*] distinguish between 'shallow' integration of the global economy (through trade in goods and services and capital, increasingly related to flows of FDI) and 'deep' integration (which they call globalisation) which occurs at the level of production. Cross-border activities within multinational corporations and within networks established by them have reinforced linkages between national economies to the extent that intra-firm trade is estimated to account for around 40 per cent of global trade [*ibid.: 6*]. They acknowledge that government policy can foster 'deep' integration but imply that the multinationals are the main actors. They state, '[i]t is the multinationals that have more often been the major impetus for globalisation, which in many instances has led, rather than followed, government policy actions' [*ibid.: 10*], with an accompanying reference to the 1993 UN World Investment Report (p.113). Perhaps UNCTAD was intent on emphasising that same distinction between 'shallow' and 'deep' integration when it chose the wording of UNCTAD IX held in South Africa in May 1996 as 'Promoting Growth and Sustainable Development in a *Liberalizing and Globalizing* World Economy' (my emphasis). In the pre-conference text, it draws a distinction between 'the globalisation of production and the liberalisation of trade' [*UNCTAD, 1996a: 10*].

But liberalisation also includes liberalisation of investment and capital flows, that is, the activities of multinational corporations and financial markets. Perhaps, it would make more sense to define globalisation as including both the 'shallow' and the 'deep' dimensions? Later, in the same text, UNCTAD seems to come nearer to this interpretation. It sees the process of globalisation as being manifested 'in the internationalisation of production and markets' [*ibid.: 33*]. The text also includes a section which describes the complex interlinkages between liberalisation, globalisation, competitiveness and global governance when it states:

> Globalisation is the product of liberalisation. But it has also set in motion forces working to accelerate liberalisation. As firms increasingly see transnational production as necessary for their competitiveness and profitability, they are exerting more and more pressures on governments to provide conditions that will allow them to operate worldwide. This involves not only further liberalisation of international trade but also freedom of entry, right of establishment and national treatment, as well as freedom for international financial transactions, deregulation and privatisation [*UNCTAD, 1996a: 7*].

Hirst and Thompson [*1996*] are convinced that, while increased internationalisation and integration have been occurring, globalisation is largely a myth. They begin by describing a simple but extreme version of an 'inter-national' economy – in which the principal entities are national economies. Interdependence between nation states within such a system remains of the 'strategic' kind, that is, it implies the continued relative separation of the domestic and the international frameworks for policy-making and the management of economic affairs, and also a relative separation in terms of economic effects. They contrast the inter-national economy with a stylised globalised one, within which, they state, distinct national economies are subsumed and rearticulated into the system by international processes and transactions. One of the many consequences of a globalising international economy, in their view, would be the transformation of MNCs into genuine TNCs as the major actors in the world economy.

Having examined the historical evidence, Hirst and Thompson conclude that there is nothing very new about the present internationalised economy. On the contrary, they argue, it is one of a number of distinct conjunctures or states of the international economy that have existed since an economy based on modern industrial technology began to be generalised from the 1860s. They even go so far as to state that in some respects, the current international economy is *less* open than the regime that prevailed from 1870 to the outbreak of the First World War. They also claim that genuinely transnational companies (TNCS) appear to be relatively rare; most companies, they state, are nationally based and trade multinationally on the strength of a major national location of production and sales. Further, they argue that capital mobility is not producing a massive shift of investment and employment from industrialised to developing countries; indeed, with the exception of a small number of NICs, the Third World remains marginalised in both investment and trade.

Hirst and Thompson conclude that the world economy is far from being genuinely 'global'. Instead, they claim, trade, investment and financial flows are concentrated in the Triad of Europe, Japan and North America and this dominance seems set to continue. And, finally, they claim that these major economic powers, the Triad or G3, have the capacity, especially if they coordinate policy, to exert powerful governance pressures over financial markets and other economic tendencies. They conclude that '[g]lobal markets are thus by no means beyond regulation and control' [*ibid.: 3*].

While it is important to know whether the governments of the G3 are powerless in the face of globalisation, or whether they can still exercise 'governance pressures over financial markets', what is even more important, in relation to human security, is the extent to which all governments, of both powerful and weak countries, can influence events to improve the lives of local populations and, even more important, whether individual people can do so in any meaningful way.

Nevertheless, the importance Hirst and Thompson attach to the historical perspective is a genuinely useful contribution to the debate. Bairoch and Kozul-Wright [*1996: 4*] also describe globalisation as a myth and they also find the historical approach useful in the interests of extracting 'some useful lessons for understanding the current wave of globalisation'. They examine a study by Sachs and Warner [*1995*] which describes the period between 1860 and 1914 as one characterised by low trade barriers and capital mobility, technological progress in long distance transportation and communications, the adoption of appropriate legal institutions, as well as the spread of the gold standard, convertible currencies and capitalist institutions. Sachs and Warner conclude that these were the factors that together promoted international trade (which had a strong North–South dimension) and capital flows and stimulated strong growth throughout the world, and the rapid spread of industrialisation beyond the core North Atlantic economies. Moreover, claim Sachs and Warner, this was a period of rapid economic convergence as poor economies grew faster than rich ones largely because of the trade stimulus. They find many parallels between that period of 'globalisation' and the present one and conclude that convergence is also likely 'for the countries that join the system' today provided they make 'appropriate policy choices' (Sachs and Warner [*1995: 61*] cited in Bairoch and Kozul-Wright [*1996: 5*]).

Bairoch and Kozul-Wright reject the thesis of Sachs and Warner, claiming that they have misinterpreted the earlier period of globalisation ('a collection of myths and realities') and have drawn false conclusions and policy implications from it for today's world. Bairoch and Kozul-Wright argue that, while international production and financial activities were evolving rapidly up to 1914, their development was very uneven both geographically and by sector and that international capital flows, like international trade flows, were highly concentrated. Moreover, they claim, convergence occurred only between a small group of rapidly industrialising economies; most parts of the world were unable to industrialise or, as colonies, were prevented from doing so. They also claim that the evidence from historical studies shows that TNCs were a more prominent feature of the pre-1914 international economic landscape than has been recognised. However, their contribution to economic growth was not as significant as was that of technological change.

In explaining the sources and spread of technological change, Bairoch and Kozul-Wright argue that the role of the state was extremely important. Not only did governments organise national transportation and telecommunication networks and create demand for technology through arms purchases, but they also provided significant amounts of direct funding for technical education and research activity (Hobsbawm [*1994*]; Freeman [*1989*], both cited in Bairoch and Kozul-Wright [*1996*]). They conclude that the evidence presented in their paper confirms their sceptical view of an altogether new globalising world. However, in view of the profound social, political and economic changes that have characterised the period between 1914 and the early 1990s, they would equally dismiss the notion that we are 'simply recovering a trend of global economic integration broken by two world wars and a perverse era of State management' (Bairoch and Kozul Wright [*1996: 26*]).

Thus, the world today (whether we describe it as globalised or not) is not totally new; neither is it simply the same as the previous period of widespread internationalisation, described by some as a previous era of globalisation.

Whatever the similarities or differences, it is important to acknowledge that governments still played a large role in the pre-1914 period. Even the Gold Standard did not operate as 'automatically' as is often claimed. As Bairoch and Kozul-Wright [*ibid.: 26*] put it, '[t]he dynamic processes that underlie investment and innovation are neither abstract nor spontaneous, but channelled and shaped by particular institutional arrangements and policy interventions'. Hirst and Thompson [*1996: 17*] come to much the same conclusion when they state '[t]here are real potentialities for developing regulatory and management systems (and) the international economy is by no means out of control' but 'the political will is lacking at present to gain extra leverage over undesirable and unjust aspects of international and domestic economic activity'. Or, finally, as Wolf [*1996*] puts it, '[p]olicy matters. On their own or together governments can do a great deal. The debate should be over what they should do, not over whether they can do anything at all.'

To sum up, it matters less how we define globalisation than that all participants in the debate are clear about the definitions that they and others are using. Those who deny that the world is globalised are probably defining the term in its 'deep' meaning. Those who claim that globalisation is already a reality are probably employing the looser and broader interpretation of the term. Yet even they still acknowledge that the process only extends as yet to a minority of peoples, most of whom live in the Triad composed of Europe, North America and Japan. However, not all who live in the Triad are capable of benefiting from globalisation and the global competitiveness which drives it, and is in turn driven by it. The poor, the unskilled, the long-term unemployed, together with the majority of the populations of the Third World remain largely marginalised from its benefits but are open to being influenced by its negative effects. The perception that the costs of globalisation and competitiveness among nations is much greater than had earlier been acknowledged is quite widespread now in both poor and rich countries.

## GLOBALISATION, COMPETITIVENESS AND HUMAN SECURITY: CAN IT BE A POSITIVE-SUM GAME?

Analysts of current developments at the world level hold conflicting views on the implications of globalisation and competitiveness for human development and for reduction of human insecurities. The 'optimistic' school of thought argues that globalisation will lead to a greater integration of developing countries into the global economy, to net benefits and to convergence at the global level. The 'pessimistic' view sees globalisation as being largely confined to the North, as widening existing inequalities and further marginalising the vast majority of developing countries – a process of divergence which is set to continue. What is particularly interesting about the more recent debate is that the pessimists now include a wide range of people in the North.

Perhaps the most pessimistic is Lester Thurow. He claims that, since the fall of communism, the capitalist system no longer has a competitor to curb its excesses, especially the tendency of the new technologies to lead to job losses and cause downward pressure on the wages of the unskilled. Many companies are 'ripping up the implicit social contracts'. He sees growing inequalities between rich and poor both inside and between countries, large-scale unemployment, increased homelessness and the breakdown of the family leading to a 'vicious circle of individual disaffection, social disorganisation and a consequent slow downward spiral' [*Thurow, 1996: 7*]. He warns that the very poor will become socially excluded and will retreat into religious fundamentalism or extremism. As a result, capitalism itself is doomed.

Kapstein is equally gloomy. He claims that the 'postwar bargain' has been broken. The global economy 'is leaving millions of disaffected workers in its train. Inequality, unemployment, and endemic poverty have become its handmaidens' [*Kapstein, 1996: 16*]. The forces acting on today's workers 'inhere in the structure of today's global economy, with its open and increasingly fierce competition on the one hand and fiscally conservative units – states – on the other' [*ibid.: 17*]. Governments are supposed to act as protectors of the weak. 'Easing pressures on the "losers" of the new open economy must now be the focus of economic policy if the process of globalisation is to be sustained' [*ibid.: 17*]. But 'systemic pressures are curtailing every government's ability to respond with new spending. Just when working people most need the nation-state as a buffer from the world economy, it is abandoning them' [*ibid.: 16*]. This poses a challenge not just to policy-makers, he states, but to modern economics as well. The outlook is bleak. He sees the possibility of the world 'moving inexorably toward one of those tragic moments that will lead future historians to ask, why was nothing done in time?' [*ibid.: 18*].

This is not the first time that the end of capitalism has been predicted – and yet it has survived. But perhaps the 'announcement effect' of Marx's *Das Kapital* induced it to reform only when communism became a reality? Do the effects of human insecurity have to cause social disintegration before their 'announcement effect' causes public and private actors to intervene this time?

However, one does not have to belong to the ultra-pessimist school to be concerned about the effects of globalisation and increased competitiveness on jobs. The overall theme of the G7 Summit held in Lyons in June 1996 was globalisation. The intention was not to attempt to halt the process but, in the words of President Chirac, 'how to ensure that it will benefit everyone' (*Financial Times*, 27 June 1996). There was some agreement at the meeting on the importance of 'the security of employability over individuals' working lives' [*ibid.*]. There was less agreement regarding labour standards. The US Labour Secretary, Robert Reich, confirmed that the US intends to press hard on the issue at the World Trade Organisation but the UK and others have been opposing this move for some time – as have developing countries who fear that it is a protectionist ploy aimed at them.

Concerns about protectionism and social conflict within Europe because of persistent unemployment is a cause for concern at the EU level. A report, prepared by the Competitiveness Advisory Group – consisting of top industrialists, trade unionists and academics – was presented to the heads of state and government at the EU Summit in Florence in June 1996. The report called for national social pacts between employers, trade unions and government in order 'to counter the threat of disruption' (*Financial Times*, 12 June 1996). Mr Jacques Santer, the President of the European Commission, presented his own 'Confidence Pact for Jobs' to the Lyons Summit. This is largely a reworking of the ideas contained in the 1993 Delors white paper on Growth, Competitiveness and Employment, the main intention of the modifications being to improve the chances of its job-creating elements being implemented (*Irish Times*, 6 June 1996).

One of the more outspoken expressions of concern about the likelihood of social disruption arising from globalisation and competitiveness is to be found in a newspaper article by Klaus Schwab and Claude Smadja, president and managing director respectively of the WEF. In their words,

> [t]he lightening speed at which capital moves across borders, the acceleration of technological changes, the rapid evolution of management and marketing requirements increase the pressure for structural and conceptual readjustments to a breaking point. This is multiplying the human and social costs of the globalisation process to a level that tests the social fabric of the democracies in an unprecedented way [*Schwab and Smadja, 1966*].

It is certainly surprising to read the following extracts from the two people at the top of the organisation which produces the annual 'Global Competitiveness Report'.

> The megacompetition that is part and parcel of globalisation leads to winner-take-all situations; those who come out on top win big, and the losers lose even bigger… [and] … The way transnational corporations have to operate to compete in the global economy means that it is now routine to have corporations announce new profit increases along with a new wave of layoffs … [and] … For those who keep their jobs, the new sense of insecurity means the demise of corporate loyalty bonds. It is not yet clear that corporations have fully realised the consequences that this

will have on their future performance (*International Herald Tribune,* 1 Feb. 1996).

Schwab and Smadja, no less than the leaders of the G7 or the EU, are concerned to ensure the survival of the 'new global capitalism' and that it does not become synonymous with 'free market on the rampage, a brakeless train wreaking havoc'. They call for action from both governments and corporations. Their policy advice to governments sounds like business as usual: they are exhorted to improve training and education, communications infrastructures, 'entrepreneur-incentive fiscal policies', and to 'recalibrate social policies'. Corporations are advised to look to their 'social responsibilities'.

According to Suzman the notion that businesses have formal social responsibilities, in addition to their contractual ones to employees and shareholders, has been spreading in recent years, largely spurred by the spectre of growing social exclusion (quoted in *Financial Times*, 17 June 1996). Suzman reports on a new organisation, the European Business Network for Social Cohesion, which has been formed to encourage companies throughout the EU to take seriously the issue of corporate involvement in the community and, in particular, job creation through investment in training and economic regeneration projects. Two US reports, commissioned by the White House's National Economic Council, one by a business group and the other by labour, have concluded that the social contract between business and its workers had been 'falling apart under the strains of competition'. They both reported that 'companies have less room for manoeuvre in the competitive global environment' [*ibid.*]. It is appropriate to note that these views come from the country that ranks number one in IMD's world competitiveness report, number five in that of WEF, number one in the rankings of the Fortune 500 global corporations and of *Business Week*'s global 1,000 corporations, and number two in the HDI rankings of the UNDP.

The UNDP itself sees globalisation, not necessarily as a positive-sum game, but as 'a two-edged sword ... with winners and losers' [*UNDP, 1996: 59*]. Divergence, rather than convergence, is the result in many cases: 'Income inequality is clearly on the rise in many countries that have opened their economies' [*ibid.: 59*]. It tries to present both sides. 'Some developing regions owe their current prosperity and human development to international trade. But others have been vulnerable to its vagaries' [*ibid.: 103*]. It adds, that '[t]he risk is not just that the benefits of globalisation will bypass these nations. The risk is that these countries will become increasingly marginal as their shares of world trade and international capital flows continue to decline' [*ibid.: 103*].

UNCTAD is also concerned about the danger of marginalisation. Liberalisation and globalisation

> are giving rise in many countries to new uncertainties and anxieties regarding growth and prosperity and the distribution of their benefits. This is particularly the case for developing countries, where there are grounds for anxiety if a country is being drawn rapidly into the globalizing world economy, and equal – or greater – grounds for anxiety if it is not' [*UNCTAD, 1996b: 40*].

In the 'Midrand Declaration' issued at the end of UNCTAD IX, it stated:

> Our economies continue to be unified by flows of trade, finance, information and technological change. This increased interdependence is a powerful impetus to liberalisation of these flows. Competitive pressure on all economies has increased, and market forces play a pivotal role ... However, we must recognise that countries enter this system from very different starting points. Accordingly the impact of globalisation and liberalisation is uneven ... The least developed countries, particularly those in Africa, and other developing countries remain constrained by weak supply capabilities and are unable to benefit from trade. Marginalisation, both among and within countries, has been exacerbated [*UNCTAD, 1996c: 3*].

UNRISD [*1995: 4*] also acknowledges that some people, and some countries, have gained enormously from globalisation but claims that, in many parts of the world, it has contributed to 'increased impoverishment, inequalities, work insecurity, weakening of institutions and social support systems, and erosion of established identities and values'. It argues that one of the most complex challenges of our times has thus become the provision of a modicum of universal social and economic security 'in an era of open markets, fierce competition, rapid technological change and instant communications' (p.v).

There is a huge research agenda waiting to be tackled on the convergence/divergence implications of globalisation in both its shallow and deep forms. Within this area, the costs (and benefits?) of marginalisation call out for investigation. For example, the South Centre questions whether African economies have suffered from being marginalised from the international economy – and whether they need to rectify the situation. It argues that the economies of Southeast Asia, whose success is attributed in many quarters to moderate government involvement in the economy and the openness of their economies, instead implemented vigorous state-directed industrial policy and 'instead of close and unfettered integration with the world economy, these countries only integrated to the extent and in directions in which it was beneficial for them to do so, pursuing ... strategic integration' [*South Centre, 1996: 4*].

UNRISD argues that the dominant processes underpinning globalisation are likely to be irreversible and thus they call for new approaches to tackle social problems. Much can be done, it states, to refurbish inherited institutions 'but because institutional changes come about through complex interactions between markets, technology, ideology, and social needs and pressures, it is difficult to predict what new configuration of institutions will emerge' [*UNRISD, 1995: v*].

## SOME IMPLICATIONS FOR DEVELOPMENT POLICY AND INSTITUTIONAL CHANGE

It is not necessary for all participants involved in the globalisation debate to use the same definition of the concept. However, when it comes to the policy debate, all participants must understand the distinction between 'shallow' and 'deep' integration. If it is agreed that the world is still only shallowly integrated, then there is no argument about the capacity of governments to intervene via policies and institutions. If, on the other hand, it is agreed that at least some parts of the world, either territorially or in relation to specific sectors or both, are 'deeply' integrated, then there may be some constraints on the ability of individual governments to make policy interventions. This is particularly true of small and poor countries. It is not true in the case of powerful countries, especially those in the Triad. And, it is in the interests of some global actors (especially the truly transnational corporations) that the myth of governmental policy impotence should obtain. In any case, the existence of 'constraints' is quite a different thing from a total incapacity to act. And, of course, if governments act in concert, using (reformed) international, regional, and inter-governmental institutions set up by them specifically for that purpose, then all governments have the capacity for policy interventions. What is needed is the political will – and some reform of the existing global institutional framework. In order to ensure that the outcomes are positive in relation to human development and human security, the participation and agreement of populations at all the various appropriate territorial levels would be required. Thus, the first step is to affirm that governments can act, that they can act in concert, and that international institutions can be used by them for policy interventions.

Beginning at the global level, the United Nations and its various agencies have long been acknowledged to be in need of reform. As Griffin and Khan put it:

> If at one extreme globalisation (in combination with subnationalism) has weakened the ability of the state to manage its national economy, at the other extreme it has begun to raise questions about how best to manage a truly global economy in the interests of participating countries, or more

accurately in the interests of the world's people, as a whole – some of whom are very poor [*Griffin and Khan, 1992: 52*].

They argue that, because existing international institutions are intergovernmental agencies rather than supranational ones, they were designed to serve a system of nation-states which were assumed to be capable of exercising sovereignty over their economic affairs. If the governments within the Triad perceive the world economy as 'deeply' globalising (or becoming so), they may consider it opportune to resurrect the proposals for Codes of Conduct for TNCS. There is nothing to stop them from doing so.

Most of the proposals for new initiatives are already well known. They include a UN Economic Security Council, a World Social Charter and a UN Agency for Women. Existing agencies in need of strengthening and revamping include the UN Industrial Organisation and the UN Environment Programme. Suggestions for mergers between existing institutions include those relating to trade and investment (WTO, UNCTAD, World Intellectual Property Organisation); development policy (World Bank, development related activities of the International Monetary Fund); and banking and finance (Bank for International Settlements and remaining activities of the IMF).

At the national level, one of the most important policy initiatives that governments of all countries, developing and industrialised alike, could take in the interests of promoting human security would be to incorporate into national policies all the relevant elements of the '20–20 compact' agreed at the Social Summit in Copenhagen in 1995, as well as those agreed at the Alma Ata ('Health for All by 2000') held in 1978, the Jomtien Conference ('Education for All') in 1990, the UN Environment Conference in Rio in 1992, and the UN Women's Conference in Beijing in 1995. The OECD/DAC has already established 'policy markers' to help track the compliance of DAC donors with the commitments they made at Rio, Copenhagen and Beijing. To date, it is only in relation to Copenhagen and the '20-20' compact that the policy marker has been quantified. It is appropriate for all governments to comply with the commitments that they made at these conferences – and for an international organisation to start tracking expenditures at national level through appropriate policy markers.

Another area where government policy is needed in a liberalising and globalising world economy is regulation. As privatisation expands and the state reduces its role as producer and provider, its role as protector becomes even more important and necessary. Stephens [*1996*] argues that the world has become very complex and even 'mystifying' for most people, such that 'scientific advance leaves us ignorant of how our food is produced, technology has injected permanent insecurity into our working lives ... [and] the pace of change leaves most of us unable to evaluate the risks' (*Financial Times*, 30–31

March 1996). Consequently, government must interpose itself and 'the state as provider is replaced by the state as regulator' [*ibid.*]. Moreover, as governments trim down the size of the public sector through privatisations, the need for regulation increases. Relating his argument to the UK, Stephens states: 'When water, gas and telephones were dispensed by public enterprises there was no need for regulators. Now we must have Ofwat, Ofgas, Oftel and a host of other regulators who oversee the private utility companies' [*ibid.*].

Although not *directly* involved in policy-making, the private sector (corporations, farmers, professional organisations) expends significant resources in all countries trying to influence government decisions and policies affecting their individual activities. In order to make the private sector (especially one operating in an environment that is increasingly privatised and deregulated) more accountable to people, increases in other forms of regulation are necessary. As also noted earlier, there are some moves afoot to persuade the corporate sector to become more accountable, not just to their employees and shareholders, but to the wider public. According to Dickson, one of the main leaders of the US corporate governance movement, the business sector's vast expenditure on Congressional lobbying, its ability to bend accounting rules and the legal system to its demands, and rocketing executive pay, all point to a lack of control (*Financial Times*, 15 July 1996). However, because he rejects government 'interference', he suggests that long-term institutional investors, particularly pension funds, should become 'corporate monitors'. Such an approach might be helpful in a large country like the United States, but in small countries, where there is a very limited pool of potential 'monitors' because of cross-cutting directorships as well as FDI in the corporate sector, it would be of limited use. The corporate sector and especially TNCs should certainly be strongly encouraged to become more responsible and sensitive to human security concerns, but if they fail to do so voluntarily, the 'encouragement' would need to be more regulatory in approach. More pressure would need to be applied by governmental and non-governmental actors to force the corporate sector to become more accountable.

Finally, community groups and the non-governmental organisations (NG0s) are an increasingly powerful force in national and international affairs. They span the whole spectrum of issues relating to human security concerns. Their views are routinely taken into account by the UN organisations when they are *planning* global conferences, as witness the 'parallel' NGO conferences at Rio, Copenhagen and Beijing. But these groups are dispersed, disconnected and fragmented. Despite some notable exceptions (for example, at Rio and Beijing), their successes tend to be rather limited at the *post*-conference stage, largely because of a lack of leverage at this stage when agreed resolutions are being considered (or ignored) in terms of implementation. Thus, another fruitful area of research could be an examination of the conditions which increase such leverage since it is only when all groups and classes are involved at the implementation stage, that human security concerns can be fully taken into account in a globalising and increasingly competitive world.

## REFERENCES


Bairoch, Paul and Richard Kozul-Wright, 1996, 'Globalisation Myths: Some Historical Reflections on Integration, Industrialisation and Growth in the World Economy', *UNCTAD Discussion Papers No.113,* March.

Bornschier, Volker, 1992, 'The European Community's Uprising: Grasping Toward Hegemony or Therapy against National Decline in the World Political Economy?', paper presented at the First European Conference of Sociology, Vienna, 26–29 Aug.

Buendia, Hernando Gomez, 1995, *The Limits of the Global Village: Globalisation, Nations and the State,* The United Nations University, World Institute for Development Economics Research, World Development Studies 5, Helsinki.

Business Week, 1996, 'The Business Week Global 1000: The Globetrotters Take Over', *Business Week,* 8 July 1996, pp.47–84.

Camdessus, Michel, 1996, as reported in *IMF Survey,* 1 July 1996, Washington, DC: IMF.

Cook, Paul and Colin Kirkpatrick, 1996, 'Globalisation, Regionalisation and Third World Development', mimeo, University of Manchester and University of Bradford.

Day, George and David Reibstein, 1996, 'Keeping Ahead in the Competitive Game', *Financial Times,* Mastering Management No.18, 1995–96.

Dickson, Martin, 1996, 'Solutions to a Global Problem, *Financial Times,* 15 July.

Economist, The, 1996, 'The C-word Strikes Back', *The Economist,* 1 June, p.84.

European Commission, DG VIII – Information/Documentation, 1996, 'The Way Europeans Perceive Developing Countries in 1995', April.

Federation of Swedish Industries (FSI), 1996, *Market Access in High-growth Asian Markets,*(by Thomas Hagdahl and Hans Ekdahl), Study No.3, Stockholm, 21 June.

Financial Times, 1996a, 'G7 Summit to Focus on Global Lack of Jobs', *Financial Times,* 1 April.

Financial Times, 1996b, 'Outlook for Jobs Remains Poor, Says OECD', *Financial Times,* 16 July.

Fortune, 1996, 'The Fortune Global 500: A Bigger Richer World', *Fortune,* 5 Aug., pp.71–121.

Freeman, Christopher, 1989, 'The Third Kondratieff Wave: Age of Steel, Electrification and Imperialism', in Kihlstrom *et al.* (eds.), *Festschrift in Honour of Lars Herlitz,* Gothenburg.

Friedman, Thomas, 1996, 'Revolt of the Wannabes: Globalisation Suffers a Backlash', *New York Times,* 7 Feb.

Galtung, Johan, 1976, 'Towards New Indicators of Development', *Futures,* June.

Griffin, Keith and Azizur Rahman Khan, 1992, 'Globalisation and the Developing World: An Essay on the International Dimensions of Development in the Post-Cold War Era', *Occasional Papers No.2,* Human Development Report Office, UNDP.

Hirst, Paul and Grahame Thompson, 1996, *Globalisation in Question,* Cambridge: Polity Press

Hobsbawm, Eric, 1994, *Age of Extremes: The Short Twentieth Century, 1914–1991,* London: Michael Joseph.

IMF, 1966, *IMF Survey,* Washington, DC, 1 July.

International Institute for Development Management (IMD), 1996, *The World Competitiveness Yearbook 1996,* IMD, Geneva.

Kapstein, Ethan B., 1996, 'Workers and the World Economy', *Foreign Affairs,* Vol.75, No.3, May–June.

Krugman, Paul, 1996, *Pop Internationalism,* Cambridge, MA: MIT Press.

McGrew, A., 1992, 'The Third World in the New Global Order', in T. Allen and A. Thomas (eds.), *Poverty and Development in the 1990s,* Oxford: Oxford University Press in association with the Open University.

O'Hearn, Denis, 1993, 'Global Competition, Europe and Irish Peripherality', *The Economic and Social Review*, Vol.24, No.2, Jan., pp.169–97.
Oman, Charles, 1994, *Globalisation and Regionalisation: The Challenge for Developing Countries*, Paris: OECD.
O'Neill, Helen, 1993, 'The Atlantic as a Moat: Are Europe and America Building Fortresses in a Regionalizing World Economy?', paper presented at an international conference on the North American Free Trade Area, Cormier Centre, Bishops University, Canada, 30 April.
Porter, Michael, 1990, *The Competitive Advantage of Nations*, London: Macmillan.
Sachs, Jeffrey and A. Warner, 1995, 'Economic Reform and the Process of Global Integration', *Brookings Papers on Economic Activity No.1*.
Sandholtz, Wayne and John Zysman, 1989, '1992: Recasting the European Bargain', *World Politics*, Vol.42, No.1, Oct., pp.95–128.
Schwab, Klaus and Claude Smadja, 1996, 'Start Taking the Backlash Against Globalisation Seriously', *International Herald Tribune*, 1 Feb..
Simai, Mihaly, 1995, 'Preface' in Buendia [*1995*].
Simai, Mihaly, 1996, 'Globalisation, Multilateral Cooperation and the Development Process: The UN Agenda and End-of-Century Realities', *Working Papers No.63*, Institute for World Economics, Hungarian Academy of Sciences, April.
South Centre, 1996, 'Liberalisation and Globalisation: The Issues at Stake for the South and for UNCTAD', *South Letter*, Vol.1, No.25.
Stephens, Philip, 1996, 'The Dangers of Deregulation', *Financial Times*, 30–31 March.
Suzman, Mark, 1996, 'Europe Gets Inclusive', *Financial Times*, 17 June.
Thurow, Lester, 1996, *The Future of Capitalism*, London: Nicholas Brealey.
United Nations, 1993, *World Investment Report*, New York, UN.
UNCTAD, 1991, 'Informal Encounter on International Governance: Trade in a Globalizing World Economy', Jakarta, Indonesia, 19 and 20 June.
UNCTAD, 1995, 'Environment, International Competitiveness and Development: Lessons from Empirical Studies', Report by the UNCTAD Secretariat, TD/B/WG.6/10, 12 Sept.
UNCTAD, 1996a, 'Promoting Growth and Sustainable Development in a Globalizing and Liberalizing World Economy', Pre-conference text, TD/367, 3 April.
UNCTAD, 1996b, *Globalisation and Liberalisation*, Report of the Secretary-General to the Ninth Conference.
UNCTAD, 1996c, 'Ninth Session of the United Nations Conference on Trade and Development (UNCTAD 1X): Midrand Declaration', *UNCTAD Bulletin*, April–June, p.3.
UNDP, 1994, *Human Development Report*, Oxford: Oxford University Press.
UNDP, 1996, *Human Development Report*, Oxford: Oxford University Press.
UNICE, 1994, 'Making Europe More Competitive: Towards World-Class Performance', *The UNICE Competitiveness Report 1994*.
UNRISD, 1995, *States of Disarray: The Social Effects of Globalisation*, Geneva: United Nations.
Wolf, Martin, 1996, 'The Global Economy Myth', *Financial Times*, 13 Feb., p.22.
World Economic Forum (WEF), 1996, *The Global Competitiveness Report 1996*, World Economic Forum, Geneva.

APPENDIX 1

COMPETITIVENESS RANKINGS OF SELECTED COUNTRIES BY IMD AND WEF, AND HDI RANKINGS BY UNDP FOR THE SAME COUNTRIES 1996

| Country | Competitiveness | | HDI |
|---|---|---|---|
| | IMD | WEF | |
| United States | 1 | 4 | 2 |
| Singapore | 2 | 1 | 34 |
| Hong Kong | 3 | 2 | 22 |
| Japan | 4 | 13 | 3 |
| Denmark | 5 | 11 | 17 |
| Norway | 6 | 7 | 5 |
| Netherlands | 7 | 17 | 4 |
| Luxembourg | 8 | 5 | 27 |
| Switzerland | 9 | 6 | 15 |
| Germany | 10 | 22 | 18 |
| New Zealand | 11 | 3 | 14 |
| Canada | 12 | 8 | 1 |
| Chile | 13 | 18 | 33 |
| Sweden | 14 | 21 | 9 |
| Finland | 15 | 16 | 6 |
| Austria | 16 | 19 | 13 |
| Belgium | 17 | 25 | 12 |
| Taiwan | 18 | 9 | * |
| UK | 19 | 15 | 16 |
| France | 20 | 23 | 7 |
| Australia | 21 | 12 | 11 |
| Ireland | 22 | 26 | 19 |
| Malaysia | 23 | 10 | 53 |
| Israel | 24 | 24 | 24 |
| Iceland | 25 | 27 | 8 |
| China | 26 | 36 | 108 |
| Korea | 27 | 20 | 29 |
| Italy | 28 | 41 | 20 |
| Spain | 29 | 32 | 10 |
| Thailand | 30 | 14 | 52 |
| Philippines | 31 | 31 | 95 |
| Argentina | 32 | 37 | 30 |
| Colombia | 33 | 40 | 49 |
| Czech Republic | 34 | 35 | 37 |
| Turkey | 35 | 42 | 84 |
| Portugal | 36 | 34 | 35 |
| Brazil | 37 | 48 | 58 |
| India | 38 | 45 | 135 |
| Hungary | 39 | 46 | 46 |
| Greece | 40 | 39 | 21 |
| Indonesia | 41 | 30 | 102 |
| Mexico | 42 | 33 | 48 |
| Poland | 43 | 44 | 56 |
| South Africa | 44 | 43 | 100 |
| Venezuela | 45 | 47 | 44 |
| Russia | 46 | 49 | 57 |
| Jordan | * | 28 | 70 |
| Egypt | * | 29 | 106 |
| Peru | * | 38 | 91 |

* not included in rankings

*Sources:* IMD, *The World Competitiveness Yearbook*, 1996; WEF, *Global Competitiveness Report*, 1996; UNDP, *Human Development Report*, 1996.

# Globalisation and Regional Integration

SANDRO SIDERI

*Globalisation represents the most significant aspect of current international relations. Yet, a shift towards regionalism and bloc formation is increasingly apparent. This study considers the impact of globalisation on the nation-state, the emergence of regionalism, and the complications created by the rising demands of devolution at sub-national level. A review of regional integration shows that whilst regionalism protects against the worst effects of globalisation and unites countries, it also encourages sub-national movements, thus heightening the dangers of national divisiveness. Yet the alternative to globalisation mitigated by regionalism and devolution is either unfettered 'global neoclassicism' or feuding trading blocs, both of which mean further marginalisation for the developing world as well as for some economic sectors and social groups in the developed countries.*

Alongside globalisation and its accompanying effects, a shift towards regionalism is also occurring. It is our intention to analyse these two seemingly contrasting phenomena, assess their relevance and their eventual connection. Section I addresses globalisation and its impact, particularly on the nation-state. Section II considers the emergence of regionalism, its causes, and the complications created by the rising demand of devolution. A number of case studies of regional integration – Europe, North America, Asia, Latin America and the rest of the Third World – are analysed in depth. Some reflections and tentative conclusions are presented in section III.

## I. GLOBALISATION AND ITS IMPACT

Globalisation is essentially a process driven by economic forces. Its immediate causes are, in this order, the spatial reorganisation of production, international trade, and the integration of financial markets. It affects most capitalist

---

Sandro Sideri, Professor of International Economics, Institute of Social Studies, The Hague, The Netherlands. E-mail: Sideri@ISS.NL. The author wishes to thank Professor J. Hilhorst and two anonymous referees for their helpful comments on an earlier draft.

economic and social relations and represents by far the most significant aspect of current international relations.[1] Being largely responsible for the end of the cold war and therefore for universalising the operations of capitalism, albeit if unevenly, globalisation is reorganising power at world level as well as at national or sub-national levels. The apparent universalisation of capitalism justifies the contention that there is a single path of economic, political, and social development for the entire world – free markets and political liberalism. Hence Fukuyama's contention of 'the end of history'.

By allowing nations to specialise in different branches of manufacturing and even in different stages of production within a specific industry, international trade has contributed to the creation of the present global manufacturing system. This dispersion of production capacity to a wide number of developed countries (DC) and developing countries (LDC), each performing tasks where it has a cost advantage,[2] has been made possible both by new forms of investment and financing, promoted by specific government policies, and by technological advance. The latter has prompted that 'knowledge era' in which the creation, storage and use of knowledge are becoming the basic economic activity. The result is distinctive patterns of spatial and social organisation.

Globalisation implies both multilateralism (mainly multilateral trade liberalisation and trade policy) and micro-economic phenomena, particularly firms' competitiveness at the global level and the profound transformation of work organisation.[3] In fact, the creation of a world market for labour and production has been made possible by the segmentation of the manufacturing process into multiple partial operations which, combined with the development of cheap transportation and communications networks, has brought the increasing division of production into separate stages carried out in different locations. This massive industrial de-location or redeployment of productive activities ('global localisation' is the expression coined by Sony's boss Akio Morita), supported by direct foreign investment, has made it possible 'to explode the value-added chain' and the creation of the multinational corporation (MNC), causing, in turn, large-scale migratory flows and the feminisation of labour. As domestic industries transfer a growing amount of their production abroad, land becomes less valuable than technology, knowledge and direct investment, and 'the function of the state is being further redefined' [*Rosecrance, 1996: 46*].

Clearly, globalisation is affecting the class structure, the labour process, the application of technology, the structure and organisation of capital, family life, the organisation of cities and the use of space. The spatial reorganisation of production has also been enhanced by the need to cope with exchange rate fluctuations resulting from financial deregulation. The world economy is therefore characterised by a growing share of GDP depending directly on international trade (the share of trade in world output increased from 7 to 20 per cent between 1950 and 1995 [*Boltho, 1996: Table 2, 256*]) and foreign capital and globalisation indicates the integration of free markets, financial flows, trade and information.[4]

The quickening of international competition and the transformation of production systems are fast creating a truly international labour market 'and workers are more likely to be in the service sector, working part-time or engaged in informal sector activities' [*UNRISD, 1995: 9*]. Hence the risk that globalisation and technological change penalise and marginalise the less educated and less skilled labour – the poor in the US and the unemployed in Europe – while economic growth and expansion of firms no longer imply increased employment. Having established a very powerful set of rules and standards for how countries must behave if they are to attract investment capital, globalisation causes higher remuneration of capital because of its greater global mobility[5] compared to labour.

Labour reductions, made possible by technological and organisational changes, also contribute to the higher remuneration of capital. Clearly productivity increases no longer necessarily translate into more jobs and higher wages. Whilst in the past 'higher profits meant more job security and better wages', global competition 'tends to delink the fate of the corporation from the fate of its employees' [*Schwab and Smadja, 1996*]. Nor is it any longer possible to assume that jobs which are eliminated in advanced economies end up in LDCs, since their opening up to world commerce – synonymous with integration – attracts not only investment but also world-competitive imports which destroy local manufactures. Contrary to what is happening in the traditional industrial countries, the linkage between growth of real output and employment and labour income remains an important aspect of the pattern of development and industrialisation in Asia, and particularly Asia Pacific.

The emergence of a global economy entails the diffusion to distant countries of identical consumer goods, including consumerism, patterns of demand and the homogenisation of market rules and structures. It also entails the spread of values, such as the dominance of market forces, and a preference for liberal democracy, even though this is more contentious than the preeminence of the market. The growing exchange of goods across frontiers also involves that of 'bads' such as narcotic drugs, pollution, etc. [*Griffin and Khan, 1992: 63*]. The phenomenon of globalisation is necessarily a 'totalising or homogenising force' whose scope extends beyond the realm of economics to embrace science, politics, culture and life styles. Whilst it 'articulates with local structures in diverse ways' and allows 'distinct regional divisions of labour', globalisation enables 'the economy, politics, culture and ideology of one country to penetrate another', and distinct regional divisions of labour are still 'ultimately subordinate to the globalisation process' [*Mittelman, 1994: 428, 430*].

The analysis of the effects of globalisation is much helped by the discussion on whether growing globalisation leads to an international economy or to a really global one. According to Hirst and Thompson [*1992: 358-60*] a world-wide international economy is one centred on nation-states, their growing strategic interdependence built first around the importance of international trade (the volume of world trade continues to expand at roughly twice the rate of growth of world production), but progressively replaced by foreign investment. In this system the 'international and domestic policy fields either remain separated as distinct levels of governance or, allegedly, they work "automatically"', that is, under the impact of unorganised or spontaneous market forces, as with the Gold Standard with its overt domestic policy interventions. The development of the current system is largely the result of the absence of a global hegemony and of political resistance to delegating authority to a supranational authority capable of generating a more disciplined order.

Within this world-wide international economic system, the MNC has arisen and matured. Like most companies trading from their bases in distinct national economies, the MNC has not necessarily lost a national identity, a fact which explains why it seems inappropriate to call it a Transnational Company (TNC).[6] Since 'national policies remain viable, indeed, essential in order to preserve the distinct styles and strengths of the national economy base and the companies that trade from it', so the nation-state's regulation of business and negotiation of trade agreements provides some governance to the international economy [*Hirst and Thompson, 1995: 424, 408; 1992: 393*]. An important characteristic of the current international economic system, which is not entirely new,[7] is the bias to disinflationary macroeconomic policies which the international capital market entails [*Hutton, 1995: 306*]. The following arguments can be made against the thesis of a truly globalised economy: (i) the number of genuine TNCs is small, most of what appears as supra-national being due to the rapid growth in inter-firm partnerships and joint-ventures; (ii) both foreign trade flows and patterns of foreign direct investment are highly concentrated in DCs and a few Newly Industrialised Countries (NIC); (iii) financial markets are not necessarily beyond regulation, as demonstrated by the success of the Plaza and Louvre accords; and (iv) even the rapid development of some areas of the Third World is not unprecedented and often depends on an authoritarian government's ability to repress political protests.

The world-wide economy is instead 'an aggregate of nationally-located functions' of truly global markets and production, as 'distinct national economies are subsumed and rearticulated into the system by essentially international processes and transactions' dominated by international financial markets and trans-national companies. National policies become then 'futile, since economic outcomes are determined wholly by world market forces and by internal decisions of trans-national companies'. The transformation of the MNC into the TNC makes it a major player in the world economy, a player that cannot be controlled or constrained by the policies of particular national states [*Hirst and Thompson, 1992: 360–62; 1995: 414*].

Even if the globalisation observable today is considered to be still quite limited, the scope for state autonomy is certainly reduced since its control of economic and social processes within its territory has become less exclusive, and its ability to maintain national distinctiveness and cultural homogeneity has been curtailed. Once considered the basic unit of geopolitics, the dominant role and independence of national states are being undermined by diverse challenges, all connected to the process of globalisation. According to *The Economist* (23 Dec. 1995, p.17) these challenges come from: (i) the transportation revolution which has 'demolished any lingering belief in national self-sufficiency'; (ii) the materialisation of the third dimension -the air – in the use of force which has changed the nature of war and left countries naked to air attacks; and (iii) the information revolution and the globalisation of knowledge which are 'blurring the sense of national separateness'. By loosening the state's exclusive control of its territory, communications and information technologies are 'reducing its capacity for cultural control and homogenisation', thus making exclusion more difficult [*Hirst and Thompson, 1995: 419*].[8] Furthermore, as Griffin and Khan [*1992: 63*] rightly observe, the arms technology and the militarisation of the oceans and the outer space have made political boundaries largely irrelevant in most of the world. In the absence of an immediate enemy – as occurred at the end of the cold war when Western countries lost the common purpose under which they had co-operated for so many years – the nation-state becomes less significant to the citisen.

It seems then that the diminished role of the state is accompanied by, and results from, the emergence of a multi-layered and overlapping system of governance by often competing institutions, agencies and centres of power. This complex system entails different levels and functions which vary from the global level, to the regional, the statal, sub-national, industrial district, and 'entity' level. There is also another possible level, the trans-regional one made up of agreements between different regional groupings, for example, APEC (see later), the US and the European Union (EU) agreement reconciling different approaches to competition policy, and, even more appropriately, the proposed Transatlantic Free Trade Area between NAFTA (Northern American Free Trade Area) and the EU.[9]

Once it becomes apparent that the state has been internationalised [*Cox, 1981*] and 'no longer serves primarily as a buffer or shield against the world economy' but, instead, has become an agent in the process of globalisation

[*Mittelman, 1994: 431*], counter reactions develop: the emergence, or re-emergence, of local movements seeking autonomy or even independence from present nation-states and a rush towards regionalism10, within which the latter's sovereignty is also going to be curtailed. One manifestation of the conflict between the fragmentation and the unification generated by globalisation, a conflict that is shaping the world order, is the rapid homogenisation of markets and the rise of ethnic, cultural and regional identities, so that the conflict is then between economic integration and political separatism. Among these fragmenting tensions must be included the emergence of 'entities', such as the Palestinian Authority or the Bosnian accord. These are newly formed polities – not-quite nations, often the remnants of old nations – created by nationalist forces liberated at the end of the cold war. A phenomenon often identified with 'overlapping sovereignty', the most immediate task is to avoid further fragmentation and/or killing on large scale [*Dickey, 1995: 22, 25*]. It is also argued that as the world becomes more democratic, so it splits into smaller political jurisdictions which from an economic point of view tend to be too small. If 'democratisation leads to secessions' – that is, 'too many nations may emerge as democracy spreads' and separation 'is to produce government policies that are "closer to the people"' [*Bolton et al., 1996: 701*] – economic integration also tends to encourage smaller entities to go it alone. Thus 'political separatism should go hand in hand with economic integration' [*Alesina and Spolaore, 1995: 2–3, 22*]. Since national self-determination derives its legitimacy from the notions of democracy and cultural homogeneity, when the state pushes its rights to the limits, devolution is no longer considered sufficient and secession becomes associated with freedom and democracy.

The various governing powers 'need to be tied together'. 'Gaps' between different agencies and dimensions of governance must be closed by what Hirst and Thompson [*1995: 423*] aptly call a process of 'suturing'; a process to which regionalisation may effectively contribute. The more extreme globalisation theorists, like Ohmae [*1993*], consider any attempt to build an institutional architecture to govern this complex system to be unnecessary, either because they believe it to be ungovernable, or because they see the market as a satisfactory mode of governance.[11] Yet, markets and companies cannot exist without the protection of the public power (even deregulation requires the active intervention of the state), just as 'the open international economy depends ultimately on Western (particularly US) force and upon active public regulation backed by legal enforcement', i.e. by nation-states [*Hirst and Thompson, 1995: 427*]. Like the national market, the international one must be 'embedded' in a context of non-market social institutions and regulatory mechanisms, lest instability and inefficiency prevail [*Polanyi, 1957: Chs. 5 and 6*]. Only the most extreme advocates of economic liberalism, or 'global neoclassicism' (see later) deny that a free market is not a state of nature, but a state which must be produced and regulated, just as property rights, without which there is no market, are not endowed by nature. Market and civil society cannot develop spontaneously, as the liberal myth assumes, but are moulded by the state and their effectiveness is not necessarily proportional to their utilisation of democratic practices. Yet the global economy appears 'increasingly disembedded from the domestic social compact between state and society on which the political viability of the post-war international order has hinged' [*Ruggie, 1995: 525*]. Gilpin [*1987: 389*] also argues that the growth in global interdependence has undermined 'the postwar "compromise of embedded liberalism" and the clash between domestic autonomy and international norms reasserted itself in the major economies of the international system'.

While international markets have eroded political sovereignty, the state is increasingly unable to act unilaterally on economic matters and achieve its objective. In fact, the globalisation of currency markets has made it more difficult for central banks to control money supply; that of bond markets has made it more difficult for the state to determine nominal rates of interest; transfer pricing by MNCs has made it easier for them to shift their profit tax liabilities from high to low taxation countries; and the ability of large firms to locate their fixed investment almost anywhere in the world has reduced the power of the state not only to regulate industry through taxation, but also to impose minimum wages, environmental controls, health and safety standards, or anything else [*Griffin and Khan, 1992: 61*]. The sise and behaviour of MNCs[12] have radically undermined conventional approaches to industrial theory and policy, while their rising importance has enhanced their influence over governments and their action in defence of the global market, making them into formidable obstacles to the protection of sectors less able to cope with global competition.

The erosion of national borders is being accelerated by the emergence of global collaborative R&D programmes, including Europe's supra-national research schemes. The globalisation of R&D facilities is expected to continue at a fast pace for three main reasons [*Sigurdson, 1996: 25*]: (i) the ongoing process of mergers and acquisitions naturally leads to more and more R&D facilities being controlled by companies with their manufacturing and/or headquarters in another country; (ii) the need to adapt increasingly sophisticated products and systems to local conditions requires the localisation of R&D; and (iii) more and more companies are sourcing their knowledge generation in countries and regions where such resources can more easily be obtained and where the costs may be considerably lower.

If there has been a strengthening of the government's influence on the location of economic activity by international companies, the emphasis of government actions has shifted from removing structural distortions in domestic markets to facilitating the supply capabilities of their own firms 'by lowering transaction-related barriers, and by fostering the upgrading and structural redeployment of the assets within their jurisdiction' [*Dunning, 1993: 10–11, 345*].

Leaving aside the question of survival, the legitimacy, relevance and effectiveness of the nation state are seriously challenged by the growing need to establish some form of governance of the globalised economy.[13] This governance, however, cannot be assured by the existing set of international institutions which, being mostly intergovernmental rather than supranational agencies, are being rendered ineffective and obsolete by the weakening of the state through globalisation. The task of global governance is, however, complicated by the realisation of the difficulties inherent in any attempt to regulate global markets and that growing interdependence might even cause disintegration.[14] In addition, there is the problem posed by the diseconomies of scale, which would certainly affect the management structure required by such a task, and at the same time the growing demand for more citisen participation which requires some decentralisation of the decision-making process [*Arndt, 1993: 280–81*]. Furthermore,

> there is now no doctrinally grounded and technically effective regime of macro-economic management that can produce sustained expansionary effects, [since] neither the financial markets not the Brussels bureaucracy ... can impose or secure the forms of social cohesion and the policies that follow from them that national governments can [*Hirst and Thompson, 1992: 371–2*].

Meanwhile the growing degree of internationalisation of business forces governments as well as firms, particularly in industries dominated by MNCs, to adopt globally oriented macro-organisational strategies and micro-economic policies respectively, which, in turn, require a reappraisal of available policies [*Dunning, 1993: 9*].

Undoubtedly, growing globalisation will focus increasing attention on the issue of international governance in the future [*Griffin and Khan, 1992: 83*][15] for the good reason that global integration has seriously changed the rules of macroeconomic policy or rather 'the timing and the severity of the consequences' should these be ignored (*The Economist*, 7 Oct.1996, p.14).

The demise of the Bretton Woods system and the shift to floating exchange rates has accelerated the internationalisation of capital markets, the expansion of international lending and security dealing, and the development of several new instruments to cope with the associated risk. This has caused a shift of power from policy makers to financial markets, weakening both the policy choices available to governments and the effectiveness of the instruments they can use.[16] But globalisation has also made financial markets much more volatile and local capital vulnerable to the strategies of corporate raiders. Hence the need for new norms for this market, or even an institutional framework. This need derives from an imbalance between the global dimension of the problems and the national dimension of the government structure of each economy. It remains unsatisfied because it requires co-operation among the principal governments.

Although many governments insist on merely addressing national political agendas, it is 'the present urge to deregulate the state out of existence' which threatens international co-operation in many areas of macroeconomic policy [*Boltho, 1996: 259*]. This significant change in the regulatory climate, with emphasis on competition and internationalisation, reflects a distinctly anti-Keynesian view (namely that governments had the duty and the power to enhance national welfare through discretionary policy action) which Schor [*1992*] aptly refers to as 'global neoclassicism'. The same change in the regulatory climate militates against the institutionalisation of international co-operation, making it more difficult and less effective.[17]

A similar process of deregulation and globalisation has occurred within related professional activities. Greater competition in these services has led to the creation of new categories of specialists, such as 'design professionals' and to the emergence of 'mega firms' and 'factories'. In the field of law, globalisation is stimulating a process of homogenisation and interconnection between national legal systems. Alongside the necessary technical communication infrastructure, particularly the global mass media, these developments raise 'the spectre of cultural homogenisation often in the form of "cultural imperialism" or "Americanisation"' [*Featherstone, 1990: 10*].

In the present context of internationalisation of economic activities,[18] companies strive to improve their overall competitiveness in major global and regional markets. The need to pool high risks and costs, to reduce time spent on research and development for product development, and to gain access to markets, drives them into finding global partners so as to mesh industries into networks with a strategic and long-term nature. Consequently, 'the modern globalising company has more and more taken on the character of a network or set of networks in which different types of co-operation, and forms of agreement, have become an integral part of the company itself [*Sigurdson, 1996: 3–4*].[19] Since even the largest MNCs find it increasingly difficult to remain sufficiently competitive in all parts of the value-added chain, strategic alliances offer the option of concentrating on core competencies and of accessing remaining inputs from partners. The expansion of strategic alliances, a transborder corporate superstructure which mix and match nationalities, erodes the possibility of controlling the national system of innovation.[20]

As 'economic globalisation changes the spatial dimension of MNCs and creates a need for more flexible production and marketing systems, and new forms of organisation' [*Dunning, 1993: 202*], the global MNC is becoming a down-sised, outsourced and largely stateless web of cross-border corporate alliances, spanning different industries and countries. The companies entering these strategic alliances, held together by common goals, act almost as a single firm, the so-called 'relationship-enterprise'. Such an arrangement is also useful for side-stepping controls, like anti-trust laws, which governments place on companies; controls which even MNCs have not yet been able to escape since the home base maintained by most of them makes them less global than they appear (*The Economist*, 6 Feb. 1993, p.65). By the same token, however, the globalisation of markets mainly takes place within a market structure characterised by clear oligopolistic features such as high concentration, instability and asymmetry, and by the convergence of consumer needs and preferences' at similar income levels [*Dunning, 1993: 202*].

If the process of globalisation has surely quickened the pace of change, economic as well as political, the speed and complexity by which capital, goods, services and people are moving around makes it difficult to predict even the immediate future. Hence the prevailing sense of a 'great global uncertainty' [*Robertson, 1990: 16*]. This uncertainty is further fuelled by the fact that

> political maps are being drawn and redrawn as myriad ethnic or political groups emerge to make new claims and stake out new territory. These changes have generated enormous social tensions that development policies have failed to tackle head-on [while] power has been transferred to institutions that have consistently ignored the social implications of their actions [*UNRISD, 1995: 8*].

One of the most dangerous temptations of globalisation correctly identified by Griffin and Khan [*1992: 66*] is the tendency 'to skimp on higher education in order not to lose resources through brain drain and to run a low wage, low human development economy in order to keep costs low and international competition at bay'.

In support of the recurring suggestion that globalisation fosters inequality among countries and affects some countries' ability to achieve higher incomes, Krugman and Venables [*1995*] have developed a formal model which explains how the differentiation of countries into a rich core and a poor periphery takes place only after the world economy has reached a certain critical level of integration. Afterwards the rise of the core's income is partly at the expense of the periphery – the 'unequal development' of the 1960s and 1970s. Only when the process of integration has proceeded far enough to erode the advantages of the core, does the periphery's income start to rise 'may be partly at the core's expense'.

In addition, two issues contribute towards increasing hostility to globalisation: (i) cultural diversity, outside the Western world; and (ii) fears of a loss of social cohesion and economic well-being in the Western countries. Differences in cultural preferences are brought to the fore by the acceleration of globalisation and the inclusion of former Socialist countries and larger Asian economies into the process. The danger of 'cultural pollution' has been attributed to audio-visuals and foreign companies' access to the print and film media, including conditions for television transmissions, and also to advertising, retailing and banking. Even the harmonisation of standards, which facilitates international exchange and renders products and services cheaper, becomes objectionable when one considers that it also erodes distinctions between societies. The cry of clash of values or ethics becomes unavoidable when attempting to build mechanisms to secure compliance with labour practices, human rights or environmental protection, by means of measures such as sanctions.

The accommodation of different business practices between countries whose approach to environmental protection and restrictions on child labour are sharply at odds is intrinsically hard and conflictive, such that it may generate a backlash against the process of trade liberalisation. Even defining minimum international standards relating to the terms and conditions of employment, and the environment,[21] generates resistances and requires interventionist measures that contradict the process of globalisation. The West's fears relate to the depressing effect that international trade may have on the real wages of unskilled workers. Hence the demand for restrictions on 'unfair trade'.[22] Populist hostility to globalisation has begun to materialise as well as to regional agreements with less developed economies, for example, American opposition to NAFTA and European dissatisfaction with EU's eventual inclusion of Eastern European countries, and international agencies like WTO. Hence the preference for regional arrangements between rather similar economies which, being able to compete constructively, could avoid the destructive social consequences caused by a global system of unrestrained competition, largely influenced by the MNCs' increasingly warlike fashion behaviour, which 'leads to winner take-all situations': those who come out on top win and those who lose risk becoming the left-behinds [*Schwab and Smadja, 1996*]. If competition between firms in different countries can never be 'fair', it may be so when taking place in the same country or within a regional bloc. In the last resort, the integration of different economies into a single market transforms international trade into a domestic exchange.

Notwithstanding the fact that 'the politics of managing globalisation will not be easy' [*Cable, 1996: 246*], globalisation is clearly here to stay and will exercise an increasing influence on the pace and pattern of growth of the world economy and hence on the distribution of income and wealth. The large-scale disruptions arising from the process of globalisation are generating, in turn, sustained pressure for self-protection; a contradiction that clearly characterises a process as complex as globalisation, and which simultaneously leads to opportunities and challenges.

An important phenomenon which accompanies, or is caused by, the process of globalisation, is the rise of regional trading blocs,[23] which pose a special challenge to the multilateral system, hence to the global economy. This does not imply, however, that trade blocs will necessarily reverse globalisation, but they may, ultimately, contribute to its development. In both DCs and LDCs regionalism appears as a response to the declining effectiveness of the state and the need to shield some sectors and some areas from the less desirable effects of growing global competitiveness among nations. Hence, states try to control at regional level (for example, by industrial policy) what they find increasingly difficult to manage at national level and impossible at global level (notwithstanding the efforts to promote international co-operation based on home country control of MNCs).

Despite the claims of the globalisation enthusiasts, nation-states and, increasingly, trade blocs appear to remain the dominant players in a fragmented and unstable world characterised by free trade within each of these blocs and managed trade between them and other countries [*Sideri, 1993*]. And while the end of bipolarism, following the dismissal of the Cold War, heightens the danger of continuous frictions and tensions,[24] 'paradoxically, globalisation engenders the regionalisation of conflict' [*Mittelman, 1994: 440*], even though it seems very unlikely that regional arrangements could spark a global trade war [*Perroni and Whalley, 1996*]. Undoubtedly, integration of nations has ambiguous economic benefits and certainly carries political costs, both largely related to the level of development of the country in question.

## II. THE RESPONSE OF REGIONALISM

In general, the need to adapt to the evolution of the world economic and political system explains the renewed interest in the potential of intra-regional co-operation through formal regional integration agreements (RIA), both multilateral and bilateral, or through different kinds of informal arrangements. For most DCs the aim of regionalism is 'to recapture collective autonomy in relation to the United States, and to begin to organise a competitive response to the Japanese challenge' [*Streeck and Schmitter, 1991: 149*]. In the case of many LDCs the need to adapt to globalisation is complemented by the fact that the previous industrialisation strategy, namely import substitution, has come to be considered inadequate and to be replaced by one centred on exporting finished products and international competitiveness.[25]

Naturally, the constraints imposed by the process of globalisation matter much more for medium and smaller countries than for the major powers.[26] In the global, multilateral economy market sise strongly defines a country's negotiating power; thus the potential contribution of regional groupings [*Oman, 1994: 29*] in order to overcome the limitations faced by each country separately. Furthermore, as it is now widely recognised that economies of scale and the need to limit international labour mobility imply large nations (although large sise also brings costs in the form of a large heterogeneous population), regional integration enables both objectives to be met whilst allowing greater autonomy to sub-national entities (and so reducing the costs of heterogeneity).

The proliferation of RIAs which started in the early 1980s represents the third wave of regionalism in this century, following that of the 1930s and the 1950–60s. Whereas the RIAs of the 1930s largely aimed to help countries withdraw from the world economy, and those of the second wave among LDCs were closely related to import-substitution strategies,[27] the present wave is driven by the desire to facilitate participation in the world economy. Hence the declared aim of these arrangements is to pursue liberalisation and export- and foreign investment-led strategies. Whilst the second wave of regional integration represented an attempt by LDCs to find an alternative to closer links with the industrial world, the present wave is seen as an attempt to strengthen the vertical as well as the horizontal links. Furthermore, present RIAs are characterised by broader scope and tend to involve North and South economies. At any rate, more than 60 per cent of world trade now takes place within regional integration schemes.

Since the overall objective of these RIAs is to enhance good and factor mobility while at the same time limiting the threat to territorially defined markets, most of them embody principles of managed as opposed to totally free trade. Hence the problem is how they can represent a route to multilateral free trade and the WTO's ultimate objective, that is, whether regionalism ultimately complements the process of trade liberalisation or leads to the fragmentation of the world economy into feuding trading blocs.[28] A real paradox is that while LDCs have finally come to accept the case for free trade, DCs have been gradually turning away from it through various forms of creeping administrative protection. The current movement towards regional trading blocs is a culmination of this trend towards so-called managed trade [*Lal, 1993: 352*].[29]

Yet, such fragmentation may reduce but not necessarily stop the process of globalisation, because important progress in liberalising world trade has been made through unilateral actions and bilateral and regional agreements, particularly in the EC and NAFTA [*Boltho, 1996: 250*]. If bilateral and regional agreements are a potentially useful means of reducing trade barriers, competition between regional blocs may increase the danger of global conflict, whose origin may lie in instability in the marginalised Third World (hence Mittelman's [*1994: 441*] 'truncated globalisation'); instability caused by poverty and undemocratic rule, but also by deeper cultural and political prejudices in antagonistic blocs.

By eroding national sovereignty, growing globalisation and interdependence help to unleash demands emerging, or re-emerging, from below.[30] The forces of cultural pluralism and of the so-called 'sub-nationalism' [*ibid.: 432*], grow stronger with the weakening of the state, but also in reaction to the homogenisation accompanying globalisation. Although it takes many forms, at the most general level sub-nationalism 'can be seen as manifestation of a search for community or identity different from the community or identity offered by shared citisenship of an existing state'. Yet, the search is sometimes accompanied by intolerance since these movements, when carried to excess, become 'narrow and exclusive, socially divisive and sources of communal strife' [*Griffin and Khan, 1992: 75, 77*]. This means that while globalisation is accompanied by widespread acceptance of the forms of democracy, the resistance to globalisation by the growing number of left-behinds, who experience the broadening of the distance between themselves and the force thy are ruled by, may turn rather undemocratic. In fact, as widening globalisation causes growing internal marginalisation, widening democratisation offers undemocratic and/or religious parties the means to exploit this coincidence to take power. This allows governments to justify their authoritarian rule in order to maintain their countries' competitiveness within a global system.

Devolution of power – that is, the assignment of the responsibility for governing – to emerging sub-national entities may be easier within the context of a regional scheme than within a single nation-state. Furthermore, the negative impact of the various types of diseconomies of scale that accompany the creation of smaller organisational units may be limited or eliminated by liberalisation and the availability of a wider regional market, and by transferring some administrative tasks and responsibilities to the regional power. Channelled in a constructive direction, the forces driving sub-nationalism can achieve the community and identity they seek, while enriching the region as well.

In Europe the possibility that geographical areas which form part of the territory of EU member states could become politically independent regions within the EU framework, their citisens being citisens of Europe, is currently being discussed. The main advantages of what Drèze has called a 'Europe of regions' are that (i) more autonomy may lead to efficiency gains; and (ii) this arrangement may provide a more efficient framework for the exercise of regional autonomy than the alternatives of political independence or greater autonomy within the existing nation-state [*Drèze, 1993: 266*]. The standardisation process implicit in regional integration brings differences between regions or sub-national units to the fore, creating new opportunities for the latter's independence under the umbrella of the supranational unit. Regional integration facilitates sub-national movements because it tends to reduce the cost of secession. The transformation of these movements into autonomous entities functioning within the regional scheme could be partially or totally financed by the supra-national government, depending on whether the countries of which they were formerly a part are willing to contribute to such an arrangement.

The loss of sovereignty involved in supra-regional institutions seems more acceptable than that implied by remote international agencies in which the weight of most countries is practically nil. Considering the difficulties of creating institutionalised governance mechanisms for the world economy and the limitations of national policies, sidelined by world market forces, many countries may turn to regionalism. The latter appears in fact useful for managing both the loss of control generated by the process of globalisation and the pressures for devolution of power and diversification emanating from below [*Sideri, 1995*]. The sharing of common rules and institutions with other nation-states allows the concession of more autonomy to sub-national entities, while regional governance may also compensate for the ineffectiveness of national policies.

Also important for resorting to regionalism is a felt need, if rarely openly stated, by countries in Europe and elsewhere to avoid the establishment of a liberalised global economy in which the US, being the single hegemonic power, maintains the right to make exceptions in the pursuit of its own interests [*Bienefeld, 1994: 45*]. Such a focus may serve to strengthen the regional group's unity but is less useful for promoting international governance, including the re-regulation of the international economy.

Yet even Ohmae [*1993: 78, 81*], who considers the nation-state to be 'an unnatural, even dysfunctional, unit for organising human activity and managing economic endeavour in a borderless world',[31] theorises the relevance of 'region states' as natural economic zones of between 5 to 20 million people, defined less by their economies of scale in production and more by their having reached efficient economies of scale in their consumption, infrastructure and professional services. Being shaped by modern marketing techniques and technologies, these 'region states' are a far cry from the present conception of the nation-state as an embodiment of common history, values and culture. What is more interesting about these 'region states' is the possibility that they represent a stepping stone not so much to globalisation but rather to trade bloc formation or, alternatively, the outcome of the breaking of a trade bloc or something in between the latter and a return to nation-states.

If national protection, especially in small countries, entails high costs in terms of the economies of scale foregone, a generally inefficient cost structure, absence of competition, and a lower and more unequally distributed income, these negative effects are lessened in regional trading blocs which become even more useful when the expansion of the world economy is only proceeding slowly.[32] This means that 'the macro-economic policies in the OECD countries are likely to determine the relative strength of the forces of globalisation and regionalisation' [*Griffin and Khan, 1992: 68–9*].

Given that regionalism seems to occur alongside the spread of globalisation, it is plausible to link these two phenomena and view regionalism as an attempt to reduce the pace of globalisation and/or to minimise the cost and pain of the latter. This does not imply that steps towards greater regional integration are always defensive in nature; they can also be stepping stones to a more open world economy. Regionalism is not a process with uniform characteristics, but one occurring in many shapes and sises and responding to a variety of forces. Yet whether or not globalisation continues and if it does how it will develop, will depend largely on what happens to regionalism. There are those who already fear that 'the world trading system is currently in danger of entering the zone of excessive regionalisation' [*Frankel et al., 1995: 92*].

As to the effects of preferential trading arrangements (PTA) on the level of welfare and on the drive towards multilateral liberalisation, the traditional theory, based on the second best approach, provides no definite answers. The net effect of the reduction or removal of trade barriers owing to PTAs on member countries' welfare is an empirical problem whose solution depends on the relative sise of 'trade creation' and 'trade diversion', the two main static effects recognised by these agreements. At any rate, when less efficient producers within PTAs replace more efficient ones outside it, world welfare declines.

Only with the addition of dynamic effects [*Baldwin, 1989*] can it be argued that the increase of member countries' income more than offsets trade diversion, hence raising outside welfare. Therefore, the impact of PTAs on multilateral liberalisation largely depends on the rules governing their formation. It has been shown [*Kemp and Wan, 1976*] that in order to improve external welfare it is sufficient to offset any potential trade diversion created by a PTA by reducing external tariffs. This can be considered as an incentive to expand membership until multilateral free trade is reached; the first best that maximises global welfare. Yet the rules of the General Agreement on Tariffs and Trade (GATT) 'ignore the issue of trade diversion and make no attempt to implement rules based on the Kemp/Wan insights' [*Lawrence, 1994: 369*]. GATT article 24 allows the formation of PTAs provided that external tariffs are not raised and barriers are removed on substantially all trade between member countries, i.e. no selective liberalisation. The chance of trade diversion being larger than trade creation is considered to be nil when the prospective members of a free trade area (FTA)[33] are close geographically [*Wonnacott and Lutz, 1989: 69*]. In this case – the EU being a perfect example at least as far as manufactured goods are concerned [*Jacquemin and Sapir, 1991: 169*] – integration is 'natural'. As members already trade a lot between themselves, integration neither causes much diversion nor penalises third parties [*Krugman, 1991a*], unless trade creation is curbed by over strict rules of origin.[34]

Yet the effects of lowering border barriers to trade clearly fail to capture the full implications of current regional initiatives aiming to reconcile or harmonise different national policies, that is, the deepening of the process of regional integration (see endnote 36), which also impinges on the role of the state *vis-à-vis* that of regional institutions. As 'not all states are effective at meeting and mediating international competitive pressures through national policy resources' [*Hirst and Thompson, 1992: 393-4*],[35] the governance of large economic areas by trade blocs allows member countries to withstand global pressures on specific policy issues and to pursue objectives, particularly social and environmental ones, that they could not attempt independently [*Hirst and Thompson, 1995: 430*]. Furthermore, the creation of regional schemes may help to lessen the effect of marginalisation – by neglect or exclusion – that globalisation apparently implies for the less developed parts of the world economy [*Sideri, 1993*]. In fact, since the benefits of global growth do not spread automatically to the poorest countries or to the poorest people, the expansion of the global economy does not translate automatically into human development for the world's poor [*Griffin and Khan, 1992: 7*]. This is well illustrated by the case of Africa (where the percentage of poor in Sub-Saharan Africa is expected to increase from 16 to 32 per cent by the year 2000 [*World Bank, 1990: 139*]) and by many enclaves in other regions of the Third World.

If regionalism seems a more potent force among DCs, this is because of their greater diversity of trade, payments and investment regimes, plus a more pronounced tendency to use protectionist measures and closer control over trade transactions which, with few exceptions, are unilaterally decided and implemented. This trend has only been reversed from the mid-1980s when regionalism started to occur in the developing world. Consequently, new and enlarged regional agreements are emerging from the process of continuing liberalisation not necessarily to halt it but to mute its negative impact and to reduce the risks implicit in the process of globalisation.

### *The European Union*

The European Community (EC) (1957) is deepening[36] relationships between its members by completing the construction of the internal market (following the 'Europe 1992' initiative) and by moving to the EU – including the introduction of a single currency – according to the Maastricht Treaty (1992).

At the same time, the EU has been widening its relations by first creating the European Economic Area and then admitting most members of EFTA (formed in 1959 by the UK, the Scandinavian countries, Switzerland, Austria and Portugal, in part reflecting 'Britain's attempt to weaken the process of EC integration' [*Boltho, 1996: 250*]). The EU has also concluded association agreements with Eastern European countries, potentially expanding the bloc sise from 370 million to more than 500 million people. These agreements are bound, however, to have a significant negative impact on exports of manufactured goods from some LDCs since both groups of countries produce and export low and medium technology products [*Sideri, 1992*].

The search for European unity seems driven by two competing visions 'both of which are based on the notion that competitiveness requires constant-wide approaches', but lead to opposite results. The first holds that market forces should operate on a continental basis, hence the process of European integration should provide greater access to third parties. The second vision insists that 'intervention and rules, the social dimension, should be likewise', leading to a Europe which is more protectionist and closed to outsiders[37] [*Lawrence, 1994: 377, 385*].

Irrespectively, Europe has not only become an 'outpost in changing globalisation trends to which other regions of the world will have to react', but also presents an 'actual example of economic integration beyond what we are used to consider an ideal' [*Bressand, 1990: 47, 63*]. With respect to the first point, the presence of the EC has forced the rest of the world to conform increasingly to its standards, to reduce their barriers to EC exports, and to seek lower barriers for their products in the EC market by concluding special association agreements with it or, where possible, to join it. As for the second point, European integration, the best example of continental economic governance, shows that trade represents only one dimension of a much more complex and dynamic economic system centred on services, technology, advanced and integrated public infrastructures and corporate cross-border networking strategies. In other words, European-based companies 'rather than simply seeking exports and economies of scale, are developing Euro-wide delivery systems, corporate alliances, production networks and electronic marketplaces'. The profound restructuring they are carrying out involves 'seeking customised, in-depth interactions with clients, suppliers and partners, through an expanding gamut of networking strategies, many of which have a strong information and advanced communication content'. In this they are strongly supported by Community programmes such as RACE, ESPRIT, EUREKA, Erasmus and Comet, and institutions like ETSI (European Telecommunications Standardisation Institute) [*ibid., 1990: 58–9*]. Furthermore, the EC has not hesitated to use sectoral protectionism, particularly towards Japan which seems to resent this measure less than the US' 'attempt to force open' its economy [*Gilpin, 1987: 405*].

The source of the renewed attempt at integration in the mid-1980s lies in the convergence of two broad interests: European firms' need to regain some of the competitiveness lost to American and Japanese producers, and the desires of state elites to recapture collectively part of their national sovereignty, particularly in respect of economic policy, eroded by growing international interdependence.

The ambitious social programme involving regional harmonisation and social homogeneity implies serious redistribution of revenue within the EU. Although this can only be done at the Community level, member states, at least the larger ones, remain crucial for constructing the *political* basis of consent needed for Community redistribution and macro-economic policies, including fiscal, regulatory and industrial policies. Nation-states will also play a substantial role in the effective establishment of sub-national governments and rules.

Since 'the concept of the nation-state shakes hands with the concept of government by consent' and 'only the nation-state possesses the necessary sense of identity'[38] (*The Economist*, 23 Dec.–5 Jan. 1996, p.20), the subsidiarity principle has been introduced to defend the identity of member nations. Drawing on this principle at the Europe's Council in Lisbon, nation states have even started to re-appropriate a substantial part of those common policies where their interests conflict most. The same principle can also be used by sub-national movements. In fact the principle of subsidiarity has inspired most Constitutions of the federal type drawn up during this century, starting with Germany's *Grundgesetz*.

The system of governance that is emerging in Europe is 'unique and uniquely complex'. Although the constituent nation states are becoming 'semisovereign', they will not disappear so that the Community's supranational institutions will have to share power with national as well as international and transnational institutions, and eventually with sub-national ones. The main problem of this systems is 'a profound *absence of hierarchy and monopoly* among a *wide variety of players of different but uncertain status*' [emphasis in the original]. The inclusion of sub-national units among the already recognised players in European politics (nations, classes, sectors, and firms – the 'regionalisation of Europe') would heighten the complexity of the system while further eroding the domestic sovereignty of nation-states [*Streeck and Schmitter, 1991: 151, 154, 156, 159*] or forcing them to bargain with the MNCs.

Coming very close to the line which separates the pooling of economic life from the merging of politics, EU member countries will soon have to decide whether they want indeed to cross it.

### *The Case of NAFTA*

The US has also reversed 'its historic antagonism toward regional arrangements' [*Lawrence, 1994: 366*] and concluded FTA agreements with

Canada (1988) and Israel (1989), and negotiated NAFTA with Canada and Mexico (1992). In June 1990 it proposed a broader network of FTAs with the nations of Latin America under the 'Enterprise for the Americas Initiative'. Based on Reagan's 'Caribbean Basin Initiative',[39] this aimed to provide a framework for the creation of a series of FTAs (a system of 'hub-and-spoke' RIAs[40] in which a large economy is supplemented by smaller satellite economies) with a view to an eventual Western Hemisphere FTA (WHFTA) from Alaska to Tierra del Fuego. Since negotiations with the US will be based on bilateral reciprocity, the 'Enterprise' should facilitate the proliferation of sub-regional groupings. Along the same lines in 1994 Clinton proposed a Free Trade Area of the Americas (FTAA).

Aside from stabilising the economic and political situation in Mexico, the US aimed with NAFTA to demonstrate the feasibility of the regional option – *vis-à-vis* stagnating multilateral negotiations – and to create, together with the 'Enterprise', a show-model for the rest of Latin America and other LDCs [*Oman, 1994: 71–9*]. Canada and Mexico were eager to join having been exposed to US unilateral measures in the 1980s.

While the Canada-US FTA 'provides a vivid example of the sometimes tortuous trade-offs that the partners made between achieving their goals while simultaneously retaining their sovereignty' [*Lawrence, 1994: 377*], NAFTA is a unique achievement because it contemplates virtually complete free trade – in 10 to 15 years – between two highly developed economies and an LDC, which receives no special and differentiated treatment apart from different time-frames for the implementation of some measures.[41] Being the first reciprocal FTA concluded between DCs and an LDC, the very profound differences between these partners may make it difficult to achieve free trade and investment between them.[42] At the same time, the heralded openness of the arrangement to other partners is less certain given the vagueness of the accession clause, and the contrary mood of the US Congress. Yet, the overall effect of NAFTA will greatly depend on whether it is a closed or open arrangement and whether it admits sub-regional groupings.

In addition to the gradual reduction of tariff and non-tariff barriers, NAFTA commits all three countries to offering national treatment to investment by other members, except in a few sectors. National treatment is extended to the field of intellectual property, while financial sectors are open to enterprises from member countries. Like other regional trade blocs, NAFTA has a foreign investment code of its own. This code improves on the WTO's rules because (i) it liberalises service trade between its three members, except for specifically excluded sectors; and (ii) it allows companies, not only states, to bring cases against the host government, under the NAFTA's dispute-settlement system.

Although difficult to determine NAFTA's potential for diverting trade and investment into Mexico and away from the rest of Latin America and the

Caribbean area, it has been argued that 'the risk of trade diversion is limited given that Mexico already enjoys a rather free access to the American market' and investment diversion would also be insignificant [*Oman, 1994: 73–5; ECLAC, 1994: 29*]. Finally, NAFTA has also created supraregional institutions relating to settlement procedure, environment, and labour issues.

*Asia's Informal Regionalism cum Corporatism*

The evolution of Southern and South-East Asia emphasises two different, but not necessarily opposing, trends: the intensification of both globalisation and regional integration. In fact, developing Asia's average share of world trade increased from 7.3 per cent between 1971–80 to 16.2 per cent between 1991–94 [*ADB, 1996: 183*], while Asia-Pacific's share of world production increased from five per cent in 1960 to currently 25 per cent. In addition, developing Asia's intra-trade rose from 22.3 per cent in 1980 to 41 per cent of their total exports in 1994 [*ADB, 1996: 186-7, Tables 3.1 and 3.2; WTO, 1995: 11, Chart 1.5*]. (Official figures probably underestimate the real sise of the flow.)

It also appears that the vertical division of labour, in which Japan imported primary products from and exported semi-manufactured products to developing Asia which then re-exported many of the finished products outside the region, is being replaced by a horizontal one. This means an upswing in manufactured exports from Asia of slightly differentiated finished products together with the incorporation of China into the region's manufacturing trade. Meanwhile markets outside the region continue to absorb a large share of Asia's growing exports of manufactured goods. Since three quarters of Asian NICs' exports of finished goods are directed to the US and the EU, the region's penetration of, and dependence on, these two markets is evident (see also Yoshida et al. [*1994: 61–6, 104*]). Compared to their extra-regional trade, exchanges between Asian NICs, between the largest ASEAN economies and between these two groups remain modest. Hence, the region's economic growth, excluding Japan, continues to depend on outside markets [*Oman: 1994: 79–80*]. Trade barriers of the East-Asian LDCs remain high, so further intra-regional trade and investment liberalisation is needed. Asia's restructuring is aided by intra-regional foreign direct investment. In 1993 over 50 per cent of the total value of the stock of foreign direct capital in East and South-East Asia originated from within the Asian region, the largest source being the Asian NICs, followed by Japan, representing an important shift of these flows over time [*ADB, 1996: 196, 198-9, Figure 3.5; Yoshida et al., 1994: 71-5, 81-9*]).

Together with the expansion of trade, services and their exchange have been growing rapidly; 90 per cent of the total exports of commercial services from the region being provided by Asian NICs [*ADB, 1996: 184*]. Intra-Asian labour movements have also increased; the pattern of migration having changed with Asian migration becoming mainly intra-regional and some countries moving from a position of net emigration to one of net immigration.

The various groupings created in South-East Asia with the purpose of integration are: ASEAN, the Association of South-East Asian Nations, established in 1967 which includes Brunei, Indonesia, Malaysia, Philippines, Singapore, Thailand and, since 1995, Vietnam; ASEAN's FTA (AFTA), a 1992 proposal which becomes fully effective in 2003 with a common external preferential tariff,[43] and the ASEAN Regional Forum (ARF) concerned with security matters; SAARC (South Asian Association for Regional Co-operation) established in 1985 by Bangladesh, Bhutan, India, Maldives, Nepal, Pakistan and Sri Lanka and now moving towards the establishment of a South Asian PTA (SAPTA); APEC (Asia-Pacific Economic Cooperation) established in 1989 – on the intellectual foundations laid by the non official forum PECC (Pacific Economic Cooperation Conference (1980)) and its Pacific Business Forum – with a membership of 18 Asian and Pacific countries; and EAEC (East Asia Economic Caucus) which emerged in 1992 from the AEG (Asian Economic Group (1990)) and is formed exclusively by ASEAN, China, Hong Kong, Japan, South Korea and Taiwan; and ANZCERTA (Australia and New Zealand Closer Economic Relations Trade Agreement) founded in 1983.

The regionalism emerging in East Asia has been presented as a 'market-led' integration compared to the 'policy-driven' and discriminatory type represented by the EU. Yet the fact that Asian regionalism is market-driven does not deny the crucial role played by national governments, as well exemplified by the creation of Special Economic Zones and open areas in China and of 'growth triangles' all over Asia's Pacific Rim [*Arndt, 1993: 277*]. The inception of the intergovernmental arrangement known as APEC represents another example of how Asian national governments intervene in, and attempt to guide, the economic process. The term 'open regionalism'[44] which Drysdale and Garnaut [*1993*] attach to this phenomenon is equally misleading as is that of a 'negotiating framework consistent with and complementary to GATT' [*Yoshida et al., 1994: 105*], since this integration process is promoted if, and only if, it is consistent with GATT and is not detrimental to other economies.

Given that the successful conclusion of the Uruguay Round protects the extra-regional interests of the region, and particularly those of the NICs, Asian regionalism should not be suspected of aiming to build an 'Asian Fortress' which would damage the world trade system as well as Asia's own interests [*Tang, 1995: 18*]. More importantly, it has been argued that Japan is not so interested in forming a trade bloc in Asia because [*Langhammer, 1992: 225–6*]: (i) it would not be able 'to cope with the subtle ways of sheltering the Japanese market (e.g. the distribution system)'; (ii) the protectionist lobby 'is still stronger than that of consumer protection in basic agricultural items'; and (iii) 'there are more efficient ways for Japanese exports to enter the market of neighbouring countries'. Furthermore, until recently Japanese economic and security interests did largely coincide with the US. More recently, however, the interests of these two countries may be leading them in different, not to say conflicting, directions and the 'region is emerging as a battleground for supremacy between the yen and the dollar' [*Stokes, 1996: 285*]. Hence Japan may reconsider the project of building an Asian bloc, even if it means tackling the difficult problem of China's role in it.

The East Asian experiment is also regarded as a clear example of 'natural' regionalism, in the sense that the expansion of intra-regional trade and investment is 'a natural result of geographical and cultural proximity, not the outcome of political negotiations' [*Thomsen, 1994: 109*]. Likewise Kreinin and Plummer (quoted in Lorenz [*1993: 238–9*]) regard an economic grouping comprising ASEAN and the Asian NICs, and certainly one consisting of them and Japan, as a 'natural' bloc since it does not greatly distort its comparative advantage. In fact, East Asia's share of intra-regional trade over the region's total trade rose from 19.0 per cent in 1965 to 29.3 per cent in 1990, an increase of almost 50 per cent, even higher than the EC's 32 per cent [*Frankel et al., 1995: Table 1, 63*].

Considered by far the most successful Asian integration and co-operation scheme, ASEAN remains basically a PTA with limited industry co-operation, so much so that the level of its intra-regional trade has remained quite stable at around 17 per cent of total trade between 1970 and 1992. More relevant appear to be the following ASEAN features: (i) formulation and representation of members' common interests in foreign affairs; (ii) a common 'perception of market forces as the driving element of development'; (iii) the creation of a strong internal network of consultation and software co-operation; and (iv) a permanent dialogue with the major OECD countries [*Langhammer and Hiemenz, 1990: 54–7*].

APEC, the other major regional initiative in the Pacific, is potentially the most sweeping trade agreement ever since it involves economies that produce half the world's output. At the Bogor summit of 1994, the then 18 members (ten applications for membership having been submitted since) agreed to 'achieve free and open trade and investment in the region' by 2010 for industrial members and 2020 for the others. Even without a formal institutional framework, trade within the area covered by APEC increased from 57 per cent of its total trade to 69 per cent between 1980 and 1992.

Although one of the main advantages of APEC is the inclusion of the US, which is seen as a counterweight to Japanese preeminence, APEC is unlikely to advance towards a FTA since the sole elimination of tariffs does not guarantee that the US can penetrate more Asian economies, particularly Japan (see section III). Moreover, APEC's investment code is 'flimsy and not binding' (*The Economist*, 16 Sept.1996, p.33). Yet Bergsten's [*1996: 107*] contention that 'APEC has eliminated any possibility of the three-bloc world that was so widely feared a few years ago' does not seem very convincing.

By contrast South- and North-East Asia are involved in a strong and informal process of regionalism through the various 'growth triangles'[45] identified along the Pacific coasts. The peculiar characteristics of this process distinguish it from other attempts and make it 'a distinctly Asian form of regional co-operation which has evolved from the area's experience with export processing zones, industrial and technological parks and other subnational zones' [*ADB, 1996: 179*]. These 'growth triangles', of which 'Greater China' is the most prominent example [*Sideri, 1994*], are localised economic co-operation zones that 'exploit complementarities between geographically contiguous areas of different countries to gain a competitive edge in export promotion'. They are more export oriented than trade blocs, can be established at relatively low cost and within a short period of time, and can be expanded incrementally. Aside from enabling an increase in exports despite rising labour costs, 'growth triangles' may also serve as protection from trade blocs and from increasing protectionism in other parts of the world [*Tang and Thant, 1994: 1, 23–4*]. Rather than trading in goods and services, they are mainly focused on the transnational movement of capital, labour, technology, and information and on the inter-country provision of infrastructure. 'Growth triangles' 'emphasise the complementarities of the actual or potential resource bases of the constituent areas which arise from major differences in the supply and prices of factors' [*ADB, 1996: 179*]. The informality of these *de facto* arrangements enhances their flexibility, although the existence of an international treaty or agreement which all can read and which is more difficult to modify, would also enhance their credibility and stability and thereby attract more foreign investment [*Oman, 1994: 16*].

This rapid intensification of regional trade and investment results more from a need to compete globally and to take advantage of the various economies' complementarities and different factor availabilities rather than a need to pursue self-sufficiency. For most South-East Asia countries opening up to the world economy by means of export-oriented policies is still accompanied by a definite policy of nurturing domestic infant industries. It is difficult, therefore, to reconcile this approach with 'open regionalism' which implies a willingness to extend to all trading partners, on a most-favoured-nation (mfn) basis, regionally negotiated tariff reductions. Such an arrangement differs from both the discriminatory GATT-notified regional integration scheme or the non-discriminatory exchange of tariff reductions in the multilateral negotiations under the GATT [*ADB, 1996, 181*].

Furthermore, South-East Asia's *de facto* regional integration represents a response to the EU and to the creation of NAFTA: the more these two regional groupings become, or are perceived to become, trading blocs the stronger the pressure on South-East Asian economies to follow suit and formalise their regional arrangement. Since their regionalism is a strategy to improve participation in the ongoing globalisation, they may resist preferential arrangements for as long as feasible. 'Growth triangles' are rather dynamic institutions since both the intensity of cooperation as well as the areas included in the triangle can be adjusted and changed. This makes them a new and potentially powerful tool of economic development. Yet, the continuous inflow of foreign direct investment, including intra-Asian investment, is crucial for the future of Asian 'growth triangles', inflow which, in turn, requires the maintenance of a reasonably open global trading system and political stability. The majority of strategic alliances entered into by Western companies, mostly American, have, until recently, been with Japanese, Korean and Taiwanese firms. In order to cope with the yen's overvaluation, Japanese firms have started to relocate their manufacturing activities, a deployment which is estimated to involve one quarter of their industrial production since the end of the 1980s [*Sigurdson, 1996: 3*]. It remains to be seen, however, whether the industrialisation and the regional division of labour emerging in Asia-Pacific, under Japan's guidance, are shaped by the pattern of co-operation and economic growth evoked by the poetic image of the 'flying geese'.

The emergence of 'Greater China', the growing economic and financial integration of China's southern provinces, Guandong and Fujian, with Hong Kong and Taiwan, has been largely driven by the private sector (particularly foreign investment, seeking to exploit factor price differentials), although there has also been some government support. The result is such that the economic integration within the triangle is mainly a vertical one as the exchange of intra-industrial products and commodities is larger than that of final goods produced by the member economies themselves. As the demand and supply of 'Greater China' are generated externally, its considerable vulnerability to market conditions in the outside world justify the label of an 'outward-dependent growth triangle' [*Chen and Ho, 1994: 67*], although this arrangement has brought major net benefits to all participants. Finally, to obtain a more complete picture the triangle should be seen within the context of a larger global relationship which includes the technology of Japan and the markets of the US and other industrial countries [*Pochih Chen, 1994: 91*].

Asia's preference for this informal type of regional integration may be due to the following characteristics prevailing in the region: (i) still relatively low volume of intra-regional trade; (ii) little homogeneity of laws and regulations governing trade and investment; (iii) large differences in per capita income; (iv) wide geographical dispersion and often poor transportation and communication networks; and (v) very diverse political, social and economic systems [*Tang and Thant, 1994: 7–8*]. It is even argued [*Mittelman, 1994: 434*] that Asian regionalism 'paradoxically both shields the domestic society from and integrates it into the global division of labour'. Although the process of regional economic integration seems firmly established, and the phenomenon could be even more consistent than indicated by aggregate trade trends, the most significant obstacles to the creation of an East Asian bloc are (i) the difficulty of harmonising the interventionist policies that all these countries, except Hong Kong, have used in order to promote export-led development; (ii) the general desire of avoiding Japanese pre-eminence, but also (iii) the impossibility of reconciling the presence of two hegemonic powers like China and Japan.

Even though transnational production networks tend to weaken the role of individual governments in formulating national development policies, and in determining how these economies are going to be linked to the global economic system [*Gereffi, 1993: 53*], an important aspect of Asia's evolution, and one which strongly impinges on both national economic development and regional co-operation, relates to the so-called 'Asian corporatism'. Also referred to in the literature as 'neo-authoritarianism', this reflects an attempt to 'reconcile two apparently contradictory demands in the process of internationalisation: internal political control and external economic integration' [*Ling, 1996: 10*]. In other words, this involves unpackaging the liberal project in order to reject some components such as civil society and democracy and a minimal role for the state.

Asian corporatism, based on Confucian tradition and reflecting the developmental experiences of Meiji Japan and later Singapore, South Korea and Taiwan, offers the following alternative set of developmental rationalisations for economic growth: (i) collective individualism, the neo-classical individual is placed within some social collective; (ii) utilitarian personalism, economic individuals apply a neo-classical utilitarian logic to hierarchically-structured, historically-conditioned, family- or clan-based personal connections; (iii) *patria economicus*, Confucian family-state; and (iv) state-mobilised learning, economic development as a form of patriotism. The existence of this Asian corporatism (see particularly the case of China which presently represents the best example) 'signals the rise of an alternative, regional hegemonic order to liberal capitalism' out of which, however, Asian corporatism partly stems, so that it has also been considered 'another kind of capitalism' [*ibid., 1996: 14–5, 19*]. Although this may indicate that the spread of liberalism is not merely a one-way process and globalisation involves different communities adapting ideas and institutions to their respective needs, a sounder interpretation is that it reveals the authoritarian underpinning of the whole process and the crucial role of the state, contrary to the liberal myth propagated by international institutions [*Rodrik, 1994*]. The insistence on

'Asian values', allegedly to avoid succumbing to Western individualism and other Western excesses, in reality serves to qualify the acceptance of democracy and reflects the elite's intention of running their countries like a family business. Consequently, the applicability of the Asian model to other parts of the world is seriously curtailed.

Finally, there remains the question of whether differences in the capitalist structures of East Asia, Europe and North America are so profound as to hinder the consolidation of the global economy and harden it into regional blocs – what Gilpin refers to as 'the Japan problem', but involves the Asian NICs. At issue is the resistance caused by their insertion into the world economy. In fact, compared to that of other DCs the Japanese economy shows 'extraordinary low inward-direct-investment ratios and import penetration' which explains why 'it has hardly shared in the internationalisation of the world economy over the last decade'. Combined with a highly competitive export sector, Japan's trade surplus was assured. The export of capital, buying US debt during the 1980s, offset the trade surpluses and checked the upward movement of the yen. Yet, the net capital inflow in the US contributes to the trade deficit since it pushes up the exchange rate of the dollar and thereby reduces American competitiveness in the world market. As soon as the financial outflow declines, the US can no longer accept the trade imbalance, even though the rise in the yen reduces the competitiveness of Japanese exports.

Similar asymmetrical trade relations characterise most of East Asia: higher investment allows the region to obtain 'a rate of productivity and innovation with which European and American producers cannot compete, but access to the region's markets 'remain structurally difficult even while their own economies remain open [*Hutton, 1995: 306-7*], owing to the fact that these economies tend to be highly regulated, compartmentalised, and segmented. Rather than trade barriers the real obstacle is their firms' anti-competitive behaviour, with their exclusive supplier or distributor arrangements (vertical *keiretsu* in Japan) and domination of particular markets. Hence the problem crystallises around the meaning given to liberalisation. Given the nature of the Japanese economy, and that of other East Asian countries, liberalisation cannot mean 'simply the removal of formal, external trade restrictions and, under certain circumstances, giving foreign firms "National Treatment"' but must go deeper, thus challenging 'inherent and crucial features of Japanese culture, social relations, and political structure'. In effect, unless Japan – and the other Eastern Asian countries – 'become a liberal society in the Western sense', Europe and North America will find it increasingly difficult to maintain economic relations with them.

Hence the crucial question: 'can a liberal international economy long survive if it is not composed primarily of liberal societies as defined in the

West ... ?' [*Gilpin, 1987: 390–93*]. Reactions against the homogenisation implied by the international liberal order are the rise of economic nationalism and the refuge of regionalism. Following Gilpin [*1987: 395*], autonomy tends to gain over interdependence in order to minimise the latter's costs. If Japan decides not to open its market to the region's growing manufacturing production and not to export its capital surplus, the chances of further integration in East and South East Asia will be sharply reduced and confrontation with China may become unavoidable.

*Mercosur and Other Regional Arrangements in Latin America*

Attempts at regional integration are not new to Latin America. After the failure of the 1960 Latin American Free Trade Association (LAFTA or ALALC), the Andean Pact was signed in 1969 by an allegedly more homogeneous group of smaller countries. In 1980 the Latin American Integration Association (LAIA or ALADI) was created to consolidate and promote existing bilateral trade relations. 1960 saw also the launching of the Central American Common Market (CACM or MCCA) which turned out to be less promising than first appeared. The trade integration aspired at by the Caribbean Community (CARICOM) set up in 1973 as a successor to the 1965 Caribbean Free Trade Association (CARIFTA) has also proved unpromising. The fact that CACM and the Andean Group were specifically designed to facilitate import substitution, clear-cut examples of 'closed regionalism', is regarded to be the main reason for their failure [*Cable, 1994: 9*]. In reality, none of these schemes has flourished.

An important new initiative is the creation of the *Mercado Común del Sur* (Mercosur) founded by Argentina, Brazil, Paraguay, and Uruguay in 1991. Chile was granted associate status in June 1996 (after the latter experienced problems in being accepted into the NAFTA) as will shortly be the case with Bolivia. At the beginning of 1995 Mercosur became a customs union and promptly signed an inter-regional Co-operation Agreement with the EU, with the aim of establishing a free trade association between the two groups. Mercosur can be seen either as a rival bloc to North America or as a step towards hemisphere-wide integration consistent with Clinton's FTAA.

The desire to revive the Andean Pact has finally brought the member countries to sign the *Acta de la Paz*. This aims to implement a FTA, create a common external tariff (effective in February 1995), liberalise maritime and air transportation, and facilitate foreign investment and capital mobility within the Andean Group. In addition, agreement was reached on reorganising the Pact's institutions.

LAIA continues to provide the institutional and legal framework for all regional activities, including many recent bilateral agreements, the so-called 'second generation' economic complementarity agreements, whose objective is to conclude a free trade agreement between the Andean Pact and Mercosur. Since 1991 Colombia and Venezuela have engaged in free trade. Together with Mexico, they have agreed to establish a free trade zone by 2005.

Since 1993 a customs union has been operating between Guatemala, Honduras, El Salvador and Nicaragua. By mid-1995 CARICOM had largely eliminated barriers to mutual trade; over half of its members had adopted the revised common external tariff. In addition, agreement was close on the free movement of capital and of some labour, and the free convertibility of currencies and the abolition of exchange controls. In August 1995 25 countries and 12 territories established the Association of Caribbean States (ACS), whose headquarters are in Trinidad and Tobago.

As a result of all these endeavours, Latin American and Caribbean share of intra-regional trade grew from 16.8 per cent in 1990 to 19.2 per cent in 1994, faster than that of its exports to the rest of the world. (Between 1990 and 1995 Mercosur's share increased from 8.9 to 22.0 per cent, the Andean Pact's from 4.1 to 11.7 per cent, and LAIA's from 10.8 to 17.5 per cent.) This growth is accompanied by the flow of intra-regional direct and indirect investment. Closer relations and linkages, both vertical and horizontal, are also being developed between sectors or groups of companies (informal conglomerates) and within associations of companies and agencies of various kinds [*CEPAL 1995: 33, Tabie 7; ECLAC, 1994: 51, Table II-9, 64*].

The current wave of Latin American regionalism differs from earlier attempts and reflects a substantial change in its role. It is no longer seen as the extension of a domestic import substitution strategy to a regional level. Instead commercial integration is currently conceived as complementing the outward orientation now largely accepted by all countries, and uniting forces to increase international competitiveness and rapidly expand exports. Yet even though regional integration does not 'attempt to insulate vulnerable economies to shocks and unfavourable trends originating in the rest of the world', its success has come to depend in part on the rapid rate of growth of the global economy [*Griffin and Khan, 1992: 72–3*].

The phenomenon of *de facto* integration is also prospering in Latin America and the Caribbean. Increased regional interdependence is advanced by preferential agreements (24 bilateral agreements were concluded between 1982 and 1993) and by a series of macroeconomic and trade polices which, although non-discriminatory with respect to trade with third countries, have created similar conditions in a growing number (now a majority) of countries in the region and thereby fostered reciprocal trade and investment. As a result the MNCs' 'position as suppliers of highly protected local markets is being threatened by the prospect of international competition on both national and foreign markets', prompting the same MNCs to change their integration strategies [*ECLAC, 1994: 12, 43 Table II-5, 33*]. However, serious doubts have recently been raised about the effectiveness of regional free-trade agreements in promoting member countries' international competitiveness. According to an unpublished study prepared by A. Yeats of the World Bank, whilst Mercosur intra-trade has increased dramatically, it has kept out imports from other countries and its exports remain uncompetitive outside the regional area [*Dale, 1996*].

*The Rest of the Developing World*

The difficulties encountered by many LDCs in creating their own regional schemes are an indication that the process of globalisation does not really involve them, or does so only marginally. Africa's experience with integration schemes is no less richer than Latin America's, but its degree of failure is probably higher.

Historically, three roots of integration have been identified in Africa [*Langhammer and Hiemenz, 1990: 34–5*]: (i) groupings that represented the remnants of large colonial entities, such as the 1966 Customs Union of West African States (CUWAS, later WAEC), the 1959 Equatorial Customs Union (ECU, later CACEU), and the 1967 East African Community (EAC); (ii) various post-independence groupings, such as the 1974 West African Economic Community (WAEC/CEAO, 1973), and the 1975 Economic Community of Western African States (ECOWAS/CEDEAO, 1975); and (iii) new integration initiatives which emerged in Southern Africa with the aim of loosening commercial ties with South Africa, such as the Southern African Development Coordination Conference (SADCC) and with its PTA for Eastern and Southern African States, founded in 1981, and the Southern Africa Customs Union (SACU), founded in 1969. Then there is the Mano River Union (MRU, 1973), the UDEAC (Union Duanière et Economique de l'Afrique Centrale, 1976) and the UMOA (Union Monétaire Ouest Africaine). Most expectations created by these various schemes failed to materialise and as a result no meaningful trade integration has taken place in Africa. Yet, the continent's difficulties with regional integration are very much connected to the limited capabilities of its national states – those 'juridical states' explored by Jackson [*1987*] – to deliver a minimum of infrastructure, such as roads and electricity, and basic health and education. No wonder that foreign investment barely reached $2.1 billion in 1995, while total official aid fell from almost $17 billion in 1990 to $15 billion in 1994, notwithstanding the fact that about 40 per cent of Africa's people live on less than $1 a day. States must be effective both to be properly drawn into the process of globalisation and to resist it through regional integration.

Regional integration schemes in the Middle East have never attracted much interest and none of the various schemes among the Arab countries has lasted long or has had much impact: the Council for Arab Economic Unity (CAEU), formed in 1957: the Arab Common Market (ACM), founded in 1964 between Egypt, Iraq, Jordan and Syria; the Gulf Co-operation Council (GCC), founded in 1981 by all the Gulf Arab countries. As yet nothing concrete has come out of two new schemes set up in 1989: the Arab Co-operation Council (ACC) which comprises Egypt, Iran, Iraq, Jordan and the Yemen Arab Republic; and the Arab Maghreb Union (AMU) between Algeria, Libya, Mauritania, Morocco and Tunisia.

Iran, Turkey and Pakistan founded in 1964 the Regional Co-operation for Development (RCD) in 1964 (reactivated in 1984 as the Economic Co-operation Organisation (ECO)) to promote trade among themselves on a bilateral level and in sectors where common interests could be defined. The impact of RCD was non existent until the Gulf War and Turkey's intensification of trade with Iran.

Comparing earlier LDC regional initiatives with more recent ones, Langhammer and Hiemenz [*1990: 57–73*] identify the main differences as (i) the shift in emphasis from more formal types of internal integration to less binding project-oriented co-operation schemes; (ii) a greater scope to pursue trade liberation at different speeds; and (iii) the lower priority assigned to regional industrialisation planning or programming compared to co-operation in providing public goods, that is, building of physical infrastructure, communication, transport, and creation of software, namely training, research and technology. One important implication of these developments is that the role of supra-national authorities in the decision-making process has been curtailed as national authorities have regained or maintained their decision-making rights.

The same authors [*Langhammer and Hiemenz, 1990: 57–73*] explain the failure of many regional initiatives by LDCs in terms of internal rather than external factors, even though the negative impact of a deteriorating external economic environment is not excluded. Amongst internal reasons cited are (i) the resistance to reduce barriers to trade and factor mobility, (ii) the macro-economic policies pursued; (iii) the fear of economic domination by a large or more advanced partner country; (iv) the problems inherent to any international co-ordination, particularly when no common threat exists; and (v) the influence of vested interests. Yet the negative outcome 'did not so much result from a misperception of the potential embodied in regional integration, but from the lack of incentives to implement integration policies in the given situation'.

Furthermore, since low wages are not a sufficient attraction for MNCs' to locate labour-intensive production in countries with inadequate infrastructure and lacking in the human capital required by 'flexible production', these countries have also failed to attract direct foreign investment, except in some primary products. For the MNCs the trend is in fact to neglect the production of low-wage goods for the world market and concentrate on production and sourcing networks at the regional level [*Oman, 1994: 93*]. The lack of progress in regional integration compounds the problems of poor infrastructure and human capital, increasing the risk of marginalisation for several LDCs and for large sections of some continents.[46]

What emerges is that although globalisation tends to marginalise the less developed parts of the Third World, their capacity to react by forming regional groupings of their own is limited, mainly because the central institutions of government are crumbling. Their prospects are no better if the world economy comes to be dominated by trade blocs [*Gilpin, 1987: 40; Sideri, 1993*]. Although their chances of obtaining some economic support may be improved in the latter case so does their dependence on one of the trade blocs. Whereas globalisation implies their marginalisation with neglect, a system of trade blocs means total dependence: an unenviable predicament.

## III. CONCLUDING REMARKS

The globalisation process is creating a world economic system which is mainly private, fast-paced and largely averse to government action, particularly when perceived as interference. It is regarded as a reversible phenomenon only by a few.

The existence of the world market renders the nation-state unable to deliver such valued benefits as job security and rising living standards to its citisens. Neither can regional integration necessarily accomplish this, yet it may be better at reconciling global competitiveness with a heightened sense of social solidarity, and possibly, democratic legitimacy. National sovereignty is no longer the valuable commodity it once was; capital markets increasingly exercise their veto power over the economic decisions of all states. If political independence does actually offer people less control over decisions that crucially affect them, the search for protection from globalisation becomes unarresting. This explains why in many countries deregulation often stimulates increased protection of domestic markets [*Gilpin, 1987: 407*].

Economic globalisation is entering a critical phase as the backlash against its effects is growing, primarily in the DCs. This, and the new brand of populism generated by globalisation is propelling the search for alternative solutions which retain most of the achievements of globalisation, but minimise its disruptive impact on economic activity and social stability.

For DCs, regionalism appears as a means of protecting them from the risk of de-industrialisation. More importantly, regional integration is seen as reducing the impact of political or cultural globalisation, both still less advanced than economic globalisation yet no less threatening. However, the forces opposing the process of globalisation, namely nationalism and powerful sectional interests, are the same forces which regionalism must overcome, while the end of the Cold War has further contributed to the fragmentation of people's horizons [*Bliss, 1994: 134*].

LDCs also regard regional integration as a useful instrument for achieving those economies of scale required to increase their participation in international trade [*Krugman, 1988: 42*]. With respect to the least developed countries, regional integration may not be a viable option, mainly because their state machinery is unable to provide the necessary backing for the establishment and functioning of a regional scheme. Nevertheless, many LDCs are currently reconsidering regional integration which, coupled with a significant degree of trade liberalisation as required by structural adjustment programmes, they see as helping to test their firms' competitiveness regionally, before being fully exposed to the more taxing global environment. Since it remains doubtful whether LDCs' segmented and unstable markets will become homogeneous and stable as assumed by structural adjustment policies, trade liberalisation, privatisation and deregulation should focus on productivity and production in enterprises which serve the domestic market and the regional one, rather than on exporting production to the global market. Outward-oriented development strategies in particular require measures which encourage the emergence of entrepreneurial capabilities. These developments involve education and training, favourable legislation, and close co-operation with the enterprises of neighbouring countries through regional integration, as well as with more advanced countries in order to gain access to their larger markets. Both types of co-operation should be facilitated by globalisation. By contributing firm and committed finance, which is unavailable locally and centrally, foreign aid would provide incentives for rational economic behaviour not determined by market prices.

LDCs' rather negative experience of regional integration contrasts with that of DCs, notably the EU, and even with that of some groupings in the developing world, namely ASEAN, 'Greater China', and Asian 'growth triangles' [*Sideri, 1994*]. Many LDCs, and particularly the least developed ones, lack the ingredients needed for the successful formation of a trade bloc or even a trade interest group, such as the Cairns group. They lack the impetus of shared political objectives and their interests often diverge as soon as one gets down to details. More generally, large variations in their economic circumstances militate against the formation of a united front and they often lack cultural, political and historical closeness essential to any common endeavour. For large sections of the developing world the road to liberalisation passes necessarily through that of regionalism, that is, if they could 'regionalise regionalism' this would help to strengthen their state's effectiveness and credibility and enable them to 'globalise globalisation', to adopt Oman's expression.

In the face of strong external pressure, the need to redefine one's identity is more pressing so that economic globalisation has gone hand in hand with political nationalism – the ideology which is probably easiest to transplant globally. To check the growing forces of disintegration, a structure must be built between national and sub-national levels and the world system. Without denying that a regional framework tends to foster movements towards autonomy and even secession, it appears as the only instrument able to address the destabilising and destructive charges emanating from both globalisation and nationalism. In addition, regional integration agreements, even the most open and liberal with respect to trade and investment, may enable groups of countries with close political and cultural ties to establish the free movement of, and equal opportunities for, people within the region, whilst restricting rights of entry, residence, and citizenship for outsiders. Particularly in post Maastricht Europe, regionalism is re-centralising state power at the regional level, eroding economic nationalism and increasing awareness of economic interdependence. It has become a useful laboratory for new approaches to deeper integration which can be applied multilaterally; it eases negotiations by reducing the number of players; and it encourages the codification and formalisation of rules and regulations affecting trade, making them more transparent and less discretionary [*Cable, 1994: 12*].

It follows that regionalism has two different meanings. On the one hand it protects against the worst effects of globalisation and unites countries. On the other hand it encourages sub-national movements, thereby heightening the dangers of national divisiveness. However, as the contradictions of globalisation become clearer – depletion of resources and the environment, reduced capacity of the state to provide public goods while 'many of the neoliberal forms of state have been authoritarian' [*Gill, 1995: 419–20*] – regionalism emerges as the stronger and more pervasive influence on the course of international policies.

The traditional analysis of RIAs which focuses on the effect of lowering border barriers to trade, fails to capture fully the implications of current regional initiatives which aim to achieve deeper integration by means of the harmonisation and reconciliation of domestic policies between member countries. The pressure of growing globalisation is forcing countries into regionalisation, but it is the latter which makes it necessary to address problems arising from different regulatory policies and to reduce differences by means of mutual recognition and a supra-national mechanism for implementing common policies. The level of policy decision and implementation can, however, vary. It can be transferred to the regional level but also to the sub-national level. Hence the problem of assigning authority for the different levels of the policy-making spectrum, that is, subsidiarity in general and fiscal federalism in this specific sector, with which to keep centrifugal forces together and retain an overall identity against the enveloping globalisation. The latter involves extending consumer choice, or wild consumerism, but it also entails market volatility, concentrating power in private hands and the deflationary bias – monetarist preferences – generated by the current international financial and trading system. In sum, it means the prevalence of the values of finance over those of production and employment, as underlined by many observers.

In addition MNCs, particularly those most competitive globally, are much more interested in intra-regional rather than inter-regional trade liberalisation. When MNCs invest in other regions, they organise their activities on a regional and fairly autonomous basis, regardless of the existence of a regional integration scheme. Since 'in those sectors in which MNCs are important, intra-firm trade[47] already appears to be a regional affair' [*Thomsen, 1994: 123–5*], MNCs would only object to an increase in the barriers to inter-regional investment, an eventuality considered unlikely even if the world economy becomes fragmented into a series of trading blocs. In any case large MNCs from the OECD area are relatively sheltered from such a fragmentation since the redeployment of labour-intensive production to low wages countries has become less relevant (see note 3). Furthermore, by multiplying international joint ventures, encouraging linkages among MNCs of different nationalities, and strengthening crosscutting interests, sectoral protectionism may reduce the risk of destabilising conflict inherent in a system of regional blocs [*Gilpin, 1987: 404*].

As regionalism mitigates the negative effects of unfettered globalisation, the system of small and medium enterprises (SME) can likewise help to re-assert the value of co-operation without reducing efficiency. The success of SMEs and the growth of sub-regional economies is connected to the overall process of globalisation as they can cope better with shifting and volatile patterns of international demand through their diversified and flexible production. By clustering together, by sharing work, expertise, collective services, and risk, inter-firm SMEs have demonstrated their superior ability to resist market shocks and adapt to rapid changes than large firms hierarchically organised.

Clearly, SME inter-firm relationships are typified by a mixture of competition and co-operation, in which the co-operative aspects help to minimise the disadvantages of small sise and the competitive aspects, along with specialisation, convey the dynamism and flexibility that are often lacking in large, integrated firms. SMEs' flexibility and strength is greatly enhanced by the development of a low-cost financial sector closely connected to the local economy and the sub-national governance. Being sheltered from some of the negative effects of globalisation, SMEs would support international openness whilst helping to retain some manufacturing activities. By allowing sub-national areas enough autonomy, the system of SMEs may develop and prosper, reducing both separatist pressures and tensions between the national level and the global one. Grafted onto the economic, political and social system, likely through decentralisation, federalism or even the recognition of sub-national entities' role and place, the system is 'embedded' in rules, norms conventions established by trade unions, the state, political parties, religious affiliations and more informal community-based institutions. The result is a 'social market' which rests as much on economic forces as on solidarity.

Alternatives to a globalisation mitigated by regionalism and devolution are 'global neoclassicism' or feuding regional blocs. Neither of these will be able to provide a stable, secure and environmentally friendly world order. Both will involve more marginalisation for the developing world and also for some economic sectors and social groups in DCs.

## NOTES

1. This globalist view satisfies the Right's anti-political liberalism, since trade, transnational companies and capital markets are freed from the constraints of politics and labour organisations, operations made more secure also by the emergence of a de-militarised world, therefore denying 'both the need for strong international governance and the possibility of national level action'. The globalist view also satisfies the Left, since 'globalisation proves the reality of the world capitalist system and the illusory nature of national reformist strategies, even if this intellectual certainty is bought at the price of political impotence'. Both 'can thus mutually celebrate the end of the Keynesian era' [*Hirst and Thompson, 1995: 424, 414*]. A rather different distinction involving globalism sees it either as 'a Kantian-Grotian-Hegelian reasoning that promotes the rule of international law, universal human rights, a global ecological order, and other concerns of a liberal world order' or as a 'Gramscian international political economy where a capitalist "world-hegemony" turns states inside-out ... to service the needs of international production', what Cox [*1981: 44–6*] calls 'the internationalising of the state'. 'Both strands of globalism share a common conviction: international relations is homogenising ... and internationalisation ultimately leads to globalisation: that is, one world order' which basically is Western-led [*Ling, 1996: 1–2*].
2. The growing practice followed by domestic firms of importing intermediate inputs is called outsourcing, simultaneously an effect and a cause of globalisation. This phenomenon is considered to be responsible for the reduced demand for less skilled labour as firms respond to import competition from low-wage countries by moving non-skill-intensive activities abroad. By internationalising the labour market, technology has created what for practical purposes is an inexhaustible labour pool at the disposal of manufacturers. As a result trade reduces the wages of less skilled labour and shifts employment towards skilled workers within, rather than across, industries [*Feenstra and Hanson, 1996: 240*]. Hence, LDCs' concern that globalisation may actually worsen their economic perspectives, or at least those of some of them, has been followed by DCs' fear that trading with LDCs will depress their own wages and standard of living.
3. Oman [*1994: 57–8*] sustains that the diffusion of the 'flexible production' system and the crisis of 'fordism' are shaping the dynamics of the present wave of regionalism. The 'flexible production' system implies a complete overhaul of the value added chain based on simultaneous engineering, continuous innovation, extensive use of general or multi-purpose machinery and skilled workers, and team work which closely integrates manual and mental tasks. This allows differentiated products and small batches of production for niche markets. Competition is combined with co-operative links among firms: the horizontal integration of production is based on thick networks among firms and sub-contracting relations – the 'just-in-time' organisation.

The response to falling markets is also very flexible and variegated, namely diversification of production, innovation, sub-contracting and lay-offs, while the 'forms of social regulation are mainly established at a local level, with an important role of specific local institutions' [*Garofoli, 1992: 3*]. The other system, namely Fordism, concerns mainly mass-production of standard goods in big plants in which economies are obtained through fixed capital and labour productivity increases within the production process. 'The prevailing form of the market is the oligopolistic one and the management of the economy is organised at the national level, especially with the goal to offset the immanent tendency to over-production.' The resulting pattern of production is therefore determined by the combination of Taylorism and the Keynesian state [*Garofoli, 1992: 3*]).

The main problem with this new system is that it is less 'robust', or more 'fragile', than Fordism owing to its dependence on reliable communication and transportation structures and on the quality of labour. This makes the flexible specialisation system less feasible for LDCs and explains the growing structural unemployment of DCs. Furthermore, since the 'flexible production' system tends to reduce the importance of the cost of labour – its share of variable production cost declining – the need to move production into LDCs in order to exploit their comparative advantage becomes less pressing (see also note 2). Much more relevant is proximity, due to the synergic character of the relationship between firms, suppliers and clients. Hence the creation of production networks in each regional market, that 'global localisation' which contributes to current regionalism. This also explains why MNCs are often more interested in regional integration and less worried about commercial obstacles to inter-regional exchanges [*Oman, 1994: 86–91*]. Flexible production is also identified with global capitalism, that is, a capitalism which is no longer nationally based but has been deterritorialised and located in the narrative of MNCs.

4. Over the past decade international trade has grown twice as fast as output (currently more than $4 trillion per year), while foreign direct investment has risen three times as fast. International capital markets' turnover is now close to $100 trillion and foreign exchange transactions approximate $1.3 trillion per day.
5. Not everybody is pleased with the mobility achieved by capital and the World Bank [*1989: 4*] warns that excessively unregulated markets 'can be unstable and susceptible to fraud', which justifies the call for 'a greater degree of control by international agencies and governments than the financial liberalisation literature suggests' [*Collier and Mayer, 1989: 11*]. Some emphasise the need for capital to become socially rooted again, because 'only when those who allocate a society's investible resources are full and responsible members of that society is it possible to strike a reasonable balance between politics and economics' [*Bienefeld, 1994: 39*]. Furthermore, *The Economist* holds that 'the international competition for capital is fiercer, and this is exercising a new influence (or should be) on the design of all manner of government policy' (7 Oct.1995, p.14).
6. 'Beneath the surface, many multinationals remain stubbornly monocultural. The proportion of foreign-born board members of America's 500 leading companies was 2.1 per cent in 1991, the same as ten years earlier.' There are even fewer foreigners in Japanese companies (*The Economist*, 24 May 1995, p.14).
7. Among those who maintain that the present international system has been around much longer, see Thomson and Krasner [*1989*].
8. Even though the state retains control of its borders, advanced countries seeking 'to police the movement of the world's poor and exclude them ... will not be able effectively to use as a principle of exclusion the claim to cultural homogeneity – for they are ethnically and culturally pluralistic' [*Hirst and Thompson, 1995: 420-21*].
9. Given that 'politics is about rule' and any system of rule comprises 'legitimate dominion over a spatial extension', the territorial state is not the only form politics takes. Since 'systems of rule need not be territorial at all', they 'need not be territorially fixed' and 'need not entail mutual exclusion', it is likely that 'the modern system of states may be yielding in some instances to postmodern forms of configuring political space', the best example of which is the EU. This 'may constitute nothing less than the emergence of the first truly postmodern international political form', somewhat similar to the situation prevailing in its medieval past when there was a 'patchwork of overlapping and incomplete rights of government which were intrinsically

superimposed and tangled' [*Ruggie, 1993: 144, 148–9, 140*].

10. Broadly defined, regionalism refers to preferential trade agreements among a subset of nations [*Bhagwati, 1993: 22*]. Lorenz [*1992: 84*] distinguishes, however, between regionalisation, that is, 'the outcome of a natural location phenomenon leading to close economic ties within a region' and regionalism which refers to 'the creation of preferential-trading arrangements'. He also considers regionalisation a more 'neutral' and adequate term for focusing 'on the rising intra-regional interdependence (cluster) of trade and other economic activities such as direct investment etc., as the *natural* outcome of the regional development process' without government-initiated RTAs [*Lorenz, 1993: 256*]. The present continent-wide regionalisation needs, however, 'a broader framework of analysis and reference than traditional reallocation analysis: it must include a broader perspective that encompasses geography and social values' [*Lorenz, 1992: 87*]. Nevertheless regionalism is used throughout this study in the interests of clarity and brevity. As for 'natural' arrangements, see section II.
11. Most international investment house bond dealers and MNC treasurers are not easily persuaded that the current financial order is unstable or economically inefficient [*Hutton, 1995: 305*].
12. The total value of MNC production began to exceed the total value of world trade in the late 1970s; in 1992 the sales of MNCs' foreign affiliates was $5.8 trillion against $3.7 trillion of world trade. Meanwhile the share of intra-firm trade in world trade increased from 20 per cent in the early 1970s to more than one third in the early 1990s. Since the late 1960s the number of the world's MNCs is estimated to have increased from 7,000 to some 40,000, with 250,000 foreign affiliates. Overall they employ 12 million workers in the developing countries and 61 million in the developed ones [*UNCTAD, 1995: xx–xxi*]. The combined global employment of the top 200 firms is estimated at 18.8 million, whereas their total sales add up to more than a quarter of the world's output, an amount larger than the combined economies of all countries minus the biggest nine [*Anderson and Kavanagh, 1996*].
13. The term global governance has not yet acquired a fixed meaning. To define it one can use either a Gramscian or a Weberian approach. In the former, global governance consists of the creation of ideological consensus and its propagation by international organisations so as to secure the reproduction and worldwide extension of industrial capitalism. Amongst the few existing Weberian definitions, the most recent is that adopted by the Carlsson-Ramphal's 'Commission on Global Governance' in which global governance is the outcome of a partnership between the agencies of the UN system and the network of worldwide civil society.
14. Although economic integration, to the extent that it occurs, brings greater economic interdependence, the two may not always coincide. Two or more countries may reach simultaneously a high degree of integration and a low level of interdependence, for example, Australia and New Zealand, and *vice versa*, the European countries before the development of EU [*ADB, 1996: 209*].
15. In respect of global economic management three broad possibilities are considered by Griffin and Khan [*1992: 84–6*]: (i) given its reduced domination of the world scene, the USA could continue to withdraw gradually its financial and political support from the existing international organisations, causing the disintegration of the present system of international governance; (ii) the major powers could tacitly agree to bypass established institutions and attempt to resolve problems as they arise on an *ad hoc* basis. This is the 'international governance by plutocracy' which considerable evidence indicates has been happening; and (iii) the emergence of a consensus in favour of reforming the existing institutions, and if necessary creating new ones, in order to strengthen the multilateral approach to international governance.
16. Fierce international competition for capital has made financial markets judge and jury of economic policy-making, making it much more difficult for governments to determine interest rates, exchange rates or even tax rates. To assuage bond holders, inflation must be checked at any cost, including excessive deflationary policies. At the same time, changes in interest rates or government borrowing have a smaller impact on the economy since firms have access to a global financial market and to the vast array of new financial instruments. (See the excellent Survey 'The world economy' in *The Economist*, 7 October 1995 which holds that 'on the whole, markets take power away from governments that do the wrong things: borrow recklessly, run inflationary policies or try to defend unsustainable exchange rates'.) As for LDCs, 'the basis for supporting financial liberalisation is weak' and its 'benefits ... can at best be described as

unproven ... The case for controls on capital inflows comes from the fact that the first stage of development involves governments in establishing reputation for pursuing sound growth strategies' [*Collier and Mayer, 1989: 10*]. Regional integration can help by enhancing the credibility of member countries' financial systems.

17. Whereas Bretton Woods established a system – the government-led international monetary system (G-IMS) – 'with a built-in asymmetry between an integrating world market for goods and commodities and domestically insulated, government-regulated financial markets', the rise of international financial markets brought the current market-led international monetary system (M-IMS) which is 'the converse of the preceding one'. Since 'the M-IMS has eroded the power of national central banks and the effectiveness of their instruments', in order to ensure monetary and financial stability 'a more complete set of policy functions' and some institutional requirements are required that may 'tend to resemble more the framework applying *within* a single nation-state than the loose arrangements applying today *among* nation-states' [*Padoa-Schioppa and Saccomanni, 1994: 264, 237, 240–41, 263, 262*].
18. The role of technology is crucially important in fostering the internationalisation of economic activity for four reasons: technology is generally internationally mobile; the escalation of product costs or process innovation forces firms to seek world markets to sell their products and to form strategic alliances with other firms; the rapid increase of intra-industry trade among industrial countries, so that no nation has technological hegemony; and, such technology has extended the geographical boundaries of both firms and markets [*Dunning, 1993: 11*].
19. These 'network enterprises' utilising the 'flexible production' system can be divided into two large categories: (i) the Northern German big enterprises or the Japanese *keiretsu*, which network internally; and (ii) the 'industrial district' of Northern Italy, Southern Germany and Denmark, that is, a large number of interconnected small enterprises [*Oman, 1994: 94–5*].
20. In the case of the EU, member countries' ability to design and implement effective science and technology policy or industrial policy is seriously undermined by the rapid expansion of strategic alliances, as companies seek to reduce their financial and technological risks, and, simultaneously, by the emergence of the Community's initiatives for global science and technology programmes. As a result while the national economies' competitiveness is enhanced, national policies and controls become obsolete.
21. Lal [*1993: 356*] expresses concern about 'a contemporary movement in the West – the global environmentalists – who might trigger another round of imperialism in the name of saving Spaceship Earth', since 'ominous is the Greens' desire to dictate environmental policy to the rest of the world'.
22. To insist that free trade requires all countries to have similar labour and environmental standards is like demanding that all comparative advantages be eliminated before international trade begins.
23. The term 'trade bloc', or 'trading bloc', is not only ill-defined [*Henderson, 1994: 183*], but its definition is 'problematic' [*Bliss, 1994: 1*] as 'ambivalent has been economists' attitude to this phenomenon [*Lal, 1993: 349*]. So, while the latter author considers all common markets and regional FTAs as trade blocs, for Wolf (1994: 13, quoted by Henderson) there are only two trade blocs: EU and NAFTA. Bliss [*1994: 6*] thinks that 'the evidence in favour of widespread block formation among the world's trading nations is not as impressive as many accounts would lead one to expect', but in the end recognises that 'trading blocks have come into being and are being developed and extended' [*ibid.: 136*], while Henderson [*1994: 184*] admits that 'the significance of regional agreements has increased in recent years'.
24. A recent contribution to the international relations literature warns, however, that models of multipolarity are both empirically and conceptually too narrow to provide a comprehensive and compelling account of the disparity of power in the contemporary international order. In fact, while bipolarity rested on a relative cohesion between the capacity to define purpose and generate military and economic power, the end of bipolarity and the consequent 'loosening' of world order has seen the decoupling of purpose and power. This divergence between purpose and power finds its strongest and most visible expression in the contrast between the rapid globalisation of markets and the rise of ethnic, cultural and regional identities [*Laïdi, 1995*]. The essential characteristic of the present system has been effectively rendered by a Japanese diplomat: 'The multilateral trade system is really the trilateral trade system.' From which

follows a simple negotiating dynamic: 'If you can get an ally on an issue, you win 2–1' (*International Herald Tribune*, 29–30 June 1996).

25. Another reason for LDCs' revived interest in regional integration is to establish 'a defence mechanism to offset some of the costs of even greater isolation resulting from any increase in protectionism in DCs' [*ECLAC, 1994: 11*]. Finally, a reason that applies to both DCs and LDCs is the frustration caused by the slow progress of multilateral trade negotiations under GATT, although the creation of the WTO may ease this problem.
26. According to Kapstein [*1994: 20*] the major powers may view globalisation 'as being in their national interest'. Yet 'small country firms will see a decline in their relative cost disadvantage and will be the main beneficiaries of the enlargement of the trade bloc', and 'neither the theory nor the data indicate any asymmetric economic gain in favour of large countries as such' [*Casella, 1996: 412*].
27. During the 1960s neo-functionalism's interest in regional integration in Latin America, Africa and South-East Asia reflected the American government's expectation that regional integration would provide a non-interventionist model for the containment of communism in the Third World.
28. See the various contributions in De Melo and Panagariya [*1993*]. The World Bank estimated that if the Uruguay Round had collapsed, losses resulting from a trade war between rival trading blocs would have amounted to 3–4 per cent of world output [*World Bank, 1991: 29*].
29. Among the initiatives that have contributed to the fragmentation of the world market and the movement towards regionalism, Langhammer includes (i) the Global System of Trade Preferences (GSTP) established since the early 1970s in order to facilitate trade between developing countries, an arrangement that 'has all the flows of regional integration schemes plus those of ineffectiveness due to a large membership and problems of "balancing" the concessions in a group of heterogeneous economies'; and (ii) the trade preferences unilaterally offered to developing countries by OECD countries, including several General System of Preferences (GSP) [*Langhammer, 1992: 217–23*].
30. Huntington [*1973: 365*] identified this phenomenon more than two decades ago: 'while functional imperatives seem to be making transnational organisations bigger and bigger, cultural and communal imperatives seem to be encouraging political units to become smaller and smaller. "Tribalism" in politics contrasts with "transnationalism" in economics.' That the nation-state and the transnational organisation coexist confirms that 'the existence of one not only implies but requires the existence of the other'. By tribalism is meant 'the retreat by individuals into communities defined not by political association or by the state borders that enclose a political nation, but by similarities of religion, culture, ethnicity, or some other shared experience. The retreat is driven by fear and confusion, and fed by the reassuring "sameness" of others in the group' [*Horsman and Marshall, 1994: x*].
31. It is, however, only in Western Europe that there is a seriously conceived plan to dissolve existing nation-states into something bigger (*The Economist*, 23 Dec. 1995–5 Jan. 1996, p.18).
32. Slow growth in DCs may in fact cause '(a) a deceleration of growth of production and trade worldwide; (b) depressed levels of output, capacity utilisation, investment and employment in a great many parts of the world; (c) a further decline in the commodity terms of trade of primary products; and (d) extraordinary high real rates of interest, a level of indebtedness in a score of countries that clearly is beyond their capacity to repay and a continuation of the large net transfer of resources from poor countries to rich' [*Griffin and Khan, 1992: 68*].
33. PTAs and FTAs refer to different kinds of 'partial regionalisation'. PTAs reduce the tariff level among partners without necessarily eliminating them, as happens with FTAs
34. Krugman [*1991b*] has also demonstrated that world welfare is lower with a few trading blocs than with the extremes of one or many; three being the worst possible number of blocs as they would be protectionist.
35. 'The emerging forms of governance of international markets and other economic processes involve the major national governments but in a new role; states will come to function less as "sovereign" entities and more as the components of an international "polity" – that among the central functions of the nation state will be those of providing legitimacy for and ensuring the accountability of supra- and sub-national governance mechanisms', mechanisms which tend to develop together. Yet, if sovereign power within a territory is the essence of the notion of a

nation, nationalism, and to that effect democracy as well, imply that 'political power should reflect *cultural* homogeneity'; hence nationalism cannot but render international co-operation more difficult [*Hirst and Thompson, 1995: 409, 411*].

36. 'Deep integration', as opposed to 'shallow integration', refers to an integration process which goes beyond a concern with tariffs. It involves a comprehensive, all-embracing, approach to liberalisation and compels governments to surrender more sovereignty, both in terms of national norms and procedures and of dispute settlement, and to transfer institutions to a supranational level, that is, institutional integration. Monetary union is required more for political union than for economic integration. This is demonstrated in Asia, where even in cases of deep integration as in 'Greater China' and the Singapore-Johr-Riau 'growth triangle' (see later) there is no plan to move towards monetary union because there is no desire to achieve political unity [*Arndt, 1993: 276*].
37. Theoretically, the main reason why blocs are expected to be more protectionist is that their larger sise allows them a higher level of optimal tariff, i.e. to turn the terms of trade to their advantage, although Whalley [*1985: 173, Table 9.6*] has estimated that the optimal tariff for the USA, the EU and Japan, assuming no retaliation, is 160, 150 and 175 per cent respectively. That FTAs may not be necessarily inferior, this being dependant much more on their design, is demonstrated by the fact that large-scale economies 'may improve efficiency even if it [the FTA] is predominantly trade diverting' [*Wonnacott and Lutz, 1989: 63*].
38. Furthermore, the nation-state still controls the army and, through taxation, a large share of GDP.
39. The Caribbean Basin Initiative (1983) allows US apparel manufacturers to ship fabric for sewing to low-wage factories in the islands and reimport the finished goods with substantial tax breaks. The *maquiladora* factories in Mexico have a similar preferred status.
40. Hub and spoke arrangements 'are worse than is often recognised' because 'each spoke thinks it is participating in regional trade liberalisation – and it is, but only with the hub ... facing damaged trade with all other spokes' [*Wonnacott, 1996: 65*].
41. The rules of origin applicable to goods benefiting from free trade, especially textiles, clothing and automotive products, could even be contrary to the spirit of GATT [*Hufbauer and Schott, 1993: 5-6, 11*].
42. Robson [*1993: 340*] rightly points out that one of the most important potential advantages of such an arrangement is the boost in credibility that LDC members derive from it. Langhammer [*1992: 213*] takes a more critical view of the FTAs negotiated by industrialised countries with some LDCs, a sort of 'minilateralism' [*Yarbrough and Yarbrough, 1987: 2–6*] with the danger of trade-diverting effects. For an analysis of the prerequisites required for free trade arrangements between DCs and LDCs, see Langhammer [*1992: 223–5*].
43. The common effective preferential tariff was initially restricted to manufactured and processed agricultural products, but in 1995 it was agreed to reduce the exclusions, to extend the commodity coverage to services, and to accelerate the timetable. Furthermore, earlier ASEAN-4 agreements related to the distribution of investment in specific sectors.
44. According to the 1994 report of the Eminent Persons Group to APEC, open regionalism is a process of regional co-operation the outcome of which is both a reduction of intra-regional barriers and of external barriers to economies that are not part of the regional arrangements. In this sense, open regionalism is consistent with and equivalent to multilateralism and the GATT agreement. Drysdale and Garnaut [*1993: 188*] hope that through open regionalism national governments will enjoy the 'prisoner's delight' of experiencing the beneficial effects of each country's liberalisation on its own trade expansion, rather than being caught in the prisoner's dilemma of negotiated concessions. Yet since any form of regionalism cannot fail to discriminate in favour of its members, open regionalism remains a contradiction in terms.
45. Several 'growth triangles', aside from the more formal groupings, are emerging within the region. Particularly suited to countries in transition from a closed and rigid economic system to an open and market-oriented economic system, a 'growth triangle' is a scheme to promote and rationalise direct investment as well as to build up infrastructure linkages within the area. Although it presents an export-oriented structure, it is not a mechanism solely to promote free trade and it does not imply discrimination as far as a third party is concerned [*Tang, 1995: 19–20*]. The most important of these triangles are 'Greater China' (starting to emerge since the early 1980s) (Southern China, Taiwan and Hong Kong), 'Northeast Asia' (Japan, South and

North Korea, Northeast China and Far East Russia), 'Greater Mekong' (established in 1991) (Cambodia, Laos, Myanmar, Thailand, Viet Nam and China's Yunnan Province) and some 'growth triangles' involving localised arrangements which cover selected areas of a few countries, like the 'Singapore-Johor-Riau Growth Triangle' (1989) between Singapore and Malaysia's and Indonesia's provinces; the 'Tumen River Area Development' (established in 1991) between North Korea, China and Russia; the 'East ASEAN Growth Area' (established in 1994) between Brunei, Indonesia, Malaysia and the Philippines; and 'Indonesia, Malaysia-Thailand Growth Triangle' (established in 1993).

46. Against the World Bank view, forcefully presented in De Melo and Panagariya [*1993*], a view is emerging with respect to the possibility of implanting regional integration even in Africa and the least developed countries, using structural adjustment programmes (SAP) to facilitate the pursuit of integration. Only by reducing its own costs from non-integration, can Africa hope to attract the inflows of foreign investment and technology and cross-border investment on which its development continues to depend [*Robson: 1993: 340*].
47. Intra-firm trade represents 40 per cent of US total trade, a percentage that may rise to two-thirds if the term 'related party' is more loosely defined [*Ruggie, 1993: 149n*].

## REFERENCES


Alesina, A. and E. Spolaore, 1995, *On the Numbers and Size of Nations*, Working Paper No.5050, NBER, Cambridge MA, March.

Anderson, S. and J. Kavanagh, 1996, 'Corporate Power Isn't Discussed', *International Herald Tribune*, 23 Oct.

Arndt, H. W., 1993, 'Anatomy of Regionalism', *Journal of Asian Economics*, Vol.4, No.2, pp.271–82.

Asian Development Bank (ADB), 1996, *Asian Development Outlook. 1996 and 1997*, Oxford: Oxford University Press.

Baldwin, R., 1989, 'The Growth Effects of 1992', *Economic Policy*, Vol.9, Oct., pp.247–83.

Bergsten, C.F., 1996, 'Globalising Free Trade', *Foreign Affairs*, Vol.75, No.3, May/June, pp.105–20.

Bhagwati, J., 1993, 'Regionalism and Multilateralism: An Overview', in J. De Melo and Panagariya [*1993*].

Bienefeld, M., 1994, 'The New World Order; Echoes of a New Imperialism', *Third World Quarterly*, Vol.15, No.1, pp.31–48.

Bliss, C., 1994, *Economic Theory and Policy for Trading Blocks*, Manchester: Manchester University Press.

Boltho, A., 1996, 'The Return of Free Trade?', *International Affairs*, Vol.72, No.2, April, pp.247–59.

Bolton, P., Roland, G. and E. Spolaore, 1996,'Economic Theories of the Break-up and Integration of Nations', *European Economic Review*, Vol.40, Nos.3–5, April, pp.99–104.

Bressand, A., 1990, 'Beyond Interdependence: 1992 as a Global Challenge', *International Affairs*, Vol.66, No.1, pp.47–65.

Cable, V., 1994, 'Overview', in Cable and Henderson (eds.) [*1994*].

Cable, V., 1996, 'The New Trade Agenda: Universal Rules amid Cultural Diversity', *International Affairs*, Vol.72, No.2, April, pp.227–46.

Cable, V. and D. Henderson (eds.), 1994, *Trade Blocs? The Future of Regional Integrations*, London: The Royal Institute of International Affairs.

Casella, A., 1996, 'Large Countries, Small Countries and the Enlargement of Trade Blocs', *European Economic Review*, Vol.40, No.2, Feb., pp.389–415.

CEPAL, 1995, 'Preliminary Overview of the Latin American and Caribbean Economy', *Notas Sobre la Economia y el Desarrollo*, 585/86, UNECLAC, Santiago, Dec.

Chen, H. and A. Ho, 1994, 'Southern China Growth Triangle: An Overview', in Myo Thant, Min Tang and Hiroshi Kakazu (eds.), *Growth Triangles in Asia. A New Approach to Regional Economic Cooperation*, Oxford: Oxford University Press.

Collier, P. and C. Meyer, 1989, 'The Assessment: Financial Liberalisation, Financial Systems and Economic Growth', *Oxford Review of Economic Policy*, Vol.15, No.4, Winter, pp.1–12.

Cox, R., 1981, 'Social Forces, States and World Orders: Beyond International Relations Theory', *Millennium*, Vol.10, No.2, pp.126–55.

Dale, R., 1996, 'Nobody Gains From Trade Fortresses', *International Herald Tribune*, 12 Nov.

De Melo, J. and A. Panagariya (eds.), 1993, *New Dimensions in Regional Integration*, Cambridge: Cambridge University Press.

Dickey, C., 1995, 'Junk Nations', *Newsweek*, 27 Nov.

Drèze, J., 1993, 'Regions of Europe: A Feasible Status, to be Discussed', *Economic Policy*, Vol.17, Oct., pp.266–93.

Drysdale P. and R. Garnaut, 1993, 'The Pacific: An Application of a General Theory of Economic Integration', in C. F. Bergsten and M. Noland (eds.), *Pacific Dynamism and the International Economic System*, Washington, DC: Institute for International Economics.

Dunning, J. H., 1993, *The Globalisation of Business: The Challenge of the 1990s*, London: Routledge.

ECLAC, 1994, *Open Regionalism in Latin America and the Caribbean, Economic Integration as a Contribution to Changing Production Patterns with Social Equity*, Santiago: UNECLAC.

Featherstone, M., 1990, 'Global Culture: An Introduction', in Featherstone (ed.) [*1990*].

Featherstone, M. (ed.), 1990, *Global Culture: Nationalism, Globalisation and Modernity*, London: Sage.

Feenstra, R.C. and G.H. Hanson, 1996, 'Globalization, Outsourcing, and Wage Inequality', *American Economic Review Papers and Proceedings*, Vol.86, No.2, May, pp.240-5.

Frankel. J., Stein, E. and Shang-jin Wei, 1995, 'Trading Blocs and the Americas: The Natural, the Unnatural, and the Super-natural', *Journal of Development Economics*, Vol.47, No.1, pp.61–95.

Garofoli, G., 1992, 'Endogenous Development and Southern Europe: An Introduction', in G. Garofoli (ed.), *Endogenous Development and Southern Europe*, Aldershot: Avebury.

Gereffi, G., 1993, 'Global Sourcing and Regional Division of Labor in the Pacific Rim', in A. Dirlik (ed.), *What Is In A Rim? Critical Perspectives on the Pacific Region Idea*, Boulder, CO: Westview Press.

Gill, S., 1995, 'Globalisation, Market Civilisation, and Disciplinary Neoliberalism', *Millennium*, Vol.24, No.3, pp.399–423.

Gilpin, R., 1987, *The Political Economy of International Relations*, Princeton, NJ: Princeton University Press.

Griffin, K. and A.R. Khan, 1992, *Globalisation and the Developing World, An Essay on the International Dimensions of Development in the Post-Cold War Era*, Geneva: UNRISD.

Henderson, D., 1994, 'Putting "Trade Blocs" into Perspective', in V. Cable and D. Henderson (eds.), *Trade Blocs? The Future of Regional Integration*, London: The Royal Institute of International Affairs.

Hirst, P. and G. Thompson, 1992, 'The Problem of "Globalisation": International Economic Relations, National Economic Management and the Formation of Trading Blocs', *Economy and Society*, Vol.21, No.4, Nov., pp.357–96.

Hirst, P. and G. Thompson, 1995, 'Globalisation and the Future of the Nation State', *Economy and Society*, Vol.24, No.3, Aug., pp.408–42.

Horsman, M. and A. Marshall, 1994, *After The Nation-State, Citizens, Tribalism and the New World Order*, London: HarperCollins.

Hufbauer G. and J. Schott, 1993, *NAFTA, An Assessment*, Institute for International Economics, Washington, DC.

Huntington, S.P., 1973, 'Transnational Organisations in World Politics', *World Politics*, Vol.25, No.3, April, pp.333–68.

Hutton W., 1995, 'A Postscript', in J. Michie and J.G. Smith (eds.), *Managing the Global Economy*, Oxford: Oxford University Press.

Jackson, R., 1987, 'Quasi-states, Dual Regimes, and Neoclassical Theory: International Jurisprudence and the Third World', *International Organisation*, Vol.41, No.4, pp.519–49.

Jacquemin, A. and A. Sapir, 1991, 'Europe post-1992: Internal and External Liberalisation', *American Economic Review Papers and Proceedings*, Vol.81, No.2, May, pp.166–70.

Kapstein, E. B., 1994, *Governing the Global Economy*, Cambridge, MA: Harvard University Press.

Kemp, M.P. and H.Y. Wan, 1976, 'An Elementary Proposition Concerning the Formation of Customs Unions', *Journal of International Economics*, Vol.6, No.1, pp.95–7.

Krugman, P., 1988, 'La Nueva Teoría del Comercio Internacional y los Países Menos Desarrollados', *El Trimestre Económico*, 40, 217, Jan./March, pp.41–66.

Krugman, P., 1991a, 'The Move Toward Free Trade Zones', in *Policy Implications of Trade and Currency Zones*, A Symposium sponsored by the Federal Reserve Bank of Kansas City, Jackson Hole, Wyoming, 22-24 Aug..

Krugman, P., 1991b, 'Is Bilateralism Bad?', in E. Helpman and A. Razin (eds.), *International Trade and Trade Policy*, Cambridge, MA: MIT Press.

Krugman, P. and A.J. Venables, 1995, 'Globalisation and the Inequality of Nations', *The Quarterly Journal of Economics*, Vol.101, No.4, Nov.

Laïdi, Z., 1995, 'Introduction', in Z. Laïdi (ed.), *Power and Purpose After the Cold War*, Oxford: Berg.

Lal, D., 1993, 'Trade Blocs and Multilateral Free Trade', *Journal of Common Market Studies*, Vol.31, No.3, Sept., pp.349–58.

Langhammer, R. J., 1992, 'The Developing Countries and Regionalism', *Journal of Common Market Studies*, Vol.30, No.2, June, pp.211–31.

Langhammer, R.J. and U. Hiemenz, 1990, *Regional Integration Among Developing Countries*, Tubingen: J.C.B. Mohr.

Lawrence, R. Z., 1994, 'Regionalism: An Overview', *Journal of the Japanese and International Economies*, Vol.8, No.4, pp.365–87.

Ling, L. H. M., 1996, 'Hegemony and the Internationalising State: A Post-colonial Analysis of China's Integration into Asian Corporatism', *Review of International Political Economy*, Vol.3, No.1, Spring, pp.1–26.

Lorenz, D., 1992, 'Economic Geography and the Political Economy of Regionalisation: The Example of Western Europe', *American Economic Review, Papers and Proceedings*, Vol.82, No.2, May, pp.84–92.

Lorenz, D., 1993, 'Europe and Asia in the Context of Regionalisation: Theory and Economic Policy', *Journal of Asian Economics*, Vol.4, No.2, pp.255–70.

Mittelman, J. H., 1994, 'The Globalisation Challenge: Surviving at the Margins', *Third World Quarterly*, Vol.15, No.3, Sept., pp.427–43.

Ohmae, K., 1993, 'The Rise of the Region State', *Foreign Affairs*, Vol.72, No.2, Spring, pp.78–87.

Oman, C., 1994, *Globalisation and Regionalisation: the Challenge for Developing Countries*, Paris: OECD.

Padoa-Schioppa, T. and F. Saccomanni, 1994, 'Managing a Market-Led Global Financial System', in P. B. Kennen (ed.), *Managing The World Economy, Fifty Years After Bretton Woods*, Institute for International Economics, Washington, DC.

Perroni, C. and J. Whalley, 1996, 'How Severe is Global Retaliation Risk under Increasing Regionalism', *American Economic Review, Papers and Proceedings*, Vol.86, No.2, May.

Pochih Chen, 1994, 'Foreign Investment in the Southern China Growth Triangle', in Myo Thant, Min Tang and Hiroshi Kakazu (eds.), *Growth Triangles in Asia, A new Approach to Regional Economic Cooperation*, Oxford: Oxford University Press.

Polanyi, K., 1957, *The Great Transformation: The Political and Economic Origins of Our Time*, Boston, MA: Beacon Press.

Robertson, R., 1990, 'Mapping the Global Condition: Globalisation as the Central Concept', in Featherstone (ed.). [*1990*].

Robson, P., 1993, 'The New Regionalism and Developing Countries', *Journal of Common Market Studies*, Vol.31, No.3, Sept., pp.329–47.

Rodrik, D., 1994, 'King Kong Meets Godzilla: The World Bank and the East Asian Miracle', CEPR, Discussion Paper Series No.944, London, April.

Rosecrance, R., 1996, 'The Rise of the Virtual State', *Foreign Affairs*, Vol.75, No.4, July/Aug., pp.45–61.

Ruggie, J.G., 1993, 'Territoriality and Beyond: Problematising Modernity in International Relations', *International Organisation*, Vol.47, No.1, Winter, pp.139–74.

Ruggie, J. G., 1995, 'At Home Abroad, Abroad at Home: International Liberalisation and Domestic Stability in the New World Order', *Millennium*, Vol.24, No.3, pp.507–26.

Schor, J. B., 1992, 'Introduction', in T. Banuri and J. B. Schor (eds.), *Financial Openness and National Autonomy*, Oxford: Clarendon Press.

Schwab, K, and C. Smadja, 1996, 'Start Taking the Backlash against Globalisation Seriously', *The International Herald Tribune*, 1 Feb.

Sideri, S., 1992, 'European Integration and the Third World', in S. Sideri and J. Sengupta (eds.), *The 1992 Single European Market and the Third World*, London: Frank Cass.

Sideri, S., 1993, 'Restructuring the Post-Cold War World Economy', *Development and Change*, Vol.24, No.1, Jan., pp.7–27.

Sideri, S., 1994, 'The Economic Relations of China and Asia-Pacific with Europe', ISESAO, Università Bocconi, Milan.

Sideri, S., 1995, 'Globalizzazione, Devoluzione ed Integrazione Regionale: la sfida dell'economia mondiale e il caso italiano', *Economia e banca*, Vol.17, No.3, pp.261–93.

Sigurdson, J., 1996, 'Globalisation and Corporate Strategic Alliances – A European Perspective', unpublished paper presented at the Second International Forum on Asian Perspectives jointly organised by the Asian Development Bank and the OECD Development Centre, Paris, June.

Stokes, B., 1996, 'Divergent Paths: US-Japan Relations Towards the Twenty-First Century', *International Affairs*, Vol.72, No.2, April, pp.281–91.

Streeck, W. and P. C. Schmitter, 1991, 'From National Corporatism to Transnational Pluralism: Organised Interests in the Single European Market', *Politics and Society*, Vol.19, No.2, June, pp.133–64.

Tang, Min, 1995, 'Asian Economic Co-operation: Opportunities and Challenges', in K. Fukasaku (ed.), *Regional Co-operation and Integration in Asia*, Paris: OECD.

Tang, Min and Myo Thant, 1994, 'Growth Triangles: Conceptual and Operational Considerations', in Myo Thant, Min Tang and Hiroshi Kakazu (eds.), *Growth Triangles in Asia: A New Approach to Regional Economic Cooperation*, Oxford: Oxford University Press.

Thomsen, S., 1994, 'Regional Integration and Multinational Production', in V. Cable and D. Henderson (eds.), *Trade Blocs? The Future of Regional Integration*, London: The Royal Institute of International Affairs.

Thomson, J.E. and S.D. Krasner, 1989, 'Global Transactions and the Consolidation of Sovereignty', in E.-O. Czempiel and J.N. Rosenau (eds.), *Global Changes and Theoretical Challenges*, Lexington, MA: Lexington Books.

UNCTAD, 1995, *World Investment Report: Transnational Corporations and Competitiveness*, New York: United Nations.

UNRISD, 1995, *States of Disarray, The Social Effects of Globalisation*, London: UNRISD.

Whalley, J., 1985, *Trade Liberalisation Among Major Trading Areas*, Cambridge, MA: MIT Press.

Wonnacott, P. and M. Lutz, 1989, 'Is there a Case for Free Trade Areas?', in J.J. Schott (ed.), *Free Trade Areas and U.S. Trade Policy*, Institute for International Economics, Washington, DC.

Wonnacott, P., 1996, 'Free-Trade Agreements: For better or Worse?', *American Economic Review Papers and Proceedings*, Vol.86, No.2, May, pp.62–6.

World Bank, 1989, *World Development Report 1989*, Oxford: Oxford University Press for World Bank.

World Bank, 1990, *World Development Report 1990*, Oxford: Oxford University Press for World Bank.

World Bank, 1991, *World Development Report 1991*, Oxford: Oxford University Press for World Bank.

World Trade Organisation (WTO), 1995, *International Trade, Trends and Statistics*, Geneva: WTO.

Yarbrough B.V. and R. Yarbrough, 1987, 'Cooperation in the Liberalisation of International Trade: After Hegemony, What?', *International Organisation*, Vol.41, No.1, Winter, pp.1–26.

Yoshida, M., Akimune, I., Nohara, M. and K. Sato, 1994, 'Regional Integration in East Asia: Special Features and Policy Implications', in Cable and Henderson (eds.) [*1994*].

# Development, Security and World Order: A Regionalist Approach

BJÖRN HETTNE

*This study contains both a methodological and a theoretical argument, and the two are closely linked. The methodological argument is that a merger between International Political Economy and Development Theory would reduce weaknesses particular to these social science traditions. A 'combined approach', with a focus on development for 'the excluded', which is the particular concern of Alternative Development Theory, is applied to the current regionalisation of the post-Westphalian world order and the structural relations between various types of regionalisms: 'neo-liberal regionalism' in the Core, 'open regionalism' in the intermediate regions, and 'security and development regionalism' in the Periphery. The author interprets regionalisation, and this is the theoretical argument, as a counter-movement in a global context, where the 'political' reappears in the form of popular resistance to globalisation, as well as in a 'new regionalism'; both reactions to the social disruption implied in the uneven and selective globalising market exchange.*

## INTRODUCTION

This study argues that development theory as a state centric concern lacks relevance and, in order to regain its earlier importance, it needs to be merged with International Political Economy (IPE). IPE, on the other hand, would be enriched by the more dynamic and normative concerns central to Development Theory, particularly Alternative Development Theory (ADT). Such a merger may ultimately strengthen an emerging 'critical political economy', dealing with historical power structures, emphasising contradictions in them, as well as change and transformation expressed in normative terms (development).[1]

---

Björn Hettne, Department of Peace and Development Research (PADRIGU), Göteborg University, Sweden. The study draws on findings from a UNU-WIDER research programme on the New Regionalism on which the author is project director. The author wishes to acknowledge contributions from all project participants for the ideas developed here, and also appreciates the destruction and reconstruction of a first version by Ph.D. students at the IPE-seminar at Padrigu. Encouraging comments from an anonymous reviewer were also crucial.

The advantages of such a merger would be a two-way traffic. It can be described as filling a theoretical vacuum constituted by at least two problematic gaps. The first is between the growing irrelevance of a 'nation state approach' and the prematurity of a 'world approach'. The second is between immanence, that is, a theorising about development as 'inherent' in history, an approach which tends to generate amoral passivism, and, intention, a political will to 'develop', which may breed excessive normativism and unrealistic voluntarism, particularly as development has become globalised and out of reach for the main actor, that is, the state.[2]

The first gap corresponds to the transition between what can be termed a 'Westphalian' and a 'post-Westphalian' world order. By 'Westphalian' we imply an interstate system with the following characteristics: the sovereign independence of states; each state motivated in its international behaviour by a consistent national interest; the interstate system regulated by a balance of power among the principal powers.[3] There is a specific political rationality underlying this behaviour, a Westphalian rationality taking the nation state as the given guarantee for security as well as welfare. What lies 'outside' the secluded and protected nation state territory is perceived as chaos and anarchy. The disorder, turbulence and uncertainties people experience today come with the realisation that this guarantee can no longer be taken for granted, and the confusion is only magnified when the two political rationalities are mixed, a merger typical for periods of historic transition. The Westphalian political rationality is, furthermore, perverted into forms of pathological Westphalianism, such as irrational bloody wars for pieces of land upon which to build mini-states. A 'post-Westphalian' logic rests on the contrary assumption that the nation-state has lost its usefulness, and that solutions to emerging problems must increasingly be found in transnational structures.

One cause of conflict and turbulence is probably the antagonistic coexistence of the two rationalities. I consider a 'new regionalism' to be a possible way out of this dilemma. The regionalist approach can thus be seen as the compromise between Westphalian and post-Westphalian political rationality, and, in terms of development principles, between territory and function.[4] The world order is increasingly regionalised, and in this process of ongoing global fragmentation, one can discern a core–periphery structure, characterised by 'neo-liberalism' in the core regions, 'open regionalism' in what I call the 'intermediate regions', and by new experiments with 'security regionalism' and 'developmental regionalism' in the peripheral regions. These experiments are seemingly undertaken to arrest the growing North–South polarisation and may even serve the purpose of avoiding the ultimate collapse of world order.

Evidently, these regionalist trends have a novel quality. Some notable differences between 'old' and 'new' regionalism are that current processes of regionalisation are more from 'below' and 'within' than before, and that ecological and security imperatives as well as economic ones push countries and communities towards co-operation within new types of regionalist frameworks. The actors behind regionalist projects are no longer states only, but a large number of different institutions, organisations and movements. Furthermore, today's regionalism is extroverted rather than introverted, which reflects the deeper integration of the current global economy and interdependence among its parts. The 'new regionalism' is thus one way of coping (offensively or defensively) with global transformation, as an increasing number of states are realising that they lack the capability and the means to manage such a task on the 'national level'. Finally, one of the defining characteristics of the New Regionalism is that it takes place in a multipolar global order, whereas the old regionalism was marked by bipolarity.

The current phenomenon of regionalism has so far been discussed mainly with regard to its impact on the pattern of trade, despite the fact that the new wave of regionalism is often defined by its comprehensiveness and multidimensionality, ranging from shared ecological threats to regional security crises, for which the region, in a world where multilateralism is in a deep crisis, has to assume more responsibility. This is due to the ridiculously small (and even diminishing) amount of resources devoted to the unprecedented global problems facing 'world society'. We can, for the sake of argument, assume that there is such a thing as 'world society' with an at least embryonic system of governance, as well as a world population facing a large number of more or less shared problems. What strategies can be conceived of to solve these problems? This question relates to the second gap referred to above; how to intervene in a development process that is no longer national, and on what moral/ethical grounds to do this.

Intervention is often reactive rather than proactive. Karl Polanyi argued that societies which have become completely dominated by the market principle, implying that land, capital and labour have been commodified, are a recent historical phenomenon. Two other economic mechanisms played a more important role in earlier western economic history as well as in many non-Western cultures: reciprocity and redistribution. The former concept refers to the socially embedded forms of exchange in small-scale symmetric communities; the latter refers to politically determined distribution in stratified societies marked by a centre–periphery structure. Both modes of distribution were critically undermined by the increasing prevalence of market exchange. However, as the market principle came to penetrate all spheres of human activity, thereby eroding traditional structures and creating social turmoil, redistribution had to be reinvented in order to provide displaced people with the necessary social protection. Polanyi called this phase of market expansion, followed by another phase of reaction on the part of society, the 'double movement'. Protectionism was in this historical perspective not inherently bad, as the conventional economic wisdom described it. Modern society is both a result of market expansion ('the first movement') and the self-protection of society against the disruptive and destabilising effects of the market ('the second movement'). This was the 'Great Transformation' [*Polanyi, 1957*].

Society is continuously being transformed in accordance with the double movement, so that, in its second phase, the economy becomes re-embedded – typically through state action – in society, like the genie who is forced back into the lamp. As market exchange can only be amoral, it is for the political regime to deal with the social disruptions of an unregulated market. In the Polanyian tradition, the political, redistributive logic (historically, the logic of the state) stands out as less destructive than the anarchist logic of the market itself. The preferred alternative to liberal capitalism on a world scale after the Second World War was therefore regionalism and planning.[5] Polanyi developed this regionalist scenario, against what he at the time feared was going to be a new hegemonic world order or 'universal capitalism'. This early and little known argument for a regionalised world system and a 'new protectionism' is still relevant and forms the theoretical hypothesis of this study. Previously, the protection of society was carried out by the state in accordance with the redistributive logic. The current phenomenon of regionalism could be seen as a manifestation of the second movement, the protection of society, on the level of the macroregion, as a political reaction against the global market expansion which gained momentum in the 1980s. Thus we can speak of a 'Second Great Transformation'.

Owing to the decline of the nation-state, the retreat of the state, and the consequent unlikeliness of a conventional redistributional solution on the national level, the potential of civil society is increasingly often mentioned as a means for the powerless and the poor to protect themselves. The response to globalism will thus contain other elements than transnational redistribution, for instance local solidarity structures based on the principle of reciprocity as new forms of self-protection of civil society. In this study the focus is on political structures of redistribution in the form of a new regionalism.

## THE INTERNATIONAL POLITICAL ECONOMY OF ALTERNATIVE DEVELOPMENT

For a decade or more, Development theory (DT) has experienced a fatal crisis emanating from its exclusive concern with the way nation states should manage 'their' economies and promote 'their' national developments, as if they were independent universes. In the earlier theoretical phase, dominated by the modernisation paradigm, the external context of development was largely neglected. Development towards ultimate international interdependence was by the modernisation theorists seen as an inbuilt tendency in the market logic. According to this thesis, modern economic history embodied the evolution of the market system, both in terms of vertical deepening and horizontal expansion. Dependency theory, in contrast, did emphasise the role of external structure, and was particularly concerned with its assumed perverting effects on dependent countries, which thereby became 'underdeveloped'. The global economy was in this perspective simplistically analyzed as a centre-periphery structure with an inherent polarising tendency between states. This approach did not provide any basis for sound development strategies, which is the ultimate rationale for development theory, concerned as it is with the task of 'developing' (intention). The raison d'etre of the dependency approach, like development theory in general, was not primarily the exploration of the nature of development (immanence), but rather to intervene in the underdevelopment process in order to achieve 'development' for the peripheries.[6]

Modern development theory was from the start both normative and instrumental. Furthermore, it was assumed that development was a process that could be steered by the state. Therefore, development has been a contested concept, and development theory an area of contending schools, modernisation theory, dependency theory and alternative theory being the most influential. The Mainstream model and the Counterpoint critique should be seen as dialectically interrelated, and as the latter is being coopted by the former, the 'actually existing development' provokes new countermovements, modifying the direction and pattern of development. Alternative development theory (ADT) deals with development in terms of how it ought to take place. Such speculative activity is not wasted, since visions of the good society influence actual development, to the extent that development is affected by political actions and human will, rather than being immanent, that is, a 'natural history'. What this ultimately involves is the inclusion of the excluded into the development process, shaped by the power structure of society. The pattern of development is a matter of power, and any modification of the pattern of development presupposes some sort of political intervention. Alternative models are, thus, not born in a vacuum, but derived from negations of existing models, from a critical debate on the reality of development, from incorporating perspectives of 'the excluded', from political struggle, and from utopian traditions. Ethnodevelopment is, for instance, seen as one counterbalance to mainstream development as cultural standardisation. Feminist critique of development theory also gradually enriched this growing tradition of critique of mainstream 'macho' development and provided further ideas for alternative sustainable ends and means.

However, long lists of preferred alternatives, to my mind, do not provide a basis for normative theory. In order to be both coherent and realistic, the alternative concepts should emerge from the fundamental contradictions of mainstream development, such as the unevenness of the development process, the homogenising impact of globalisation on cultural diversity, leading to national and subnational identity crises, and the finiteness of the resource base. Taking the most challenging problems in contemporary development into consideration, a consistent theory of alternative development should contain the following three principles:

(1) The principle of *territorialism* as a counterpoint to functionalism;

(2) The principle of *cultural pluralism* as a counterpoint to standardised modernisation; and

(3) The principle of *ecological sustainability* as a counterpoint to 'sustained growth'.

These three principles overlap to some extent but, nevertheless, highlight important dimensions of an alternative pattern of development rooted in space, culture and ecology. They constitute a package supporting each other, and derive from the same basic development philosophy, what I call the 'counterpoint' to the mainstream model. In a dialectical perspective the principles can thus be seen as correctives to the mainstream pattern. The principles are, furthermore, meant to benefit the 'non-elites', in accordance with what was said above about the sources of ADT. In the world of 'actually existing development', 60 per cent of the world's population belongs to a periphery of stagnation, marginalisation and poverty [*Friedman, 1992*]. Alternative development is therefore a cry for visibility, participation and justice, which in the current world order means large-scale (albeit not imminent) structural changes [*Hettne, 1995a*].

The stress on intention, how to design a development process, rather than immanence, the natural history of development, is arguably a major difference between development theory and IPE. The emerging Critical Political Economy is one exception, as it does share some traits with radical development/underdevelopment theory, in particular the emphasis on transformation and purposeful change.[7] The normative and voluntarist thrust is, however, on the whole conspicuously absent in the most common IPE schools, where structure typically is seen as more important than agency. The scope of action for radical reformists is thus seen as fairly limited.

IPE typically deals with the connection between politics and economics in international relations, and the particular social order which links the two. Its underlying assumption is that an economic system cannot function without a political framework of some sort. From this follows that development is structured by the social order or, if we are thinking of development in a global context, the world order. Alternative development theory, as described above, is more concerned with 'community' and 'civil society'; issues which therefore would also add more flesh and blood to a new IPE, with a higher dose of historicism, holism and normativism.

Development theory in its various manifestations can thus make significant contributions to a new IPE; contributions which are related to normative developmental issues which do not arise from pure considerations of power and welfare. By making distinctions between different paths and strategies of development, the relationship between various domestic situations and different foreign policy outcomes is highlighted. By stressing national development strategy as a special case, it is implied that one can think of other actors than the state as social carriers of development strategies, and other 'levels' of the world-system, apart from the 'national', at which these strategies can be carried out by a great variety of actors.

To understand reorientations in the process of development, the study of previously excluded actors is of particular importance. Exclusion can be analyzed both in social terms, which means class analysis in a transnational context, and in geographical terms, which means regional analysis. This paper concentrates on the latter. This perspective opens up a vast field of empirical research, case studies, comparative analysis, and middle-range theorising concerning the role of development actors in the context of a changing international political economy and world order, currently affected by the contradictory processes of globalisation and regionalisation. These terms will be further elaborated below.

## WORLD ORDER AND DISORDER

The study of world order can be regarded as IPE's distinct contribution to social science, and consequently to development theory [*Cox, 1996*]. What is meant by world order? It can be defined as the rules and norms regulating international economic transactions. Disorder consequently refers to the turbulent interregnum between world orders. Polanyi [*1957: 18!*] used to warn against what he called the 'hazards of planetary interdependence' associated with global market expansion. His sceptical view on interdependence based on the market corresponds to the contemporary neomercantilist view of the market system as a fragile arrangement in need of political control. The post-war world economy was in fact a historic compromise between international economic *laissez-faire* and a certain level of domestic control. This essentially Keynesian approach was abandoned during the 1970s and in the subsequent decade neoliberal principles became increasingly dominant, a trend that culminated when the socialist world began to disintegrate.

Amongst more radical theorists, disorder is therefore often associated with economic globalisation; the crucial question then being the return of 'the political' and the form this return will take. One possibility is regionalism, and another is a variety of alternative or 'new' social movements. These two reactions roughly correspond to the two principles of redistribution and reciprocity mentioned above. The rules in force during the postwar era constituted the Bretton Woods post-war world order, characterised by a compromise between international free trade and domestic regulation (manifested in a milder form in the capitalist countries and a more rigid form in the so-called socialist countries).[8] As long as one particular world order is maintained, the rules of the game are known. This situation generally facilitates the growth of economic interdependence. To the extent that such a situation is widely accepted, it is referred to as 'hegemony', a kind of power based on different but mutually supportive dimensions, fulfilling certain functions (the provisioning of international collective goods) in a larger system lacking formal authority structure, and, consequently, more or less voluntarily accepted by other actors.

The New World Order concept as used in the context of the Gulf War can be seen as a counter-strategy of the declining hegemon against the various challenges, for instance regionalisation, the rise of aggressive regional powers, and various kinds of 'antisystemic' resistance movements. Unilateralism is different from hegemony in being conflictive rather than consensual. The leaders of the other two regional blocs, Japan and the European Union, are the only possible hegemonic successors. There are, however, no signs that they are prepared to participate in a bid for hegemony in the foreseeable future. A more likely scenario is a territorial type of fragmentation in the form of regionalisation of the world. Regionalism and globalism will thus continue to be closely linked, both contradicting and supporting each other. It is therefore important to clarify what is implied by these two processes. Whereas 'regional' has an impressive theoretical tradition behind it, 'global' is a more recent concept in social science, often used in a rather loose and ideological sense. Globalism can be defined as programmatic globalisation, the vision of a borderless world, in which territory has lost all importance and functionalism is predominant.

As a process, globalisation indicates a qualitative change in the internationalisation process, thus further strengthening the functional and weakening the territorial dimension.[9] The contemporary concern with phenomena such as 'interdependence', 'world order' or the 'global system' is to a large extent a cognitive phenomenon; that is, it is a matter of how the world is conceived.[10] I see globalisation as a qualitatively new phenomenon. If globalisation simply implies an observed tendency towards a global social system, its origins may be traced far back in history, but one could also argue that the process reached a new stage in the post-Second World War era. The subjective sense of geographical distance is dramatically changed, some even speak of 'the end of geography'. The world is also commonly experienced as one in ecological terms. In this context we are primarily interested in the economic dimension.

Economic interdependence was made possible by the relative political stability of the American world order, which lasted from the end of the Second World War until the late 1960s or early 1970s. After the breakdown of the compromise of embedded liberalism, political control of the process was abandoned as part of the hegemonic role of neoliberalism. Globalisation in this period is therefore conceived as contradictory and 'turbulent' [*Rosenau, 1990*]. It represents the ultimate manifestation of a post-Westphalian logic. It coincides with the neo-liberal doctrine, and is typically articulating the interests of strong economic actors, the big players on the global market, but asserting, in a universalised language, the values of efficiency and competitiveness against corruption and mismanagement, described as 'rent-seeking behaviour' in neo-classical economistic terminology. Thus, globalisation represents the project of the self-regulating market in its ultimate transnational and functionalist form. The basic problem with globalisation is the selectivity of the process. Exclusion is inherent, and the benefits negatively balanced by misery, conflict and violence. The negative effects are incompatible with the survival of civil society, and thus in the longer run a threat to all humanity.

The New Regionalism, by contrast, represents a territorially based urge for control over financial and economic forces. It is similar to mercantilism, albeit relating to a completely different global context. One can think of the 'new regionalism' as a way of overcoming the contradiction between Westphalian and post-Westphalian rationality. In the era of New Regionalism, regionalisation would be a multidimensional process of regional integration including economic, political, social and cultural aspects which go beyond the free trade market idea, that is, the interlinkage of previously more or less secluded national markets into one functional economic unit. Rather, the political ambition of establishing territorial control and regional coherence cum identity (in Polanyi's terms: protecting regional civil society) is the primary goal. In the Polanyian terms presented above, globalisation, or the rise of the global market, can be seen as the 'first movement' in a second Great Transformation, initiated in the mid 1970s. We can now consequently observe the beginning of a 'second movement' in terms of popular resistance to globalisation (which can be linked to the principle of reciprocity) and the return of the political (which can be linked to the principle of redistribution), currently in the form of 'the new regionalism'. It corresponds to the concept of ADT in Development Theory in that it is basically normative (although not utopian). This means that the process of regionalisation is analysed from the point of view of its potential to change the mainstream pattern of development.

Regionalisation occurs in a global situation characterised by multipolarity, but an asymmetrical form of multipolarity. A rough distinction can thus be made between the core regions and peripheral regions, as well as an intermediate category which I shall call intermediate regions. This is the way countries used to be analysed by the neo-marxist and dependency tradition in development theory. The core regions are thus politically stable and economically dynamic and organise for the sake of being better able to control the world. The peripheral regions are defined as being politically more turbulent and economically more stagnant; consequently they organise in order to arrest a process of marginalisation. At the same time their regional arrangements are fragile and ineffective. Their overall situation therefore makes 'security regionalism' and 'developmental regionalism' more important than the creation of free trade regimes. In contrast to the Core, they strive to change the established pattern of development, simply because they have objective reasons to do so.

The Core is constituted of regions which are economically dynamic and politically capable, whether this capability is expressed in a formal political organisation or not. So far only one of the three core regions, namely Europe, displays aspirations to build such an organisation, albeit against growing nationalist resistance. The other two, North America and East Asia, are economically strong but still lack a regional political order. All three want a say in world affairs from the point of view of their distinct interests. Accordingly, G7 declarations and cooperation within organisations such as APEC, NATO, and OSCE notwithstanding, relations between them are quite tense.

Intermediate regions are those being incorporated into the Core, that is, former Eastern Europe, those waiting to join the European Union, Latin America and the Caribbean in the process of becoming 'North Americanised', and South East Asia, Coastal China, the European Pacific (Australia, New Zealand) and South Pacific, which are drawn into the East Asian economic space dominated by Japanese capital. South Africa belongs here, as may North Africa, depending on the outcome of the ongoing internal violence and the willingness of the EU to engage itself.

Remaining in a peripheral position are thus six regions: the former Soviet Union, the major parts of which are now being reintegrated in the form of the Commonwealth of Independent States, the Balkans, where the countries have lost whatever tradition of co-operation they once might have had, the Middle East, with an unsettled and explosive regional structure, South Asia, with a very low level of region-ness because of the 'cold war' (occasionally getting hot) between the major powers India and Pakistan, the non-coastal areas of China, and most of Africa, where in a number of countries the political structures called 'states' are falling apart.

## WORLD DEVELOPMENT

The world order provides the context of development. The old world order of 'embedded liberalism' thus meant very different conditions for national development strategies than the neoliberal new world order or, for that matter, a regionalised world order. Weak and strong states naturally have different stakes in different types of world orders. For instance, in a world conceived as an international welfare system, authoritative resource allocation would have a different impact from that of allocation based on market exchange, which has now become the general norm [*Strange, 1988: 208*]. There is no political authority accountable for resource-allocation and welfare in the global system. To the extent that one can talk of a world welfare system, this is therefore truly embryonic. The same can consequently be said about the possibilities of an international civil society to sustain such a system. From an IPE perspective the aid phenomenon is a mechanism of stabilisation and diffusion of strategic world order values from core to periphery. The ongoing controversy over political conditionalities, such as human rights fulfilment, armament levels, type of political system, and type of economic policies shows that norms are in fact being imposed on the dependent regions. This implies a process of homogenisation of the global political space, expressing the hegemonic value system.

More important than aid for the development prospects of the individual developing countries, is the nature of the global transaction system and the rules for trade, investment and so on which govern it. This was already discovered by the Latin American dependency school, which took the disruptive impact of the capitalist world economy on the Latin American economies for granted, and therefore urged delinking. As will be discussed below this perspective is still relevant in a modified form when analyzing world regions and their relations. The basic IPE positions regarding development are thus not unfamiliar to development theorists. What is new is the overall perspective, which transcends the nation state. The liberal paradigm in IPE is closely related to the modernisation perspective in development theory, where the gains from the international division of labour are assumed to benefit all. Consequently, outward-oriented development strategies are recommended.

This classical pattern of economically strong states pushing for free trade and 'liberalisation' is repeated in the neo-liberal regionalism among the dominant economic blocs. The crucial development issue in the neo-Marxist tradition is integration into versus delinking from the world market, or, as the question is posed in more recent contributions, the optimal combination of the two strategies in different conjunctures of the international political economy. This is reflected also in open versus introverted regionalism. The IPE approach to development, derived from so-called realist thinking, is that a national development strategy forms an integral part of the nation-state project. The commitment to 'development' is subsumed under the 'national interest' of state survival, that is, the modernisation imperative. The outstanding example of this 'realist' or 'mercantilist' approach to development is, of course, Friedrich List. Neomercantilism can be seen as transcending the nation-state logic in arguing for a world system consisting of self-sufficient blocs [*Hettne, 1993a; 1993b*]. The external environment of development undergoes continuous changes. What is more, the state operates in an equally shifting domestic context, trying to respond to political challenges from 'the excluded' in a way which optimises its legitimacy and autonomy. The state as such is not a monolithic structure but complex and continuously changing and it will also have to adapt to the international political economy. The current trend is rather the 'internationalisation of the state' [*Cox, 1996*], which means that the state does not so much protect 'its' own population as it is instrumental in its adjustment to global market forces. The main reason for this important transformation of the state is the globalisation process which transfers power from the states to global actors, exploiting the free play of market forces. Against this globalist trend, regionalisation means the return of 'the political', as stressed above. However, different regionalisms carry different political content.

## NEO-LIBERAL REGIONALISM IN THE CORE

The concept of 'neoliberal regionalism' is a contradiction in terms, since the universalist liberal doctrine is the antithesis to organised regionalism, whether leftist or rightist. Nevertheless, regional groupings may be instrumental for pursuing different types of goals, in this case non-discrimination in trade and, as is normal for proponents of free trade, access to all relevant markets and the elimination of all kinds of nationalist obstacles. This is not necessarily done in the pursuit of some kind of universal interest, but in the interest of the respective economic bloc, often headed by a rather illiberal government–corporate alliance trying to penetrate the other blocs which are blamed for being protectionist. Free trade has always been an excellent argument for top dogs in asymmetrical relationships, but love of it is seldom blind, not even in the Core. The top dog in question is, of course, the USA which, mainly for security reasons, played an important role in the development of the West European and Asia Pacific regions by 'raising' the two economic giants West Germany and Japan, often described as 'free riders' under the shield of Pax Americana. With declining US hegemony, these regional great powers are emerging as regional bloc leaders and now challenge even US supremacy on a number of issues, thus establishing what could be described as a trilateral global power structure.

Significantly, the USA is active in all regional core organisations. There is perfect compatibility between the ideology of globalism and the strategy of regionalism as far as the Core is concerned. Although the blocs in the Core accuse each other of being too closed and introverted, none of the three blocs assumes an explicitly protectionist posture. On the contrary, they compete in the praise (if not in the practice) of free trade. Europe has established a single market, but is often described as a 'fortress' by other external actors. For the USA, NAFTA was perceived as a step towards free trade – as a natural part of the GATT process and the Uruguay Round. In Asia Pacific the situation is more complex. According to a World Bank report (Sustaining Rapid Development), East Asia should strengthen regional integration through trade liberalisation and promotion of foreign direct investment within the framework of the multilateral trading system. 'A trading block would more likely foster an inward orientation, impairing the world wide search for market opportunities that has served East Asia so well' (*Bangkok Post*, 15 April 1993, p.25). The preferred regional alternative is thus the 15-member-strong forum for Asia Pacific Economic Cooperation (APEC) which was set up in 1989. It has regional and interregional trade expansion as its main goal and in no way implies regionalism of an introverted sort. APEC can thus be compared to 'the Atlantic project' in Europe. It is a transregional network providing a bridge for the USA in the area, and therefore supported by US-oriented regimes and opposed by spokesmen for a genuinely Asian regionalism (EAEC). From the US point of view, APEC – like NAFTA in the Americas – is a continuation of its strategy of bilateralism (that is, pursuing the US national interest).

## OPEN REGIONALISM IN THE INTERMEDIATE REGIONS

In the intermediate regions the prevalent economic ideology puts emphasis on 'open regionalism'. In Europe the intermediate region, Central Europe, is more faithful to neoliberal doctrines than most Core countries. The same position is now taken by Australia in the Pacific area. Australia is of course desperately anxious not to be left out of the ongoing process of bloc formation. The word 'open regionalism' is often used for regional trade arrangements that do not hurt third parties and thus are 'free trade compatible'. The idea of the slightest kind of more introvert regionalism is on the whole very controversial in the South East Asian region, being dependent on unhindered world trade. In 1990 the Malaysian Prime Minister Mahathir (in his frustration at drawn out GATT negotiations) broke this policy line and urged Japan to act as a leader of an emerging East Asian Economic Grouping (EAEG), which would create an East Asian and South East Asian superbloc with a Sino-Japanese core. EAEG (it has since been modestly renamed East Asia Economic Caucus – EAEC) would be a sort of response to European and North American 'fortresses'.

The EAEC proposal is slowly gaining support among other ASEAN countries, whereas the East Asian countries, particularly Japan and South Korea, have taken a more sceptical attitude. So has, of course, the USA and the World Bank. Thus there are two understandings of regionalism: (1) a way of managing multilateralism, and (2) a challenge to multilateralism. The first conception predominates in Asia-Pacific. In Latin America the emphasis on the whole is on 'regionalismo abierto'. This largely neo-liberal interpretation of regionalism appears to be a paradox. According to a recent ECLAC document:

> What differentiates open regionalism from trade liberalisation and non-discriminatory export promotion is that it includes a preferential element which is reflected in integration agreements and reinforced by the geographical closeness and cultural affinity of the countries in the region. A complementary objective is to make integration a building bloc of a more open transparent international economy [*ECLAC,* 1994: 12).

The concept 'open regionalism' may sound like a contradiction in terms, as having your cake and eating it. To some extent open regionalism is a way of reviving interest in an issue which has been dead for a decade in Latin America, and which in a neoliberal political context sniffs of forbidden protectionism and state-interventionism. It is also of course a recognition of the fact that the global economy in the 1990s is different from the one in the 1960s. Finally, it is a cautious strategy given the high level of uncertainty about the future development of the world economy.

> If a less optimistic international scenario should develop, open regionalism is still justifiable as the least objectionable alternative for dealing with an external environment which is unfavourable to the countries of the region, since it at least preserves the expanded market of the member countries of integration agreements [*ECLAC*, 1994: 14].

In a more negative global scenario, regionalism thus remains a second best alternative, better than a return to economic nationalism. It is also obvious that Mercosur is driven more by political ambitions than merely trade strategies. Economic nationalism is, however, not on the agenda in Latin America. On the contrary, there are strong convergencies both within Latin America and between Latin America and North America.[11]

## SECURITY AND DEVELOPMENT REGIONALISMS IN THE PERIPHERY

As an alternative to the scenario of unrestrained globalisation, interventionist regionalism is more attractive to the Periphery than to the Core.

Developmental regionalism and security regionalism constitute a package which, with varying contents, is relevant to all emerging regions, particularly the marginalised areas. Even if 'delinking' is no longer on the agenda, the general orientation may be more or less defensive and introverted.

*Security Regionalism*

In the field of conflict management and conflict resolution, the idea that conflicts within a certain region are best dealt with directly by the region concerned is not new. In the earlier debate, however, the 'region' was simply conceived as an intermediate level between the global level and the 'floor' of nation states. The region was not an actor itself, only a 'level' or 'space' of action. With increasing 'regionness' the region becomes an actor in its own right, it is being transformed from object to subject. The crucial criterion for assessing the coherence of a region is therefore its capacity for autonomous conflict management and conflict resolution.

This regional coherence can be described in terms of levels of 'regionness'. We can, with particular reference to regional conflict and conflict management, distinguish five levels. The first level is region as a *geographical* unit, delimited by natural geographical barriers and with limited and sporadic contacts between human groups. Violence is therefore limited and sporadic. The second level is region as a *social system,* which implies more dense translocal relations, constituting some kind of regional complex, what Buzan [*1991*] calls a regional security complex, in which the constituent units (normally states) are dependent, as far as their own security is concerned, on each other. The third level is region as *organised cooperation*, where region is defined by membership of the regional organisation in question. To the extent that the 'formal' region, which may be a *military alliance*, corresponds to the 'real' region (that is, the regional security complex), regional security is enhanced. The contrary would be the case where the region is divided between two military alliances, a common situation in the cold war. The fourth level is region as *regional civil society*, which will take shape when the organisational framework promotes social communication and convergence of values throughout the region, thereby transformed into a *security community.* The fifth level is region as *acting subject* with a distinct identity and interest, actor capability, legitimacy, and structure of decision-making in such crucial areas as conflict resolution (between and within former states) and welfare (in terms of social security and regional balance), as well as joint management of ecological problems. A regional organisation capable of handling this range of challenges would be like a state, a region state.

Implied in this sequence of stages (no determinism involved) is the idea that any particular region will increase the level of security and peace by raising the level of regional cooperation and move from security complex to security community (and even more integrated political structures). Paradoxically perhaps, the new type of conflicts, which are internal with respect to a particular state formation (in contrast to the interstate conflicts typical of the Westphalian world order), tend to reinforce regional security cooperation. The reason for this particular outcome is very simple. The new conflicts and the 'failed states' create security crises which (in any regional security complex) are impossible to neglect for the states constituting the complex.

To understand how and why a (national) society breaks down, one must understand what makes it peaceful in the first place, that is, how it normally functions. This would be a situation where civil society mediates between the state and the actual and potential 'primary groups'. Civil society (here used as a normative concept) is by definition open, multicultural, and facilitating communication between all groups constituting the national system. The unevenness and selectivity of the globalisation process leads to social (or ethnic) exclusion and increasing social (or ethnic) tensions. The process of erosion can be described as a transfer of loyalties from civil society to the primary group, a concept summing up both 'primordial' and 'socially constructed' groups.[12] This creates a situation in which each single group becomes responsible for its own security [*Posen, 1993*]. This breakdown of civil society leads to a regional security crisis which, if it serious enough, will lead to some kind of intervention from outside.

There is, of course, a need for legitimation in all cases of external intervention because of the sanctity of territorial sovereignty inherent in the Westphalian tradition. There are in the intervention discourse two major varieties of legitimation: (1) a conflict constitutes a threat to international peace and (2) the behaviour of the parties to a conflict massively violates human rights. The first has a clear foundation in the UN charter. The implications of elevating the second variety of legitimation to a general principle are dramatic. There is no international order that will react to all crises in a consistent and uniform way. Therefore *ad hocism* has been the rule, and will probably continue to be. Every case has its own motivations and underlying interests. External intervention can take two major forms, civil and military, with several sub-categories. Civil intervention may be preventive. It may try to influence the parties in the early stages of the conflict, by positive (assistance, encouragement) or negative (sanctions) methods. It may provide humanitarian assistance at a later and violent stage of a conflict, or it may be devoted to reconstruction and peace-building in a post-conflict situation.

There are five different modes of military interventions: unilateral, bilateral, plurilateral, regional and multilateral. The distinctions are not very clear-cut, and in real world situations several actors at different levels are involved, the number increasing with the complexity of the conflict itself.

The point to be stressed here is the increasing importance of regional interventions, and the likelihood that a combination of regional and multilateral interventions may be the preferred form in the nearest future, while in the long run the regional mode will be predominant. This implies some form of institutionalisation, which in turn means a relative strengthening of regional *vis-à-vis* national structures.

Some illustrations of the various forms of intervention can be given. The USA has carried out a large number of unilateral interventions in Latin America, most of them part of the cold war game. Other interventions were made by 'concerned neighbours' (Tanzania in Uganda, Vietnam in Cambodia, India in Bangladesh) as responses to regional security crises. (These interventions may have been multilateral or regional today.) Occasionally such interventions are based on a bilateral agreement (such as India's occupation of northern Sri Lanka). With a stronger SAARC (South Asian Association for Regional Cooperation) this particular operation might have been a regional one (which would have made more sense). Plurilateral interventions are made by military alliances (NATO in Bosnia, or the Organisation of Islamic Conference in the case of Mindanao in the Philippines) or other *ad hoc* groupings (such as the 'contact group' also in Bosnia, alarmingly similar to the nineteenth-century European Concert). They differ from regional interventions by their lack of territorial dimension.

Regional interventions are thus organised by territorially based organisations such as EU (not yet formed when the crisis in Yugoslavia started). The best example is, somewhat unexpectedly, the ECOWAS (ECOMOG) intervention in Liberia, not particularly successful but nevertheless a good illustration of the dynamics of regional intervention in local conflicts. (In making an assessment it should be kept in mind that some multilateral interventions have been catastrophic.) Multilateral intervention (Cambodia being the most quoted case although Japan and ASEAN played an important role) is still the norm and, according to many, the only legal possibility. It has therefore been used for authorisation in the case of other types of interventions. To my mind, it will be less frequent and more selective in the future. Regional interventions are necessary and inescapable in deep regional security crises, and there is reason to believe that such interventions lead to more lasting solutions, since otherwise neighbouring countries have to live with the problem and face the eruption of new violent conflicts. The record of regional intervention is recent and the empirical basis for making an assessment is fairly weak. Incidents of national disintegration can both make and break regional organisations, but the more important the regional factor in conflict resolution, the higher the degree of 'regionness' of the region in question.

*Developmental Regionalism*

The old regionalism was often imposed for geopolitical reasons, and there were no incentives for economic co-operation, particularly if the 'natural' economic region was divided in accordance with the Cold War pattern. Attempts at regional co-operation were often inherited from colonial times and did not go far beyond regional trade arrangements. Owing to lack of complementarities, such arrangements were never sufficient to realise the potentials of development regionalism. As the global pattern of uneven development was reproduced within the region, the result was political tension.

The 'new' regionalism, in contrast, is more political. Its approach to free trade is cautious, far from autarkic but more selective in its external relations, and careful to address the interests of the region as a whole, as in the case of management of natural resources or infrastructural development. Benefits with different relevance in different contexts and situations can be found in a number of areas:

(1) In a highly interdependent world the question of size has undoubtedly lost some of its former importance, but regional co-operation is nevertheless imperative in the case of micro states who either have to co-operate to solve common problems or become client states of the 'core countries' (*the argument of sufficient size*). In the Caribbean the regional organisation CARICOM (with 13 members) contains less than six million people. There are not more than 32 million people in greater Caribbean. The next step should therefore be to form a Caribbean Basin region which also includes Central America. The small Central American states also have strong incentives for regional co-operation. The change of regime in Nicaragua increased the regional political homogeneity and consequently the scope for regional initiatives. So did the settlement of the border conflict between Honduras and El Salvador and more recently the internal peace agreement in Guatemala. Thus regional conflict resolution is often the first step towards regional cooperation for development. The crucial issue is whether the countries can develop a common approach to the emerging US-Canada-Mexico bloc, or whether they will join NAFTA as individual client states, and thereby become 'North Americanised'.

(2) Self-reliance is an old development goal which rarely proved viable on the national level. Yet it may be a feasible development strategy at the regional if defined not as autarky but as coordination of production, improvement of infrastructure, and the use of complementarities in order to strengthen the position of the region in the world economy (*the viable economy argument*). In Sub-Saharan Africa there has been little regional integration, simply because

there is little to integrate in the first place. The urgent need for a broader and more dynamic concept of development, beyond 'stabilisation', is only possible within a framework of regional co-operation. The 'dynamic approach' to regional integration must be further developed. One important regional initiative is SADC (Southern Africa Development Community), originally created to reduce dependence on South Africa. Recent SADC documents indicate an awareness of the need for political intervention to prevent deepening of regional economic disparities.

(3) Economic policies may be more stable and consistent if underpinned by regional arrangements which cannot be broken by a participant country without some kind of sanction from the others (*the credibility argument*). For external potential investors the country is therefore considered more stable and safe. Political stability is of course a wider and more complex concept, as shown in the Mexican crisis, caused by the resurgence of guerilla activities (first in Chiapas, then in Oaxaca and Guerrero). Being part of NAFTA did not prevent the country from being thrown into a major crisis arising from external speculation. On the other hand, being part of NAFTA did facilitate the salvage programme that followed. For the same reason the Chiapas conflict did not grow worse, and the democratic process has been kept on the track. A more recent example (April, 1996) of the stabilising role of regionalism was the firm reaction of MERCOSUR countries to an attempted coup in Paraguay. Thus the credibility argument concerns political stability as well as economic policy.

(4) Collective bargaining at the level of the region could improve the economic position of marginalised countries in the world system, or protect the structural position and market access of new successful exporters (*the argument of effective articulation*). The countries in ASEAN are all outward-oriented, and in various phases of a NIC-type development path. Thus 'open regionalism' is a way to articulate interests from within the region *vis-à-vis* the globalisation process.

(5) Regionalism can reinforce societal viability by including social security issues and an element of redistribution and protection (by regional compensation and development funds or specialised banks) in the regionalist project (*the social stability argument*). This argument becomes particularly relevant when the degree of regionness is so advanced as to include an element of mutual solidarity among both the constituent states and their subnational regions. So far it is at the most embryonic in the peripheral regions.

(6) Few serious environmental problems can be solved within the framework of the nation-state. Some problems are bilateral, some are global, quite a few

are regional. Regional problems often relate to water: coastal waters, rivers, and ground water. Of particular importance are the South and South East Asian river systems. In the field of resource management there are strong interdependencies which up to now have been a source of conflict rather than co-operation. They may, however, also be turned into regionalist imperatives (*the resource management argument*).

(7) Regional conflict resolution, if successful and durable, eliminates distorted investment patterns as the 'security fund' (military expenditures) can be tapped for more productive use (*the peace dividend argument*). This argument carries special force in the Middle East. Stable peace would open a completely new world, and for this reason the breakthrough in the Israeli–Palestine peace process was particularly important. A regional development process based on the triangle Israel-Jordan-Palestine is essential for the consolidation of the peace process, and again for further development in the whole region.

Here the circle is closed: regional co-operation for development reduces the level of conflict and the peace dividend facilitates further development co-operation. This positive circle must not be turned into a vicious circle, where conflicts and underdevelopment feed on each other. How do these principles fit with an alternative development pattern? On the whole, developmental regionalism forms part of mainstream development thinking, just like dependency theory was a mainstream approach, albeit expressing a Southern viewpoint. However, contradiction is not the same as incompatibility. Along the dimensions of territorialism – functionalism, cultural pluralism – standardised modernisation and ecological sustainability – sustained economic growth, regionalism is to my mind situated closer to the counterpoint position than globalism.

## CONCLUSION

I have argued the methodological point that a merger between International Political Economy and Development Theory, particularly Alternative Development Theory, would reduce weaknesses particular to these social science traditions; in the first, a static amoral concern with power and wealth; in the second, an exaggerated concern with the increasingly irrelevant 'national' space, and failure to take cognisance of the implications of the globalisation of development. A development perspective on IPE would lead to a stronger focus on change and transformation, and an IPE perspective on development would emphasise the global context of development, and the way development is structured by any particular world order.

In more theoretical terms, the article has argued (with inspiration from dependency theory) that the emerging world order is regionalised, and constituted by Core, Intermediate regions and Periphery. The new regional order further generates, but also feeds on, the disorder created on the sub-national level in the wake of globalisation. Thus integration and disintegration are simultaneous processes, order and disorder paradoxically related. This is particularly evident in the peripheral regions. The ambivalent and paradoxical 'open regionalism' of intermediate regions is a contradiction in terms, revealing the completely different structure of interests between Core and Periphery. In this perspective, development should be understood as a reduction of the structural gap between Core and Periphery. The means whereby this could be achieved are Security Regionalism and Developmental Regionalism, which (in contrast with the globalist hegemony established by the Core) necessitate a substantial degree of interventionism. The New Regionalism implies the possibility of a regional formation with a distinct identity and a capacity as an actor. It does not preclude a function for the old nation-state which, for certain limited purposes, could be a useful level of decision-making. However, in many instances, the nation-state often prevents rational solutions, whereas the regional level opens up new ways of solving conflicts that have become institutionalised in the historical state formations.

This article was inspired by Karl Polanyi who was a pioneer in the more voluntaristic and development-oriented tradition of IPE. His basic theory about a 'double movement' assumed a return of the 'political', after a phase of market expansion, which according to him is bound to lead to disorder and turbulence. In what I have termed 'the Second Great Transformation', the first phase of market expansion corresponds to globalisation. Regionalism is the major reactive force in the second phase of the contemporary 'double movement'. Regions can only be defined post factum, which implies different regionalisms, supported or challenged by different ideological arguments and reflecting various positions in the world economy.

Still within Polanyi's terms, new reciprocal structures in the form of localism, local structures of self-help and solidarity could emerge as a reaction to globalisation and as a supplement to the emerging (if this study proves right) redistributive structures of a new regionalism. It will certainly be a complex system of interacting levels with a stronger role for supranational and sub-national levels, and a diminished role for the nation-state level (post-Westphalianism). This may, again in Polanyi's terms, prevent fascism (linked to a Westphalian mentality) and create 'freedom in a complex society' as the positive alternative to war among civilisations, guerilla wars without (political) purpose, urban jungles of criminal mafias, tribal wars among motorbike gangs, and other postmodern perversions so vividly and usually correctly described in neo-conservative writings, but without much indication of what should be done about it.

Regionalism is one approach to various global problems, but its content will be conditioned by the very nature of these problems. From the point of view of the Core, the function of regionalism is completely different from that of the Periphery. The peripheral regions are peripheral because they are, dependent, economically stagnant, politically turbulent and war prone, and the only way for them to become less peripheral in structural terms would be to become more regionalised, that is, to increase their level of 'regionness'. The alternative is further disintegration and the complete disappearance of the most fragile states, whose territories will be absorbed by stronger neighbours. Developmental regionalism is the appropriate response to the threatening peripheralisation of the poor regions of the world. National strategies will in the end defeat their own purpose, since no country in any particular region can be made immune to a general economic and political regional disease. Without regional co-operation, the only 'power' of these regions is 'chaos power', that is, the capacity to create problem for the Core, thereby providing some kind of engagement. For the poor areas, there are thus strong imperatives in favour of regionalism and alternative development strategies.

Such strategies, by their comprehensiveness, provide solutions to a number of problems. As should be evident from this analysis, the development issues cannot be studied apart from issues of security. When a regional security complex moves from largely negative to largely positive interdependencies (what is sometimes called a security community), such a process to a large extent coincides with what is usually called development. Conflict resolution is a necessary precondition for development, and development in turn reduces the risk of conflicts. Developmental regionalism contains the traditional arguments for regional co-operation, such as territorial size and economies of scale but, more significantly, adds some new concerns and uncertainties in the current transformation of the world order and world economy.

Thus security regionalism and developmental regionalism are mutually supportive and together form the only possible strategy to arrest the process of further marginalisation or subordination for the peripheral regions. Alternative development (defined as development for the excluded and marginalised) is not easily reconciled with the strategy of development regionalism, since this strategy implies a considerable degree of transnational coordination and the development of suprastate institutions. It could, nevertheless, be argued that the counterpoint initiatives are more easily carried out under the protective shield of developmental regionalism, than if exposed to the chilly winds of globalisation.

## NOTES

1. This problem is raised in Hettne [*1995a*] and was the theme of the special issue of *The European Journal of Development Research*, Vol.7, No.2, Dec.1995. The concept of 'critical political economy' comes from Robert Cox and is discussed in Hettne [*1995b*]. The discussion on regionalism elaborates on earlier analyses in Hettne [*1993a; 1993b*] and Hettne and Inotai [*1994*].
2. The distinction is central to the analysis of development theory in Cowen and Shenton [*1996*].
3. The definition is made by Robert Cox and summarised in Hettne [*1995b: 12*].
4. This important distinction is elaborated in Friedman and Weaver [*1979*].
5. 'The new permanent pattern of world affairs is one of regional systems coexisting side by side' [*Polanyi, 1945: 87*].
6. For an assessment of this tradition, see Blomström and Hettne [*1984*] and Kay [*1989*].
7. The intellectual father of this still rather tentative 'school' is Robert Cox, whose most important articles are found in Cox [*1996*].
8. Ruggie [*1982*] refers to this compromise as 'embedded liberalism'.
9. Whether this qualitative deepening in the process of internationalisation is significant enough to deserve a new name, that is, globalisation, is debatable [*Hirst and Thompson, 1996*].
10. Is globalisation, for instance, to be seen as a single process or is it made up of more or less interlinked sub-processes or trends? In the UNRISD study, 'States of Disarray: The social Effects of Globalisation', a distinction is made between six 'key trends': spread of liberal democracy, dominance of market forces, integration of the global economy, transformation of production systems and labour markets, spread of technological change, and the media revolution and consumerism.
11. OAS now appears less an instrument of US imperialism and more a genuine expression of the interests of most countries in the Americas. This trend towards hemispheric regionalism started in earnest with the 1994 summit of the Americas in Miami.
12. Primordial, as used here, does not define particular components of identity, but simply refers to those components which are more persistent and durable.

## REFERENCES

Blomström, Magnus and Björn Hettne, 1984, *Development Theory in Transition: The Dependency Debate and Beyond*, London: Zed Books.

Buzan, Barry, 1991, *People, States and Fear*, Boulder, CO: Lynn Rienner.

Cowen, M.P. and R.W. Shenton, 1996, *Doctrines of Development*, London and New York: Routledge.

Cox, Robert, with Timothy J. Sinclair, 1996, *Approaches to World Order*, Cambridge: Cambridge University Press.

ECLAC, 1994, *Open Regionalism in Latin America and the Caribbean: Economic Integration as a Contribution to Changing Production Patterns with Social Equity*, Santiago: United Nations Economic Commission for Latin America and the Caribbean.

Friedman, John, 1992, *Empowerment, The Politics of Alternative Development*, Cambridge, MA: Blackwell.

Friedman, John and C. Weaver, 1979, *Territory and Function: The Evolution of Regional Planning*, London: Edward Arnold.

Hettne, Björn, 1993a, 'The Concept of Neomercantilism', in Lars Magnusson (ed.), *Mercantilist Economics*, Kluwer.

Hettne, Björn, 1993b, 'Neomercantilism: The Pursuit of Regionness', *Cooperation and Conflict*, Vol.28, No.3, pp.211–32.

Hettne, Björn, 1995a, *Development Theory and the Three Worlds, Towards an International Political Economy of Development*, London: Longman.

Hettne, Björn (ed.), 1995b, *International Political Economy, Understanding Disorder*, London: Zed Books.

Hettne, Björn and Andras Inotai, 1994, *The New Regionalism, Implications for Global Development and International Security*, Helsingfors: WIDER.

Hirst P. and G. Thompson, 1996, *Globalisation in Question*, Cambridge: Polity Press.

Kay, Cristóbal, 1989, *Latin American Theories of Development and Underdevelopment*, London: Routledge.

Polanyi, Karl, 1945, 'Universal Capitalism or Regional Planning', *The London Quarterly of World Affairs*, Jan., p.87.

Polanyi, Karl, 1957, *The Great Transformation*, Boston, MA: Beacon Press.

Posen, Barry R., 1993, 'The Security Dilemma and Ethnic Conflict', in Michael E. Brown (ed.), *Ethnic Conflict and International Security*, Princeton, NJ: Princeton University Press.

Rosenau, James N., 1990, *Turbulence in World Politics, A Theory of Change and Continuity*, Princeton, NJ: Princeton University Press.

Ruggie, John Gerard, 1982, 'International Regimes, Transactions and Change: Embedded Liberalism in the Postwar Economic Order', *International Organisation*, Vol.36, No.2.

Strange, Susan, 1988, *State and Markets: An Introduction to International Political Economy*, London: Pinter.

# Globalisation: The Last Sky

ZUHAIR DIBAJA

*What makes globalisation worthy of discussion, despite the vagueness of the term, is its cultural magic. After a long history of extraordinary destruction, we are now told that all societies can become a single society. This contribution raises an important question: from where does the discourse of globalisation derive its strength? Readers will quickly discover the close link between the modernisation project and the globalisation project. An examination of globalisation shows that Western culture is disconnecting in the global field. What is also interesting to observe is that globalisation trivialises Western civilisation. The main conclusion is that globalisation neither produces useful results nor helps to advance the cause of mankind.*

## INTRODUCTION

The modernisation project has failed to Westernise the culture of the world. The discourse of modernisation – laden with ideological distortions, instrumental policies, strange concepts – has been powerless to assist. In addition, development has been a field of corruption embracing those who do not mind losing their intellectual probity. The discourse of globalisation takes its inspiration from such ruins and some professionals believe that the end of the history has arrived.

This contribution aims to question globalisation. Criticising scholarly Western relations to the world is unlikely to please contemporary conservative thinking. I draw on Roland Robertson's work quite prominently for a number of reasons. First, on account of its currency in academic institutions. Second, his analysis, made credible by its balanced tone and unstated creed of the superior West, deserves attention. Third, certain values and principles espoused by Robertson, such as his notion of 'shared values', invite further inquiry. As will be seen, a society in which individuals are formed and influenced by the values of the Industrial Revolution appears to be culturally disconnecting in the global field. Finally, I hope no one will regard me as depicting Westerners as a bunch of conquerors; I regard the West as the site of great civilisation and achievement.

---

Zuhair Dibaja, Research Fellow, Institute of Development Studies, University of Helsinki. The author wishes to thank all those who commented on this text.

## WHY GLOBALISATION?

In his prologue Roland Robertson [*1994*] writes that his work on globalisation began in the mid-1960s. Robertson then has been around for nearly thirty years. Something must have happened. At the end of his prologue, he states: 'Perhaps my dominant interest ... has been in trying to isolate the period during which contemporary globalisation reached a point when it was so well established that a particular pattern, or form, prevailed' [*ibid.: 6*]. He goes on to argue that the debate on convergence or divergence from modernity has been revived in the light of the collapse of communism in the early 1990s [*ibid.: 11*]. Thus, this implies that the concept of globalisation could not be revived if many ideological patterns exist. Robertson criticises Immanuel Wallerstein's theory of world-systems in which the world is conceived as a consequence of the capitalist system of exchange. 'The way in which I speak of globalisation is ... centred on such a conception, which involves the attempts to take the notion of globality very seriously. Much of the thrust of my own thinking centers on my attempt to depict the main general contour of the world as a whole' [*ibid.: 15*]. Robertson believes his perspective to be superior to Wallerstein's. This is quite common among social scientists who normally regard their own perspective as the best in the field and often look at other perspectives with disrespect [*So, 1990*]. Robertson believes that he employs the concept of culture more fluidly and adventurously than others. For him, culture indicates a particular way of doing sociology and not vice versa. In his representation of the global field, he stresses processes of differentiation which have implications for socialisation in the contemporary world.

Malcolm Waters [*1995: 1*] begins his text on globalisation with the following statement:

> Social change is now proceeding so rapidly that if a [social scientist] had proposed as recently as ten years ago to write a book about globalisation they would have had to overcome a wall of stony and bemused incomprehension. But now, just as postmodernism was the concept of the 1980s, globalisation may be the concept of the 1990s, a key idea by which we understand the transition of human society into the third millennium.

Accordingly, the time has come to scrutinise what mankind (humankind is preferred by Robertson) has achieved since the birth of Jesus Christ. There have been great civilisations, outstanding figures, prodigious achievements, complex events, and great intellectual consciousness. Robertson limits his enquiry, however, to Western thoughts and actions since the Age of Enlightenment.

In the works of Robertson and Waters, societies in a globalised world can draw inspiration from former experiences. Put differently, since many past events occurred in a global context, societies should affiliate globally around the society with the highest standards. Accordingly, even the US is expected to respond to Japan. If societies do not think in terms of divergence, globalisation becomes 'a social process in which the constraints of geography on social and cultural arrangements recede and in which people become increasingly aware that they are receding' [*Waters, 1995: 3*].

This process is conceived to be the fruit of modernity. Robertson remarks that there must be something after modernity. He argues that 'globalisation cannot be comprehensively considered simply an aspect of the outcome of the Western "project" of modernity' [*Robertson, 1994: 27*]. And notes: 'I also argue that globalisation is intimately related to modernity, as well as postmodernity and postmodernisation' [*ibid.: 53*]. Robertson not only believes in modernity, and its impact on the world, but comprehends gestures of anti-modernity and anti-globality as phenomena which are also modern.

Waters' definition of globalisation represents the final stage of societal integration. In order to simplify a complex argument, Robertson presents a minimal model of globalisation. Prior to that he advises us to assume a moderate stand towards Westernisation, imperialism and capitalism. Robertson's model consists of five stages, one of which recalls Rostow's model of the five 'Stages of Economic Growth' developed in the 1960s. While Rostow's imperialistic theory focused on take-off to economic maturity, Robertson's model is about take-off to globality, and is laden with instances of Western achievements. This dovetailing is not accidental, as Hans Singer commented at the 8th EADI General Conference in Vienna in 1996. In Robertson's project, Rostow's drive to maturity could be interpreted as meaning the drive to globality, in which the immature countries assume a permanent role as subservient hinterlands for the overdeveloped folk of the capitalist West.

Globalisation, according to Mittelman [*1994*], involves the dissemination of the economy, polity and culture of one sphere into another. If this is so, the human endeavour to influence or dominate has been evident throughout the ages. Robertson is, however, more concerned to create a socio-cultural system in which culture, and only culture, plays a dominant role in the world system. Economy and polity are not excluded from the world system, but help to energise it 'negatively or positively'. In such a world system, individuals, societies, the system of societies and humankind, are to be treated in terms of one coherent analytical framework. In the light of the above definition, Waters [*1995: 3*] predicts a surprising result:

> In a globalised world there will be a single society and culture occupying the planet. This society and culture will probably not be harmoniously integrated although it might conceivably be. Rather it will probably tend towards high levels of differentiation, multicentricity and chaos. There will be no central organising government and no tight set of cultural preferences and prescriptions. Insofar as culture is unified it will be extremely abstract, expressing tolerance for diversity and individual choice ... Importantly territoriality will disappear as an organising principle for social and cultural life, it will be a society without borders and spatial boundaries.

If our world turns into a sort of nightmare, our research will not be worth the paper it is written on unless Robertson is able to convince us how economy, polity and culture work together in the new world system, and particularly, why culture is superior to everything else. Lindblom [*1977: 7*] remarked that 'in all political systems of the world much of politics is economics and most of economics is also politics'. This implies that culture will inevitably dovetail with economics and polity, because culture has always been politicised, such as in Japan-US relations. Robertson, dissatisfied with the notion of economism, argues that the economisation of the world has proceeded without 'cultural guidance', and that economy and polity have not been strong enough to globalise existing reality. Robertson tries his best to depart from materialist accounts and argues that culture, via symbols and images, can play a greater part in the crystallisation of the modern world system. His argument is also charged with excessive symbols and abstractions, such as responses, presuppositions, anti-systematic movements and so on. It is a sociological approach.

What we need to do is develop a small part of Robertson's film, so that we can see some real pictures. For example, contrary to Wallerstein's view, if Islamic ideas and values press Muslims to attack the world system, we need more than a single set of alternatives to prevent the world system from being victimised; an alternative which would please major actors. That is so because it is difficult to agree that Islamic ideas and values are the best for all or vice versa. Therefore, societies must go further in dynamising a societal order in relation to a global order which 'almost automatically means that political-ideological and religious movements arise in reference to the issue of defining societies in relationship to the rest of the world and the global circumstances as a whole' [*Robertson, 1994: 71–2*].

Therefore, to be in the business of globalisation is to be in the business of culture and vice versa. In terms of culture, the process implies that Muslims, Christians, Jews, Hindu-Indians, Buddhists, and so forth, must discuss their differences and adopt alternatives which bring them closer to a single global

order. Samuel Huntington [*1993*] goes so far as to say that Islam, Confucianism and Western liberal democracy will contest each other for dominance. In terms of polity and economy, the process also involves international organisations and transnational movements whose aim is to have the upper hand rather than the advancement of humankind. Consequently, under the Western umbrella, where organisations and multinationals play a dominant role, globalisation will be no more than the disorganisation of non-Western cultures and structures.

In the light of such a global transformation, Waters [*1995*] presents a set of persuasive elements for drafting the new world. However, the intellectual thoughts which Waters and Robertson draw on are exclusively Western in origin; as if non-Western countries have produced nothing intellectually; as if they have not been part of the globe. Absent is the history and the achievements of non-Western civilisations. Western intellectuals have always felt that they exist in a sort of global space, as Julien Benda attempted to make us understand in 'The Treason of Intellectuals' written in the 1920s and quoted in Said [*1994a*]. Benda presented his views about intellectuals as if he himself lived in a globalised world. He observed that the constraints of geography (spatial boundaries) and cultural identity (ethnic identity) disappear in the minds of intellectuals. Yet, the intellectuals he approved of consisted mainly of Europeans (and Jesus) [*Said, 1994a: 19*].

One of Robertson's phrases concerning Japan reminds me of Said's 'orientalism'. Said uses the term 'orientalism' to describe Western scholars who disseminated preposterous ideas about the Orient. Robertson remarks that 'our relative inability to comprehend the "Japanese phenomenon" is that the fathers of modern scholarship did not prepare us well for this' (p.92). Robertson assumes that all real knowledge rests with the West only. Whilst both authors stress multiculturalism, rather than xenophobia and race-oriented nationalism, Said's view emphasises the interdependence of various histories whilst Robertson's thesis can be interpreted as connecting various histories under the capitalist West. Thus in camouflaged Orientalist style, Robertson assumes Western superiority.

Indeed, it seems that globalisation originated from Western thought in the same way as the discourse of modernisation. Western intellectuals still see themselves as the best in the field, despite the West's diminished capacity for spinning intellectual stories about non-Western places. Indeed, it shows that the North is more conscious about the globe than the South. This raises the question of whose influence will shape the present and future welfare of the earth's inhabitants. Robertson presents his ideas from the standpoint of one who believes in justice and freedom for all. However, the globalisation scheme will largely rest on the assumptions and echoes the voices of individuals from the West. In a globalised world, societies are invited to celebrate the arrival of the third millennium under a new banner: if you cannot become like us, you can live with/under us. Something staggering has happened. Blackwell and Seabrook [*1993: 2*] remark:

> The end of communism has been used to affirm with an even greater finality the superiority, indeed the inevitability, of the market system. The worlds of the two consciousnesses cannot, it seems, be brought together. The economy exists in one real world, and nature exists in another. No wonder we are generally happy to keep them apart in our perception, in spite of the sense of powerlessness which this creates.

Thus, global powerlessness could be changed into something useful which focuses on the global scale of current and future problems in terms of 'homogeniz[ing] lifestyle, culture, values, and the land itself', as Mander [*1993: 19]* observed, according to an overall vision for a world economy. It is a world which not only functions the same everywhere but lumps together large groups under the supervision of one group. One might ask what is special about a unified world? Can cultural guidance redeem previous sins and conflicts? In many ways this approach conceals the triumph of liberal economic thought. The significance of globalisation must be seen in terms of whether current Western liberal economic and cultural constructions can permanently survive.

But what do we care about global symbols and signals? What do we care about electronic objects, religions, international tourism or sport? What do we care about the French Revolution, the Industrial Revolution or the Copernican Revolution? Indeed, what do we care about global processes produced by earlier powers, such as the Romans, the Arabs, the Spanish and Portuguese, the British and French, the Ottomans or the Russians? All these developed in their own context of space and time. Globalisation would be senseless if the evil empire is still around. One wonders whether globalisation will work under evil imperialism, which is likewise an obstacle to economic and cultural interdependence.

The process of advocating change appears endless. For the last two hundred years 'countries which pride themselves on having reached an advanced stage of development, of being post-industrial, of being "developed", constantly require accelerating change from their privileged population' [*Blackwell and Seabrook, 1993: 3*]. But now this apocalyptical scheme seems to be the apogee of all changes since Adam and Eve, where the world of difference may/can/will find its unity and finality. In a globalised world, we should accept change in order to become a single society and culture. The strong should become global players, and the rest learn to adjust to the players' performance. The new version of change is also about competition, in which the rich alone will be rewarded and esteemed.

## MAKING THE COALESCENCE

We can proceed to examine globalisation in terms of the components which constitute its engine, namely economy, polity and culture. Robertson has formulated the project; the choice remains for us to decide whether to globalise or deglobalise. It is of great importance to note, however, that Robertson's universal plan is not as simple as presented here. His earlier training in religion may have enabled him to address globalisation more powerfully than some other writers.

Globalisation as a Western liberal project, derives its strength from the philosophy of liberal thought and the success of rationalisation. However, in order to advance a cultural world which embraces all national constituents, the adherent must not rest heavily or solely on Western conceptions of the world, unless it is to be just another imperialist and social project, such as the notorious Project Camelot in 1964 or Huntington's [*1993*] recent disheartening project. Social science and humanities departments are always financed to study programmes that assist commercial or political plans. Social sciences are always in need of new conceptual projects, and the globalisation project offers a rich and fruitful vocabulary to social scientists.

However, economy, polity and culture contain too many micro-components and in terms of interplay this interpenetration becomes problematic. The world has been strongly shaped and structured according to Western notions of globality. As Robertson [*1994: 87*] wrote this 'is not to deny that the modern global circumstance has been in large part made from the West'. The contemporary market, as he argues, involves the interpenetration of culture and economy without producing cultures affected by capitalist logic. Jameson's [*1984*] view that cultural structures and attitudes are vital responses to economy – culture is directed by the logic of capitalism – is rejected by Robertson. He also deplores the view of Christopher Chase-Dunn [*1989*], an advocate of world-systems analysis, that the USSR's and China's socialism has increased our collective knowledge. With respect to Jameson's view, Robertson is incorrect. The market economy not only directs cultures by the logic of capitalism but also tends to produce cultures in its own image. To take a simple example from Jan Munt [*1994: 51*]: 'The spread of capitalist relations of production … throughout the Third World is one of the most notable global processes … International tourism has been an important conduit of this process.' Munt notes that in terms of effect, tourism is a highly interventionist and subordinating industry; it forces recipient governments to change their cultural policies and create facilities which are compatible with the lifestyles, including sexual fantasies, of the visitors (normally new petit bourgeoisie). Robertson cites Talcott Parsons [*1979*], who argued that when the Industrial Revolution upgraded the erotic-sexual aspect of human life, the economy existed as a potentially autonomous realm.

Moreover, under globalisation, we expect the act of igniting the three energies to disrupt the world social order and to be followed by a process which moulds the final structure in the image of the stronger. In reality, while the globalisation process appears to be a homogenising force, 'it fuses with local conditions in diverse ways ... generating ... striking differences among social formations' [*Mittelman, 1995: 273*]. But are there any current signs of globalisation? Mittelman refers to globalisation in terms of the expanding export-processing plants in Mexico, and the evolving regionalism between Japan and the tiger countries (Africa, the Middle East, and the rest of Latin America are not seen as acting, or even thinking, globally).

However, globalisation is not a self-operating machine but requires a great deal of co-operation from those involved, especially when the problem relates to cultural identity. The entire project, therefore, demands a hegemonic organisation capable of diffusing, enforcing and protecting the harmonious interaction of economic, political and cultural processes. The problem is that good hegemonic power (whose goal is co-operation and liberation rather than colonisation and domination) is hard to define in the modern world, given that international relations can be easily abused and subverted for national interests. The problem in the modern world has been described by Blake and Walters [*1983: 9*] in the following terms:

> Clearly great conflicts of interest between states are inherent in this basically zero-sum view of international economic relations. Policy prescription is not universalist. Policies appropriate for rich states in the center of the global economy are not appropriate for poor states in the periphery ... The existing international economic system is not politically neutral, as the classical liberal economists argue. The policies of all the key international economic institutions and the distribution of benefits from most public and private economic transactions inherently favor rich states, ensuring their dominance in global economic and political relations.

We regard the US and its allies to be a strong hegemonic power, but not a good hegemonic power. Since the time when the US emerged as an international superpower, the principal idea adopted has been 'Divide and Rule'. This places a knife in the heart of the process of integration (unification is the term preferred by Robertson), and affects the entire range of political, economic, social, cultural and moral relationships. 'On the political side, the United States assumed the role of international policeman from the British after the interregnum of the inter-war years, and regularly intervened covertly and occasionally overtly to prevent hostile elements from coming to power' [*Marglin, 1988: 8*]. Let us broaden the concept of hegemonic power to include the allies, namely, Western Europe. In the ideological terrain, Western Europe identifies with American interests. American liberal thought dominates the cultural structure of Western Europe. Like the US, Western European policy aims to secure economic and cultural dominance over non-Western nations. The expectation of integration is belied by economic, political and cultural events.

Thus, Robertson's concept of powerful actors must be organisational, namely, the body of the United Nations. If this is the case, the choice is no better for '[n]othing can be done (or undone) in the United Nations without the US' [*Said, 1995: 85*]. The idea of globalising economy, polity and culture appears rather flimsy, because the West is already in a powerful position. Globalisation theory pays insufficient attention to the abhorrent behaviour of Western countries since the Industrial Revolution. It advocates an ideal situation in which the involved entities are globally committed to the development of human circumstances. This ideal should be addressed to the West. While acknowledging the intricacy of the problems involved, Robertson appears to believe that these can be solved through negotiation.

Furthermore, capitalism is not inspired by the notion of integration or unification, but by expansionism. These energies are not without radiating influence and it is this influence which we conceive of as a globalising force. This influence does not aim to achieve global cultural integration but to uphold processes which protect capitalist achievements. Global integration (better unification) can hardly be considered a reality. Rather there is a pattern of inconsistencies, which has erased the merits of co-operation. The process of cooperation is hampered by the fact that Western countries are not ready to accept sacrifices which may be painful to them [*Mahbubani,1994*].

Since the world has become a global market-place, the West has created a level playing field whereby every country can bargain in terms of its comparative advantage. The logic of the level playing field gives an egalitarian premise for all countries. In reality, it is owned by a capitalist elite, and access to it has never been equal. Agreements such as the Maastricht Treaty, NAFTA and GATT are no more than games which mainly favour transnational corporations (TNCs). Under the banner of free trade, TNCs extend their dominion over the global economy [*Nader, 1993*]. Fairness in trade has neither been recognised (or even agreed upon) nor does there exist a generally accepted definition of appropriate social standards [*Fouquin et al., 1995*]. This is vitally important given that globalisation is a social process.

## THE SUPERIORITY OF ECONOMISM

By culture, I refer to values, attitudes, beliefs, manners and behaviour. By the superiority of economism, I do not mean to infer that culture *per se* is empty, but that I regard cultural progress as coming from within the economy. For example, the Islamic countries lag behind Japan and Western countries in terms of scientific accomplishment and technical education. Yet aside from Islam's influence on the social, economic and political life of the Islamic world, there are many newcomers to Islam, some of Western origin. This may show that although underdevelopment prevails in the Islamic world, its repertoire of values continues to span continents with connecting effects. In addition, to be connected with Islamic values is to feel some connection with the Arabic language, with the history and culture of the Islamic civilisation. If Islam can create particular bonds across the world, why is Western culture so rampant and why does the West impose a higher standard of society? I believe that Western cultural pervasiveness is explained by its powerful economy rather than by the content of its cultural values. Despite the strength and the pervasiveness of Western culture, the West is a disconnecting culture in the global field. Huntington [*1996: 38*] rightly argues that 'the world is becoming more modern and less Western', but mistakenly continues that Western culture is partly rejected because it is Christian. As will be seen, the rejection of Western culture owes more to the subversive materialistic character of the West than to religion.

I have spent most of my life as an immigrant in Finland and have always been at odds with Finnish cultural realities. Without wanting to belittle Finnish culture, I and the majority of immigrants, have not been deeply influenced by Finnish cultural values. In other words, movements of people to Western countries are influenced more by economic, than political or cultural effects. 'Backwash effects' [*Myrdal, 1957*] continue to drain poor countries. In the United States, 'many of the new arrivals cling to their ethnic identity, preserving their customs and language, nurturing old prejudices, developing new ones, rubbing up against each other without mixing' (*Time Magazine*, 13 June 1983, p.12). This situation has not changed. This does not mean that the US cultural structure produces disconnecting irregularities. On the contrary, US society is elastic, generous and much less rigid than other Western societies. One type of 'backwash effect' is the 'brain drain', typified by the movement of skilled people to the United States, many of whom went on to enrich American universities with their talents.

In Western Europe, the protection of European culture from external threats and protectionist nationalism seems to be the order of the day. In France, this concern is focused on Muslim immigrants from Algeria, whose religion and habits are regarded as posing a threat to French culture [*Hertzberg, 1993*]. Those who refuse to become French by assimilation can be punished or even expelled [*Hoffmann, 1994*]. Alas, Huntington [*1996*] advises Western countries to do the same. In Finland, almost everything from abroad is looked at with suspicion and disrespect. Xenophobia, racism, and aggressive race-oriented nationalism characterise everyday life. For many decades Finland's major newspaper, *Helsingin Sanomat*, has undermined the integrity of immigrants. This disheartening reality makes it hard to believe that modern societies are ready for cultural integration or unification. But, it is in our interest to see the world community 'affirming the interdependence of various histories on one another, and the necessary interaction of contemporary societies with one another' [*Said, 1994b: 43*]. Having stated all this, I shall elaborate further the dilemma involved.

Robertson's project is appealing. The world needs a project which advances global cultural interdependence, eradicates the animosity between nations, and the chauvinism, racism and jingoism, which dominate modern societies. The powerlessness of cultural guidance owes much to imperialism which accompanied the early development of Western capitalism. Robertson's concept of cultural relationships aims to present a new idea of man and the future of humanity. There is nothing basically wrong with this; all societies are entitled to possess an idea of the future of humanity. The problem lies, however, in the difference between Western and non-Western levels of development, which means that economic power is concentrated in one world. As Western culture is rampant in the world, Robertson's project puts non-Western societies at the mercy of the West. The future of humanity will be determined by the economics of the strong. Hence it is a project of cultural domination.

Such a project is not only improbable but impossible since almost everything is reduced to material bonds. Such a construction is wishful thinking, especially because the project associates globalisation with the disorganisation of capitalism (see Waters [*1995*]). Robertson's thinking is more explicit when he deals with Japanese religion.

The remarkable increase in speed of all kinds of communications has created a new awareness of the world. Although the world is divided into developed and undeveloped, one can no longer speak of developing nations as before. The North as well as the South has its own repository of peculiarities, pathologies and accomplishments. Despite the differences, global connection is essential, and it is on this basis that the world must globalise. Japan presents a fascinating, but elusive, example in the field of globality.

Differences between Japan and Western countries are evident in terms of their history, geography and culture. Yet Japan is a more advanced industrial society. Robertson seems to believe that in order to understand why Japan has become globally oriented one must consider the role played by Japanese religion. He appears quite persuasive and wise in his selection of an approach to support his point of view. Robertson also believes that an understanding of the role played by Japanese religion will strengthen the view that the global field is not the outcome of capitalism, imperialism, modernity or whatever. Here, I think, Robertson's statement is lacking in power.

I have myself toyed with this issue because the cultural calibre of religion is pervasive. However, there is no clear proof that it is religion which acts as the prime mover of an economy and which contributes towards transforming the state into a giant space ship towards globality. If we take one religion as such, Islam offers the best perspective on globality. Although Japan represents a unique phenomena of rapid transformation, it has not been as globally influential as Islam or the West in the ideological terrain. Whatever the underlying reason for Japan's take-off, this should not blind us to the idea that the contemporary global field is the result of capitalism, imperialism and modernity. While world markets have been inundated with Japanese hi-tech products, the outcome has mainly been to materialise global life. As for Islam, its global influence has persisted without that materialist slant. In the case of the West, these societies have been more concerned with socialising domination, by selling instrumental modernity and imperialist policies to the undeveloped countries. The fact that Japan has attained its advanced status without imperialistic gestures does not exempt the West from having been imperial nor does it suggest that the global field is not a consequence of imperialistic capitalism.

If Robertson could demonstrate that the Japanese religion is the engine making Japan global, we could accept the power of a country's value system. In the modern world, the Japanese materialist motto tended to localise, then to internationalise, and then to globalise. But surely the ideas, information and values contained in these three processes are no more than materialistic simulations. In other words, Japanese output tends to globalise only through the emphasis put upon the material connection between countries. Thus, while Japanese religion is valuable and significant for Japan's production, its global orientation is devoid of cultural values. If Japan's success can be attributed to cultural dynamics, we would expect these to travel rather than to remain in Japan, as they have done.

Thus, what I am arguing is that religion alone is insufficient to make a country global although it can point to processes which increase our knowledge of some achievements. Ideas, information, symbols and values contained in material simulations are not sufficient to enhance cultural prevalence and the take-off to globality. Nor is culture itself sufficient to disorganise functional structures. For example, Islam spread by dissolving cultures in order to establish a single Islamic culture. During the process of Islamising everything in sight, adherents did not draw strength from existing functional structures but relied on the social/functional concepts contained in Islam. Laws, manners and attitudes were profoundly absorbed and efficiently implemented without disorganising existing functional structures. It is interesting to note that the Islamic civilisation, with its scientific progress and achievements, helped the West to emerge out of the gloom of the Dark Ages.

Japan also began to revolutionise its economy by drawing on the social/functional notions contained in the Japanese religion. The endurance of these notions may have helped modern Japan industrialise and maintain a strong functioning economy. The cause (and the confluence of several reasons) of the retreat of the Islamic civilisation lies in ignoring the importance of the same social/functional concepts which are crucial for building the economy. The fall of the economic sector crippled its capacity to engage in science and the ability to build a strong working economy [*Ghazali, 1987*]. During the Islamic era, early Muslim leaders realised the importance of economics and adopted a strong fiscal policy which kept the Islamic empire solid [*Keirnan, 1978*]. The current resurgence of Islamic groups is closely linked to the question of a troubled economy. Although these movements may seem to be an attempt to flee an outmoded superstructure, the struggle is not essentially about disseminating Islam as 'Islam is the way', but about using Islamic values towards economic recovery. Thus, a country's capacity to become global rests on its economic capacity, and religion (or culture) does not make a country global.

The process differs for Western countries. The growth of Western culture was a consequence of the functional notions contained in the Enlightenment. Culture spread from the Industrial Revolution, not from the Christian religion. Over time, Western life became merely physical growth and enjoyment. The career of the 'Western functional character' began with the Industrial Revolution which tended to operate in three directions [*Furtado, 1964: 33–4*]. The first marked the line of development in Western Europe. The second consisted of a displacement of frontiers towards unoccupied land with similar characteristics as those in Europe. The third line of expansion of the European economy was towards already inhabited regions whose economic systems were of various types.

Put differently, the West derived its functional strength from the materialistic (or capitalistic) structures which Western societies established both at home and abroad. I do not mean that they have no social values, but that their social values have always been materialistic. 'Western developmentalism takes its cue from an economic model driven by technology and market behavior rather than from existing cultures' [*McMichael, 1996: 11*]. In the old days, as Baran [*1973: 273*] remarked: 'They came to the new lands with capitalism in their bones … they succeeded in a short time in establishing … an indigenous society of their own.' They handed the Bible to the native and took the land [*Fanon, 1963*]. Then, as Crosby [*1986*] argues, the imperialist West went on materialising everything in sight. They succeeded in moulding socioeconomic structures according to set of materialistic values, with the result that the world is divided into poor and rich economies, and each side thinks about the other in terms of material gain. Robertson thinks the reason lies in 'Cherchez la Culture'. In contrast to my own view, Robertson tends to ignore the fact that one of the battles of Western imperialism was over who was to transform and mould the value system in the world according to Western values. Up to the present this has prevented dependent countries from entering the global field in the same way as Japan and the West. His view tends to blur the vital role of economic dominance in the world system.

Current Western obsession with market values is not only dispiriting, as Blackwell and Seabrook [*1993*] argue. It is also the consequence of victorious capitalism and the success of the global market economy. Globality is a consequence of capitalism, imperialism and modernity. One is tempted to ask why neither the West nor Japan have been culturally effective in the global field, and why Western countries and Japan remained culturally disconnected. In other words, the task of demonstrating that cultural guidance is not operative at the global scale is quite simple. Material simulations of all kinds are insufficient entities to globalise a culture. Industrial entities are always replaceable, changeable and perishable. Sponsored by men of capitalism, food, music, fashion, electronics and film are stupefying entertainment which destroy intelligent thought among young and old. Globalising fleeting sources of enjoyment via all kinds of industrial simulations is a fruitless effort. If we identify the strength of Western culture with these sources of enjoyment, the West would seem a trivial civilisation [*Huntington, 1996*].

The Islamic world identifies its cultural strength without these sources of enjoyment, which Muslims regard as scornful pastimes, especially during the Ramadan fasting. These artificial and trivial activities are mainly made to please the market. They seem powerful because societies have been made to understand that 'industrial society offers "a package", a totality, which is non-negotiable ... everything it produces is essentialised' [*Blackwell and Seabrook, 1993: 89*]. The current global consumer culture is dispiriting [*Waters, 1995*]. The more an industrialised economy produces material entities, the more industrialisation remains a disconnecting culture. The impact of consumer goods has resulted in the commodification of life, and industrialists have relied on the power of consumer goods to corrupt foreign regimes. Thus, one could argue that technological globalisation is not without detrimental effects, and the process makes the West appear subversive. In the West, 'this complete commodification of life is undermining what remains of democratic control by people over the conditions of their daily existence' [*Robinson, 1996: 15*]. In poor countries, the effect is crippling to a young person's growth because of the inability to demonstrate stability and homogeneity when faced with such an attack. And since the West has linked industrialisation with indoctrination in capitalistic virtues, capitalism itself becomes a disconnecting culture.

Thus, while a culture may have some global influence through permeating processes, these processes are insufficient to create a single global culture.

Culture on the global scale is not as dynamic as it may seem and culture is only operative at the national level. For example, while the Nordic societies form a regional civil society, each society within the region still identifies itself as different. According to Kemiläinen [*1994*], Swedes regard the Finns as racially inferior and non-Scandinavian. A better example to support my point is that of the relationship between the United States and France. Although the cultural and material levels of the United States and France are relatively similar, one of the cultural phobias of France is to prevent the invasion of the US film industry [*Hoffmann, 1994*]. Thus, even where both countries are culturally Western, one continues to protect its culture from the other's influence. But when culture is used by men of national culture for chauvinistic and patriotic purposes, it becomes a formidable hurdle to human-cultural-interdependence. Cultural interdependence is not supposed to yield results which undermine, change or replace another culture (as Robertson agrees), but to organise harmoniously the production of exchange that is beneficial to economic and social arrangements.

Globalisation is a necessary process for the marketing of industrial output, not the marketing of culture. Herein lies a dilemma which runs counter to the prophecy of globalisation. In a unified world system in which we 'imagine' that profit is somehow equally distributed, liberal lucrative principles become frail and powerless. But if we assume the opposite, globalisation then works mainly in favour of capitalist expansionists. Thus, in a globalised world where culture is unified, globalisation cannot flourish without economy and, moreover, is predetermined by economic forces. Hence globalisation is primarily a consequence of economic guidance, and the fate of culture is decided by the economy.

What is the upshot of this discussion? There is a tremendous falsity about this cultural consciousness. The falsest consciousness of is to believe that a society in which the individual is determined by the nature of capital is connective or oriented towards solidarity and cooperation. Its materialistic structures (see Blackwell and Seabrook's electric work) are engrossed when they create similar materialistic prerequisites around the world. In the past, Western structures were built with the sweat and blood of non-Western races [*Fanon, 1963*]. During the Cold War, the same structures were nourished by loss of money and lives in the poor world. For a few dollars more, international development projects fell into a spiral of deadly political games, bringing about the suffocation and degradation of poor communities [*Dibaja, 1993*]. Development also involved thinking about war and identifying the enemy so that the empire was always ready to strike. 'A result commonly achieved by murdering priests and union leaders, massacring peasants trying to organise, blowing up the independent press, and so on' [*Chomsky, 1993: 120*].

In a globalised world, as long as capitalist society continues to be determined by the nature of capital, it cannot transcend its nature and be replaced by a better one. It is made of 'consumerism and cut-throat individualism' [*Robinson, 1996: 17*]. Therefore, it does not hesitate to corrode the cultural structures of other societies. This is partly why Robertson could not assume that his sociocultural system would succeed in operating positively. Capitalism is a violent system. The challenge for the scholar is not to separate one society or culture from another, as Huntington [*1996*] wants to do, but to find ways of achieving the harmonious interdependence of societies. Put another way, the challenge for the scholar is not to write about globalisation as a science-fiction writer would or to preach that there will be a single chaotic and robotised society occupying the planet. Nor is it to imagine that governments will vanish, that borders and spatial boundaries will disappear, that food and sex will have a different taste, that signs and symbolic tokens will prevail. Instead of reaching for the sky let us stand firmly on the ground. Let us affirm first the interdependence of histories with one another, as Said [*1978; 1994b*] recommends. Let us develop a strategy against global capitalism or 'solutions to the plight of humanity under a savage capitalism', as Robinson [*1996: 27*] advocates. Indeed, let us understand globalisation as if people mattered.

## THE INEVITABILITY OF ANTECEDENT IRRADIANCE

Where does economy, polity and culture derive its conceptual resilience from in the model of globality? Undoubtedly, the discourse of globalisation cannot be formulated without reference to Western theoretical heritage. The reader must bear in mind that the evolutionary and structural-functionalist paradigms of the 1980s have been powerless to erase material poverty in the developing world and to confirm the validity of non-Western cultures. Yet by entering the global field, we find ourselves strolling along the same track. As Waters [*1995: 3*] puts it:

> The concept of globalisation is an obvious object for ideological suspicion because, like modernisation, a predecessor and related concept, it appears to justify the spread of Western culture and of capitalist society by suggesting that there are forces operating beyond human control that are transforming the world.

Waters mentions that forerunners to globalisation, such as Durkheim's differentiation, Weber's rationalisation and Marx's capitalist commodification, gave an enormous impulse to perspectives on the global field. Robertson denies, however, that his project is a grand account of the past, present and future, as poststructuralists and postmodernists now claim. Robertson is deeply influenced by the controversy over his own concept. As a sociologist, sociology presents him with many renowned thinkers on social theory, such as

Talcott Parsons, or Martin Levy, Neil Smelser, James Coleman, Walt Rostow and others. We would expect Robertson's argument on globalisation to draw on such thinkers, especially Parsons. This is so because modernisation professionals have presented many perspectives which connect with problems on the global scale.

Paradoxically, Robertson's dissatisfaction with his own concept stems from the fact that globalisation derives sustenance from modernisation thinking, which has not succeeded in formulating a theory which accounts for the situation of the Third World. It is also wrong to regard structural functionalism in terms of globalisation. While the views of structural functionalists may appear linked to the international system, their goal was not to promote a single society driven by Western cultural forces First, the school of structural functionalism emerged as a result of the failure of the evolutionists. Second, the functionalists were motivated by the desire to win back former colonies and replan their future. Members of the functionalist platform were not international thinkers; they were in fact nationalists (some would also say racists [*Malik, 1996; Barrat Brown, 1993: 19*]), who thought about the world system in terms of servicing national units. In their attempt to redefine human space in terms of society and man, the question of bringing back former colonies was addressed by referring to the functional structure and cultural character of the functionalists' own societies. It never occurred to these thinkers that the world consists of different modernities. Indeed, they regarded West as best. Their goal was to propagate a type of super society which deflects poor countries from thinking about their modernity. Thus, the battle of the functionalists has been ideological rather than cultural.

In his work 'Social System', Parsons [*1951*] was concerned to sustain the model of Western functional society and to deprive non-Western societies of cultural and functional identity. Similarly, the work of Levy [*1967*], Smelser [*1964*], and Coleman [*1968*] implies that Third World countries are socially and politically unstable and tyrannical, whereas modern Western society is devoid of such disturbances. Rostow's [*1960*] 'The Stages of Economic Growth' is even more dispiriting, and speaks for all the imperialists.

Likewise, although social evolutionists tended to appear as globalists, they also thought in terms of national units under the influence of capitalism. Evolutionism was a fancy intellectual idea which not only differentiated between societies but saw others through a racial lens. The extinction of the evolutionary approach is evidence of its complete ignorance and unawareness of social and cultural processes. However, the theoretical legacy of evolutionists provides globalisation professionals with ideas and information about how to comprehend the globe. (See perspectives on the evolutionary approach in Harrison [*1988*], Fägerlind and Saha [*1986*], and Spybey [*1992*]). Indeed, the deeper one probes, the further one slides into Tonnies' community and society, Durkheim's mechanical and organic solidarity, Spencer's military and industrial society, and Comte's theological, metaphysical and positive stages. According to McMichael [*1996: xv*], only when students 'do go beyond the evolutionary perspective, they are better able to evaluate their own culture ... social change, development, and international inequality'.

Whilst evolutionists were concerned with transferring laissez-faire economics into nature, and the functionalists with transferring biological evolution into the social and political sphere, economists are concerned with globalisation to transfer sociological substance into the economic sphere. This has been an ongoing process since the Renaissance. Globalisation, then, is about employing the past to serve the future.

Thus, if discussing globalisation reawakens the social legacy, discussing capitalism reawakens the economic legacy of Smith, Marx, Ricardo and others. In this sense, revitalising past discourse is banal unless 'to articulate the past historically does not mean to recognise it "the way it was". It means to seize hold of a memory [or a presence] as it flashes up at a moment of danger'(Benjamin, cited in Said [*1994a: 26*]).

## IS GLOBALISATION USEFUL?

It is beyond the limits of this study to explain in detail why globalisation is harmful. With the fall of communism, capitalism can be seen as only semi-victorious; complete victory involves absorbing all societies into a single capitalist one. This view can be observed in Robertson's work. However, the dissolution of the communist system does not imply that the capitalist system is eternal. Its survival persists only so long as societies fail to create a new ideology. Thus capitalism lives in constant fear. On the ideological terrain, men of capitalism identify Islam as the new threat. The same fears are not expressed about Japanese religion, shintoism, or the ideology of Jewish messianism [*Shahak, 1995*]. In order to secure the future of capitalism, men of capitalism seek help from the process of globalisation in which all countries are positioned in relationship to the capitalist West. In other words, capitalist countries attempt to forge a global order which protects capitalism, not culture, so that capitalism retains global influence.

So how come Robertson and other globalists are not part of the corporate ensemble? How come Robertson does not ally himself with the success of the victors? The fact that globalisation appears non-ideological is partly because Robertson's motives remain unknown to us. By this I do not mean to question his honesty and cause, but it is hard in the age of victorious capitalism to consider social integration as operating independently from system integration. It may be paradoxical to regard cultural guidance as a separate entity. As capitalism does not accept a world of mixed economies and cultures, globalisation gives men of capitalism the power to eliminate the risk of this occurring. In order to prevail globally, it has to tame and condition the world to accept its conceptual viewpoint. Mittelman [*1995*] and Fouquin *et al.*, [*1995*] argue that the Asia-Pacific region is forming a new regional economic power which poses a challenge to the US and Western Europe. Given the global pressure faced by the developed countries Fouquin *et al.* argue that these countries should be co-operatively prepared to meet the challenge.

Scholars should reject the globalisation project, as was proposed by Riccardo Petrella at the 8th EADI General Conference in Vienna in 1996, and develop a strategy or programme to tame wild capitalism, as Robinson [*1996*] suggests. In his new project, Huntington [*1996*] wants to deglobalise by isolating and uniting the West under the idea of the Great West, in the same way as the evolutionists thought about their own history, race and culture. Globalisation is not a great achievement; its cultural content is fallacious. Globalisation embodies serious economic and social problems. As a scheme for advancing the cause of mankind, globalisation raises doubts. In this case, 'Radical doubt is an act of uncovering and discovering; it is the dawning of the awareness that the Emperor is naked, and that his splendid garments are nothing but the product of one's phantasy' [*Fromm, 1971: viii*]. What we have to deal with here is the same modern West, the same modern thoughts, and the same Western relations to the world. Alas, we agree with Inkeless [*1964*] that scientific, rational, modern man is only a hypothetical figure.

## REFERENCES

Baran, Paul A., 1973, *The Political Economy of Growth*, London: Penguin Books.

Barratt Brown, M., 1993, *Fair Trade, Reform and Realities in the International Trading System*, London: Zed Books.

Blackwell, T. and J. Seabrook, 1993, *The Revolt Against Change, Towards A Conserving Radicalism*, London: Vintage.

Blake, D.H. and R.S. Walters, 1983, *The Politics of Global Economic Relations*. 2nd Edition, New Jersey: Prentice-Hall.

Chase-Dunn, C., 1989, *Global Formation*, Oxford: Basil Blackwell.

Chomsky, Noam, 1993, *Year 501 The Conquest Continues*, London: Verso.

Coleman, James S., 1968, *Modernisation: Political Aspects*, New York: Macmillan.

Crosby, Alfred, 1986, *Ecological Imperialism: The Biological Expansion of Europe 900–1900*, Cambridge: Cambridge University Press.

Dibaja, Zuhair, 1993, *Development Projects in the Third World, Success or Failure?*, Monograph 5, Helsinki: Finnish Society for Development Studies.

Fägerlind, I. and L. J. Saha, 1986, *Education and National Development, A Cooperative Perspective*, Oxford: Pergamon Press.

Fanon, Frantz, 1963, *The Wretched of the Earth*, New York: Grove Press.

Fouquin, M., Chevallier, A. and J. Pisani-Ferry, 1995, 'The New International Competition: Effects on Employment', in Mihaly Simai (ed.), *Global Employment. An International Investigation into the Future of Work*, Vol.1, London: Zed Books.

Fromm, Erich, 1971, 'Introduction', in I.D. Illich, *Celebration of Awareness, A call for Institutional Revolution*, New York: Anchor Books, pp.vii–x.

Furtado, C., 1964 [1973], 'Elements of a Theory of Underdevelopment – The Underdeveloped Structures', in Henry Bernstein (ed.), *Underdevelopment and Development: The Third World Today*, New York: Penguin Books, pp.33–43.

Ghazali, M., 1987, *Islam and Economic Conditions*, 7th Edition, Arabic version, Cairo: Dar al-Sahwa.

Harrison, David, 1988, *The Sociology of Modernisation and Development*, London: Unwin Hyman.

Hertzberg, Arthur, 1993, 'Is Anti Semitism Dying Out?', *New York Review of Books*, 24 June, No.12, pp.51–7.

Hoffmann, Stanley, 1994, 'France: Keeping the Demons at Bay', in *New York Review of Books*, Vol.XII, No.5, pp.10–16.

Huntington, Samuel, 1993, 'The Clash of Civilisations', *Foreign Affairs*, Vol.72, No.3, pp.22–49.

Huntington, Samuel, 1996, 'The West: Unique, Not Universal, *Foreign Affairs*, Vol.75, No.6, pp.28–46.

Inkeless, Alex, 1964, *Making Men Modern: Interactions, On the Causes and Consequences of Individual Change in Six Developing Countries*, New York: Basic Books.

Jameson, F., 1984, 'Postmodernism, or the Cultural Logic of Late Capitalism', *New Left Review*, 146.

Keirnan, Thomas, 1978, *The Arabs, Their History, Aims and Challenges to the Industrialised World*, London: ABACUS.

Kemiläinen, Aira, 1994, *Suomalaiset, Outo Kansa*, Helsinki: Suomen Historiallinen Seura.

Levy, Martin J. Jr., 1967, 'Social Patterns and Problems of Modernisation', in Wilbert Moore and Robert Cook (eds.), *Readings on Social Change*, Englewood Cliffs, NJ: Prentice Hall, pp.189–208.

Lindblom, Charles E., 1977, *Politics and Markets, The World's Political Economic Systems*, New York: Basic Books.

McMichael, Philip, 1996, *Development and Social Change, A Global Perspective*, London: Pine Forge Press.

Mahbubani, Kishore, 1994, 'The West and the Rest', in Uner Kirdar & Leonard Silk, (eds.), *A World Fit For People*, New York: University Press, pp.6–18.

Malik, Kenan, 1996, 'Universalism and Difference: Race and the Postmodernists', *Race & Class*, Vol.37, No.3, pp.1–17.

Mander, Jerry, 1993, 'Megatechnology, Trade, and the New World Order', in Nader *et al.*[*1993: 13–22*].

Marglin, Stephen A., 1988, *Lessons of the Golden Age of Capitalism*, Research for Action, United Nations University: WIDER.

Mittelman, J.H., 1994, 'Global Restructuring of Production and Migration', in Yoshikazu Sakamoto (ed)., *Global Transformation: Challenges to the State System*, Tokyo: United Nations University Press, pp.267–98.

Mittelman, J.H., 1995, 'Rethinking the International Division of Labour in the Context of Globalisation', *Third World Quarterly*, Vol.16, No.2, pp.273–95.

Munt, Ian, 1994, 'Eco-tourism or Ego-tourism?', *Race & Class*, Vol.36, No.1, pp.49–60.

Myrdal, G., 1957, *Lands and Poor*, New York: Harper & Row.

Nader, Ralph, 1993, 'Introduction: Free Trade and the Decline of Democracy', in R. Nader *et al.*, *The Case Against Free Trade, GATT, NAFTA and the Globalisation of Corporate Power*, San Francisco, CA: Earth Island, pp.1–12.

Parsons, Talcott, 1951, *The Social System*, Glencoe IL: Free Press.

Parsons, Talcott, 1979, 'Religious and Economic Symbolism in the Western World', *Sociological Inquiry*, Vol.47, pp.11–58.

Robertson, Roland, 1994, *Globalisation, Social and Global Culture*, London: Sage Publications.

Robinson, William, I., 1996, 'Globalisation: Nine Theses on our Epoch', *Race & Class*, Vol.38, No.2, pp.13–31.

Rostow, W.W., 1960, 'The Stages of Economic Growth: A Non-Communist Manifesto', Cambridge University.

Said, Edward, W., 1978, *Orientalism*, London: Routledge & Kegan Paul.

Said, Edward, W., 1994a, *Representations of the Intellectual*, The 1993 Reith Lectures, London: Vintage.

Said, Edward, W., 1994b, *Culture and Imperialism*, London: Vintage.
Said, Edward, W., 1995, *Peace and Its Discontents, Gaza – Jericho 1993–1995*, London: Vintage.
Shahak, Israel, 1995, 'The Ideology of Jewish Messianism', *Race & Class*, Vol.37, No.2, pp.81–91.
Smelser, Neil, 1964, *Toward a Theory of Modernisation*, New York: Basic Books.
So, Alvin Y., 1990, *Social Change and Development, Modernisation, Dependency, and World-System Theories*, London: Sage.
Spybey, Tony, 1992, *Social Change, Development and Dependency*, Cambridge: Polity Press.
Waters, Malcolm, 1995, *Globalisation*, London: Routledge.

# Equity and Growth Revisited: A Supply-Side Approach to Social Development

JAN NEDERVEEN PIETERSE

*Does combining several arguments on the relationship between equity and growth yield new insight? Redistribution with growth, prominent in the 1970s, is currently being revisited. East Asian experiences can also be considered with a view to equity. Human development makes a strong case for combining equity and growth along the lines of human capital, but leaves the social dimension unexplored. Studies of welfare states add finesse to equity-growth arguments. Sociology of economics addresses questions of embeddedness, social capital, networks and trust, which are rarely considered in this context. By adding novel elements, this exercise seeks to arrive at a new overall perspective on social development.*

On the occasion of the World Summit for Social Development in Copenhagen in 1995 such benevolent statements as 'broadly effective social progress is not possible without a socially oriented economic and finance policy' were made about the relationship between growth and equity (Development & Co-operation, Vol.1, 1995, p.12). Here an attempt is made to probe these rhetorical statements to find a core of policy relevant thinking.

'Social orientation' can have many meanings. In the framework of Copenhagen the dominant tendency has been to relegate questions of social development to poverty alleviation. It may be necessary, however, to challenge the 'Washington consensus' in development not merely in policy terms, resulting in an adjustment (but not a structural adjustment) of structural adjustment, but in intellectual terms. Revisiting Keynesian management strategies [*Singer, 1996*] may be important but one wonders whether they are a viable option in the context of accelerated globalisation. Here I explore the equity-growth argument.

First let me briefly refer to two alternative positions: *rejecting growth* or, alternatively, pursuing *equity without growth*. A prominent set of positions rejects growth for various reasons, such as ecological views, according to

---

Jan Nederveen Pieterse, Associate Professor, Institute of Social Studies, The Hague, The Netherlands; E-mail: nederveen@iss.nl. The author would like to thank Melania Portilla and anonymous referees of the EJDR for their comments.

which more is not better, and alternative development views which hold that what matters is not growth but development that is equitable, sustainable and participatory. In many instances this view is accompanied by a repudiation of growth per se. A further position is anti-development or post-development, which repudiates not only growth but also development as such. A general problem with these positions (discussed in more detail in Nederveen Pieterse [*1996*]) is that the target is too wide: arguably what should be at issue is not growth as such but the *quality* of growth. Exploring this is the point of juxtaposing growth and social development. Clearly 'growth' is a deeply problematic category. The mere question of how growth is defined and measured raises numerous problems. On the other hand, simply rejecting growth may leave us with too narrow a position and too narrow a political coalition to implement whatever policies seem desirable.

On a general level it might be argued that what many people desire is not growth but change, qualitative transformation. Marshall Berman [*1988: 47*] refers to 'the desire for development'. It seems that the point is not to go against this desire, or complex of desires, not to adopt a confrontational approach, a politics of purity or abstinence, which would invoke many resistances, but to transform and channel desire. In other words, and at risk of sounding patronising, to educate rather than suppress desire. The market place represents powerful and dynamic forces in society, which resonate with deep-seated drives, not merely to 'accumulate, accumulate' but also to 'change, change' and 'improve, improve'. Market forces as such alienate and marginalise many in society, but is the appropriate response to marginalise, alienate or ignore market forces in return? A wiser course may be to explore what common ground there may be between the market and social development, or the scope for a social market approach. Put in other words, the target is not the market but the *unregulated* market.

A different option is to pursue equity *without* growth. This kind of approach has been referred to as 'support-mediated security' [*Drèze and Sen, 1989*].[1] This may give us the 'Kerala model' – a constellation of advanced social policies and comparatively high levels of education, health and female empowerment. From the mid-1970s, as Kerala was acquiring international model status, it was slipping into a major crisis, including 'severe stagnation in the spheres of material production, soaring unemployment, acute fiscal crisis and erosion of sustainability of the social welfare expenditures' [*Isaac and Tharakan, 1995: 1995*].[2] Growing unemployment may be due to the fact that investors shun a state where the unions, with the backing of state government, are too strong, which is the position taken by the local right-wing backlash and by international press comments [e.g., *van Straaten, 1996*]. This refers us to the familiar chronicles of Western welfare states in the era of post-Fordism and globalisation and the question of 'social dumping'. Aside from the deeply politicised question of how to account for the Kerala crisis, a recent analysis concludes that 'in the absence of economic growth it is difficult to sustain, much less expand, welfare gains' [*Isaac and Tharakan, 1995: 1993*].

Thus we turn to equity with growth, summed up under the heading of social development. The point here is not to make a case for social development in *moral* terms, in the name of solidarity, compassion or decency. Thus Galbraith [*1996]* argues that, '[i]n the good society there must not be a deprived and excluded underclass'. It is not that such moral considerations are irrelevant but they are of limited purchase. Moral economies and discourses are unevenly distributed so that achieving a political consensus purely on moral grounds is unlikely. Moral arguments invite trade-offs – the appeal of moral policy may be outweighed by the importance of economic growth. Since in conventional views growth is supposed to trickle down, in time growth policies will generate moral outcomes. Hence moral considerations tend to be practically outflanked and too easily neutralised by growth policies.

Neither is the point to make a *political* case for social development. Social and welfare policies enhance political stability and legitimacy but they also invite trade-offs – between political legitimacy and political efficacy or state autonomy. Thus, a classic position is that collective demands are to be restrained so that collective interests will not crowd out state autonomy and state capacity to implement reform measures. The absence of social development may prompt uncontrolled informalisation, including ethnic and religious mobilisation and a growing underground economy. These are important considerations but they are not the main line of argument followed here.

Rather, the point is to consider the case for social development on *economic* grounds, in relation to growth itself. In other words, to examine whether, how, to what extent and under which circumstances social development is good for growth and beneficial to business. Phrasing it in contemporary language, the point is to explore the scope for a market-friendly social development. This line of thinking involves classic debates on the welfare state, on the 'big trade-off' between equality and efficiency [*Okun, 1975*], and on modernisation and equality. Here this question is revisited by considering several lines of research and bodies of literature, to review the existing scope of social development arguments and whether their combination yields new insight. This may be worth doing considering that 'there is no very strong tradition of doing macroeconomics as if poor people and social processes mattered' [*Taylor and Pieper, 1996: 93*].

Relevant lines of research include the following. (1) Redistribution with growth. Prominent in the 1970s, these views are currently being revisited. (2) Lessons from East Asia. Usually discussed in relation to the role of state intervention, they can also be considered with a view to equality and equity.

(3) Human development. This approach makes a strong case for combining equity and growth along the lines of human capital, but the social dimension and the question of social capital is left unexplored. (4) Lessons from welfare states. (5) New institutional economics provides institutional analyses and sociology of economics addresses questions of embeddedness, social capital, networks and trust. Other bodies of literature are relevant to social development – such as comparative studies of social security, the regulation school, post-Fordism, associational democracy – but fall outside this treatment. The point of this exercise is to find out what emerges when various arguments on equity and growth are grouped together and to arrive at a new overall perspective by adding novel elements which are not usually combined with social development.

## SOCIAL DEVELOPMENT

It is appropriate first to delineate in what sense social development is used here. A first and narrow meaning of social development is public welfare policies of health, education and housing. This approach, as Midgley [*1995*] points out, suffers from compartmentalisation, in particular the separation of social policies from development policies. The Copenhagen summit was not free of this tendency: social development mostly referred to or ended up in the basket of poverty alleviation [*UNRISD, 1995*]. For the same reason, the present argument is not concerned with the social economy, progressive market or socially responsible business, cooperatives or fair trade [*Ekins, 1992*]. Not because they are unimportant, but because they represent a compartmentalised or at least a partial approach. The focus is on the overall economy rather than on particular segments. Second, social development may be used in a disciplinary sense to distinguish it in particular from economic development [*Booth, 1994*]. The third option, which is followed here, is to view social development in a substantive and comprehensive manner with equal emphasis both on 'social' and on 'development', in other words as an integrated approach to social concerns and growth strategies.

A definition of social development offered by Midgley [*1995: 25*] is 'a process of planned social change designed to promote the well-being of the population as a whole in conjunction with a dynamic process of economic development'. Here the notion of planning carries *dirigiste* overtones (while in effect Midgley argues for 'managed pluralism'), which raises the question of the agency of social development.

The dominant discourse of social development as used by governments, international institutions and many NGOs is as a terrain of *social policy*. In other words, social development as a matter of social engineering, a managerial approach. This is apparent if we leaf through the various reports submitted to the World Summit for Social Development.[3] The bodies of literature reviewed here reflect this general tendency, except for sociology of economics, which follows a different track. Sociology of economics looks at the social from the ground up. We might term this a society-centred approach to social development or, possibly, social development from below. Actual social security concerns much more than state social policy, such as family and local networks [*Hirtz, 1995; DSE, 1994*]. As Ann Davis [*1991: 84*] remarks, 'Of course, social work agencies are only one way of replenishing family and friendship networks'. When social security falls outside conventional social policy, how could a conventional approach to social development be adequate? Accordingly, implicit in 'social development' are multiple layers of difference implicit in 'development': compartmentalised, or holistic; managerial, from above, or society-centred, from below; from outside and from within.

## REDISTRIBUTION WITH GROWTH

In the growth and redistribution literature of the 1970s several currents of thought came together. Adelman and Morris [*1967*] developed an approach to social development influenced by modernisation theory; their social development index may be read as a modernisation index.[4] At a time when Keynesian demand management played a prominent part, Gunnar Myrdal adopted a productivist or supply-side approach. According to Myrdal, 'welfare reforms, rather than being costly for society, actually lay the basis for more steady and rapid economic growth' (quoted in Esping-Andersen [*1994: 723*]; Myrdal [*1968*]). In presenting redistribution as a *precondition* to growth, Myrdal followed a Swedish tradition.

> The unique contribution of Swedish socialism was its idea of 'productivist' social policy. Its leading theoreticians stood liberalism on its head, arguing that social policy and equality were necessary preconditions for economic efficiency, which, in turn, was a prerequisite for the democratic socialist society [*Esping-Andersen, 1994: 713*].

The Swedish concept of a 'productivist social justice' in which 'the welfare state invests in optimising people's capacity to be productive citizens' contrasts with 'the strong Catholic influence in Continental European welfare states [which] has resulted in a policy regime that encourages women to remain within the family' [*ibid.: 722*]. The productivist approach to social justice addresses the standard criticism of Keynesian policies that they only address demand and ignore supply factors. We find echoes of productivist arguments in human development (below) and the regulation school.

In a well-known World Bank-sponsored study, Hollis Chenery and associates [*1974*] argued that egalitarian and developmental objectives are complementary. This position favoured redistribution of income and assets to the poorest groups [*Midgley, 1995: 59, 130*]. If we now reread *Redistribution with Growth*, and sequel studies such as Adelman and Robinson [*1978*], they are inspired by dissatisfaction with the mainstream course followed during the first development decade. This egalitarian alternative proposal has since been outflanked and clipped by the rise of monetarism, supply-side economics and neo-conservativism in the 1980s. Hence it makes sense to revisit these arguments, taking into account subsequent trends and addressing the misgivings about *dirigisme*, rents and rent-seeking, welfarism and dependency.

In the 1990s the idea of redistribution with (or for) growth is regaining ground in mainstream development policy, with some new inflections: a general concern with social indicators in measuring development, to the point of redefining development itself; an emphasis on human capital; and a growing critique of trickle down. A World Bank report presented at the Copenhagen summit, *Advancing Social Development*, notes: 'How growth affects poverty depends greatly on the initial distribution of income. The more equal the distribution of income to start with, the more likely it is that poverty will be reduced for a given increase in average income' [*World Bank, 1995: 4–5*]. Hence the World Bank recognition of the importance of safety nets for the poor when implementing policy reforms of deficit reduction [*ibid.: 23*]. The World Bank package presently includes 'promoting labor-demanding growth, investing in people, providing safety nets, and improving governance' [*ibid.: 48*]. In this fashion social development is assimilated as part of structural reform – as a supplementary safety net, as structural adjustment with a human face, or as 'stage two' of structural reform, as the political stabilisation of reform policies.

In view of the recognised importance of the initial distribution of income and its effect on poverty alleviation, is merely installing safety nets logical or adequate? To achieve these effects more far-reaching measures appear to be called for. In addition, what is at issue are structural reform policies themselves and their underlying economic rationale. The real challenge is to examine the nexus not merely between income distribution and poverty alleviation but between equity (or equality) and growth. Redistribution with growth, in a mix of productivist and demand management elements, now also informs South Africa's Reconstruction and Development Programme [*Moll, Nattrass and Loots, 1991*].

## LESSONS OF EAST ASIA

Equitable development policies are widely recognised as a crucial factor in East Asian development. Thus, 'there is substantial evidence to suggest that equity in income distribution and decent welfare systems are friends not enemies of growth, a pattern strikingly clear for Japan, Taiwan, Hong Kong, Korea and Singapore where equity and growth have gone hand in hand' [*Weiss, 1996: 195*]. World Bank studies acknowledge that one of the initial conditions for rapid growth in East Asia

> was the relative *equality of income* in the first generation NIEs. This factor was more of a change brought about by policy than an inheritance. Most other low- and middle-income countries were not able to achieve similar equality of income or assets. Large land reform schemes in both Korea and Taiwan, China, did away with the landholding classes and made wage income the main source of advancement. Public housing investments in Singapore and Hong Kong were early priorities of governments bent on maintaining a national consensus on development policies [*Leipziger and Thomas, 1995: 7*].

This is often noted: 'some of the advantages of the rapidly growing East Asian countries were their unusually low initial income inequality in 1960 and their labor-demanding pattern of growth, which tended to reduce income inequality over time' [*World Bank, 1995: 5*].

Education policies are part of this equation. The World Bank study on *The East Asian Miracle*

> shows that the single most important factor in launching the miracle countries on a path of rapid, sustained economic growth was universal or near-universal primary school enrolment. In 1960 Pakistan and Korea had similar levels of income, but by 1985 Korea's GDP per capita was nearly three times Pakistan's. In 1960 fewer than a third of the children of primary school age were enroled in Pakistan while nearly all were enroled in Korea [*ibid.: 34*].

Such evidence is less conclusive in relation to the late NICs in Southeast Asia. In Malaysia between 1970 and 1990 the New Economic Policy established an inter-ethnic trade-off between Bumiputras and Chinese – economic gains for the Malays and political citizenship rights for the Chinese, without infringing their economic position. This was made possible by rapid growth rates and foreign investment by MNCs, and resulted in equity among Malays and Chinese (but excluding inhabitants of Sabah and Sarawak, the indigenous Orang Asli, and Indians) [*Gomez, 1994; Jomo, 1995*]. Policies pursuing equity and growth are less evident in Thailand, play a minor part in Indonesia and are absent in the Philippines.

While the elements of equity in the growth path of East Asian NIEs are noted in World Bank and other studies, they are not often highlighted. In Leipziger and Thomas' [*1995:* 2] *Lessons of East Asia* they figure in the text but not in the 'Development Checklist', which features items such as selective industrial policies and directed credit. Debates on the East Asian NICs have concentrated on the question of the efficacy of government interventions – as the primary challenge to neoclassical economics and its emphasis on trade liberalisation as forming the clue to Asian economic success. The question of the 'governed market' [*Wade, 1990*] or 'governed interdependence' [*Weiss, 1996*] and the enduring debate on state or market [*Wade, 1996*] has tended to overshadow issues such as equity and growth. In an Asian perspective on the 'East Asian Miracle' study, equity and growth, or 'shared growth', is mentioned in passing while the emphasis is on the institutional capacities of government [*Ohno, 1996: 20*; cf. *Iwasaki et al., 1992*].

The emphasis on the authoritarian character of Asian regimes (itself a variant of the well-worn Orientalist theme of 'Oriental despotism') biases the discussion. References to Confucianism and 'Asian values' are not particularly helpful either. The first distinctive feature of East Asian authoritarian government is that it has been *developmental* – unlike, say, Somoza's authoritarianism or that of predatory states. The second is that in significant respects it has been *cooperative* in relation to market and society – unlike Pinochet's authoritarianism in Chile. A third distinctive element is that it has not only disciplined labour but also *capital*. What has been overlooked or downplayed is the coordinating character of government intervention in East Asia and the ingenious political and social arrangements which have been devised in order to effect social policies in a market-friendly fashion, or vice versa, to effect market support strategies in a society-friendly fashion [*Weiss, 1996; Ohno, 1996*]. Specific examples include state support for small and medium sise businesses in Taiwan [*Hamilton and Woolsey Biggart, 1994*], Singapore's housing policy [*Rodan, 1989; Hill and Kwen Fee, 1996*] and Malaysia's new economic policy. In addition, China's experiences in combining the market economy and social development are worth examining [*Gao, 1995*].

## HUMAN DEVELOPMENT

'Empowerment is not only democratic, it is efficient'
(Griffin and McKinley, 1994).

The human development (HD) perspective takes a further step in making a general case for the nexus between equity and growth. According to Keith Griffin [*1996: 15*], 'under some circumstances, the greater is the degree of equality, the faster is likely to be the rate of growth'. His considerations include the cost of the perpetuation of inequality and that inequality undermines political legitimacy while 'modern technology has destroyed the monopoly of the state over the means of violence'. Furthermore, 'measures to reduce inequality can simultaneously contribute to faster growth'.

> ... there is much evidence that small farms are more efficient than either large collective farms of the Soviet type or the capitalist latifundia one finds in Latin America and elsewhere. A redistributive land reform and the creation of a small peasant farming system can produce performances as good if not better than those of other agricultural systems. The experience of such places as China and Korea is instructive ... what is true of small farms is equally true of small and medium industrial and commercial enterprises. An egalitarian industrial structure, as Taiwan vividly demonstrates, can conquer world markets [*Griffin, 1996: 17*; cf. *Fei, Ranis and Kuo, 1979*].

Further elements mentioned by Griffin [*ibid.: 17*] are investment in education ('There is probably no easier way to combine equality and rapid growth. The whole of East Asia is testimony to the veracity of this proposition') and the liberation of women. 'A final example of the falsity of the great trade-off is the liberation of women. Equal treatment of women would release the talent, energy, creativity and imagination of half the population' [*ibid.: 17*; cf. *Buvini, Gwyn and Bates, 1996*].

A broadly similar case is made by ul Haq [*1995: 21–2*], who mentions 'four ways to create desirable links between economic growth and human development': investment in education, health and skills; more equitable distribution of income; government social spending; and empowerment of people, especially women. Ul Haq proposes an HD paradigm of equity, sustainability, productivity, and empowerment [*1995: 16*]. It is the element of *productivity* which sets this paradigm apart from the alternative development paradigm. This refers to the supply-side factor as the nexus between equity and growth.

This position is not necessarily controversial from the point of view of neoclassical economics. HD owes its definition to the emphasis on the investment in human resources, human capital, which is prominent in the East Asian model and Japanese perspectives on development and is now a mainstream development position. The argument that investment in human capital fosters growth is reinforced by the growing knowledge intensity of economic growth, as in innovation-driven growth and the emphasis on R&D and technopoles. ul Haq rejects the idea that adjustment and HD are antithetical, either conceptually or in policy.

> Far from being antithetical, adjustment and growth with human development offer an intellectual and policy challenge in designing suitable programmes and policies ... The challenge of combining these two concerns is like that of combining the conflicting viewpoints of the

> growth school and the distribution school in the 1970s [*ul Haq, 1995: 7–8*].

The same reasoning has informed 'structural adjustment with a human face' [*Jolly, 1986*].

It is not difficult to find confirmation for human capital arguments in neo-classical economics:

> welfare economics and human capital theory provide important market-conforming justifications for a range of social policies, most notably for public health and education ... neoclassical economics is inherently theoretically elastic. The theory of market failure may, in fact, justify a 'residual' welfare state, while information failure theory can be applied to argue for a fully fledged, comprehensive welfare state [*Esping-Andersen, 1994: 712*].

Nevertheless, the author continues, neoclassical economics emphasises the efficiency trade-offs associated with welfare policies, specifically negative effects on savings (and hence investments), work incentives, and institutional rigidities (such as labour mobility). In other words, neo-classical economics can both acknowledge and deflect welfare arguments by treating them as subsidiary to growth as the primary objective so that in the end welfare policies end up on the backburner. The key question is, rather, to zero in on those elements in the equity–growth debate which are controversial or which open up the framework of neo-classical economics.

The HD approach skirts rather than confronts this issue. This follows from the fact that HD follows the *human capital* argument which is part of the paradigm of neo-classical economics. In addition, in assuming the *individual* as the unit of human development HD shows that its intellectual roots are in liberalism.[5] HD may also be interpreted as the lessons of East Asia translated into general policy. As such one way of reading it is as a meeting point between the authoritarian state and the neo-liberal market, with the state acting as the supplier of human skills to the market, through human resource development programmes, packaged to achieve effective global competition. Merging social concerns and market concerns is excellent, but the question is, on which terms? According to ul Haq there is no contradiction in principle between structural reform and HD, it is only a matter of designing the right policy mix. This means that HD may be institutionally and ideologically acceptable to all sides. Since HD does not challenge but goes along with market logic, it does not address the problem of the unregulated market in a principled way.

HD has been inspired by Amartya Sen's [e g. *1985*] work on development as human capacitation. An obvious question here is, if following Sen's reasoning capacitation becomes the objective and measure of development, then who defines capacity, ability, or human resources? What about the disabled, single mothers, the aged? What about human traits that can*not* be translated into economic inputs, resources?[6] Besides, if capacitation and the enlargement of people's choices are the yardstick of development, as HD would have it, should we also consider, say, the Medellín Cartel as a form of capacitation and enlargement of people's choices? As Gasper [*forthcoming*] argues there is no moral dimension to Sen's approach to capacitation.

To the extent, then, that HD does not challenge neo-liberalism and the principle of competitiveness but endorses and feeds it, HD may enable development business-as-usual to carry on more competitively under a general 'humane' aura. Accordingly, social development, if sharpened, redefined and renewed in a wider framework, might be a more inclusive and enabling perspective than HD.

## LESSONS OF WELFARE STATES

Looking at social development side by side with the welfare state serves two purposes. It bridges the increasingly artificial divide between developed and developing countries and it helps to clear the path from economic generalisations to institutional and political questions. However, it might also confuse issues: equity-growth policies do not necessarily have to take the form of welfare states, which are a specific institutional arrangement.

It is not difficult to find econometric confirmation for the general positive correlation between equity or equality and growth: 'virtually every single statistical study concludes growth is positively related to equality' [*Esping-Andersen, 1994: 723*]; 'most econometric studies conclude that inequality is harmful to growth' [*1994: 72*]. However, aside from methodological limitations, a fundamental theoretical fallacy is implicit in this approach. Ironically, this echoes the fallacy inherent in neoclassical economics, namely the tendency to *abstract* economic factors from institutional and political dynamics. According to Esping-Andersen, 'the narrowly economic framework of the neoclassical model' is the reason for 'the curious gap between theoretical claims and empirical findings ... The model is consistent only when it leaves out political and social variables; studies that incorporate them invariably produce contradictory results' [*ibid.: 724*].

The welfare state may also be thought of as a particular way in which the economy is embedded in society.

> The welfare state is not something opposed to or in some way related to the economy; it is an integral element in the organic linkage of production, reproduction and consumption ... what we think of as the

> postwar welfare state is but one crucial regulatory element in the Fordist system of mass production [*Esping-Andersen, 1994: 716–17*].

The failure of welfare states lies not so much in fiscal strain but can rather be seen as a 'manifestation of a mounting incompatibility between a fossilised welfare state, on one hand, and a rapidly changing organisation of production and reproduction, on the other hand' [*ibid.: 717*]. This refers to a series of shifts – towards service production, of industrial production to NICs, from standardisation to flexibility, and from the Fordist family to women's economic independence, dual-earner households and non-linear life patterns; and towards the Schumpeterian workfare state [*Jessop, 1994*] and towards welfare pluralism [*Mishra, 1996*].

The reorganisation of production is a function of new technologies and changing consumer demand (flexible accumulation) as well as globalisation and the rise of the NICs. The crisis of welfare states, then, is in part, the other side of the coin of East Asian economic success. For instance, 'the redistributive Keynesian demand-stimulus policy, which served very well to assure adequate demand for domestically produced mass-consumption goods ... became increasingly counterproductive when such goods originated in Taiwan and Korea' [*Esping-Andersen, 1994: 717*] This suggests that the framework in which equity and growth is conventionally considered – the society or nation state – needs to be opened up, eventually to a global scope.[7]

Studies of welfare states highlight their diversity. This includes distinguishing between residual welfare states (USA), lean welfare states (Switzerland, Japan), productivist welfare states (Scandinavia), and the Rhineland welfare states which tend to uphold status differences rather than strive for equality. These distinctions may be merged with dynamic, curvilinear arguments on the relationship between equity and growth.

Arguments on the relationship between equity and growth coined in general terms are superseded by 'more complex, interactive models that posit curvilinear relationships between welfare states and economic performance' [*Esping-Andersen, 1994: 723*]. Such arguments suggest, for instance, that up to a certain point the welfare state will have a positive influence on economic growth after which it turns increasingly negative. Another curvilinear model suggests that 'full employment is best secured in countries where collective institutions (and the Left) are either very weak or very strong ... In the former case, labor market clearing is largely left to naked market forces; in the latter, to political management' [*ibid.: 724*]. Accordingly,

> the effect of a welfare state cannot be understood in isolation from the political-institutional framework in which it is embedded ... there may exist a trade-off between equality and efficiency in countries where the welfare state is large and very redistributive but in which the collective

> bargaining system is incapable of assuring wage moderation and stable, nonconflictual industrial relations. Thus, in concrete terms, a Swedish, Norwegian, or Austrian welfare state will not harm growth, while a British one will (even if it is smaller) ... if we turn to a dynamic interpretation, the evidence suggests that as long as a large and redistributive welfare state is matched by neocorporatist-style political exchange mechanisms, equality and efficiency are compatible; when the capacity for harmonious political bargains ceases to function, the same welfare state may threaten economic performance [*Esping-Andersen, 1994: 725–6*].

One line of argument is that after a certain level growth yields diminishing returns in terms of welfare and well-being [*Daly and Cobb, 1994*]. This calls to mind an earlier argument of Keynes on diminishing returns of the pursuit of surplus [*Singer, 1989*].

Similar dynamic and curvilinear arguments have been made in relation to 'social capability': 'a country's potential for rapid growth is strong not when it is backward without qualification, but rather when it is technologically backward but socially advanced' [*Temple and Johnson, 1996:* 2]. How to define and measure 'social capability'? Putnam [*1993*] looks at associational membership and survey measures; Myrdal considered levels of mobility, communication and education. Temple and Johnson [*1996: 1*] are concerned with the 'social factors that play a role in the speed of catching up' and they define social capacity narrowly as 'the capacity of social institutions to assist in the adoption of foreign technology' [*1996: 3*]. They follow the Adelman and Morris index of social development and conclude from their findings that the 'relative importance of investments in physical capital and schooling appears to vary with the extent of social development' [*1996: 41*].

## SOCIAL CAPITAL

This brings us to the wider question of the institutional embeddedness of social policies. At the end of the day arguments about equity and growth cannot be made in generic terms. They are political questions or, more precisely, for their economic rationale to be operative they depend on institutional arrangements and political settlements. New institutional economics focuses on the institutional requirements for economic growth such as legal frameworks and structures of rights, while the growing body of work on the sociology of economics examines the embeddedness of economic behaviour. The standard literature on social development is, as mentioned before, dominated by questions of social policy. The literature on economic performance increasingly turns towards social issues [*Granovetter, 1992; Stewart, 1995*], but on an entirely different wavelength. Since the two fields hardly intersect, it is an interesting exercise to consider their possible intersections. They concern two dimensions of social development: social policy and the economic significance of social networks and relations of trust, often summed up under the heading of social capital. Social capital refers to a wide range of arguments, with various possible intersections with social development, depending on which angle on social capital one adopts.[8]

A key concern of Bourdieu [*1976*] is the relations among economic, social, cultural and symbolic capital, which he regards as cumulative and interchangeable. Current interest is more concerned with social capital as a clue to economic capital, an asset in the process of accumulation. Social capital in this sense may be appropriated in a rightwing perspective, in which civil society serves as a counter (rather than as a complement) to the state. According to Fukuyama [*1995: 103*], '[t]he character of civil society and its intermediate associations, rooted as it is in nonrational factors like culture, religion, tradition, and other premodern sources, will be key to the success of modern societies in a global economy'. Building intermediate associations may be an alternative to the role of government and to 'social engineering', which are seen to be a dead end. Left-wing perspectives on social capital make a similar case, but in this case addressed to market failure rather than state failure. In view of the success of corporatist strategies in East Asia and continental Europe, various forms of 'concertation' may be recommended as a redress for market failure. Along these lines, Etzioni's communitarianism emphasises building community and civic virtue. In Britain, rethinking social democracy combines ideas about rebuilding community, the social market or social economy [*Sheffield Group, 1989*] and 'stakeholder capitalism' [*Hutton, 1995*] with the renewal of democracy, as in associative democracy [*Hirst, 1993; Amin, 1995*].

These concerns overlap with an extensive literature on industrial districts and local economic development, which goes beyond agglomeration economies and transaction cost arguments to incorporate relations of trust [*Harrison, 1992; Ottati, 1994*] and institutional densities [*Amin and Thrift, 1993*] as elements that go into the making of regional economic performance. Politics of place may also involve local culture as a dimension of economic performance [*Hanloe, Pickvance and Urry, 1990; Lash and Urry, 1994*]. Analyses of the 'Third Italy' from the point of view of associative economics also refer to local democracy as an economic asset. This may take the form of a New Left productivism, centred on 'the popular construction of cooperation through citisenship and authentic participation, in politics and the workplace' [*Amin, 1995: 13*]. In this context the informal economy may be viewed as a permanent arrangement, which may be further developed, for instance in the form of labour exchange networks (exchanging child care for gardening), in combination with an active and capacious state.

These right-wing and left-wing perspectives on social capital are both upbeat and optimistic in their view of social capital as an avenue either to outflank the state or to combine strong civil society, strong state, strong economy. Social capital has thus become a new terrain of rhetorical positioning and ideological contestation, which calls for greater analytic clarity.

Putnam's [*1993*] study of the course of administrative decentralisation in Italy since the 1970s has been quite influential in putting social capital on the map. According to Putnam, those regions in the North of Italy, which have a historical legacy of civic associations and participatory local government, have reacted well to administrative decentralisation in terms of regional government and economic performance; while the Mezzogiorno, which has historically been governed along centralised and vertical lines, shows high rates of failure both in terms of administration and economic achievement. His conclusions come down on the side of 'history as destiny' and carry a conservative bias. Putnam's work has been criticised for misconstruing 'path dependency', misreading Italian history and stereotyping the South [*Levi, 1996; Sabetti, 1996*]. In addition, this approach leaves no room for the possibility of nurturing or generating social capital. The record of several countries shows that the vicious circle can be broken. Notably in East Asia policy interventions have been able to create economically enabling political and institutional conditions within reasonably short time spans, even countries that had been used to vertical and centralised government. In other words, levels of trust are not simply historical givens but can be fostered through an appropriate policy mix. Policy performance can be a source of trust, not just a result.

Notions such as social capital and the social market carry a double meaning. They refer both to the socialisation of the market and to the instrumentalisation or commodification of social relations. The notion of 'trust as a commodity' exemplifies this double move [*Dasgupta, 1988*]. Likewise there are different dimensions to embeddedness. At a general level the point is that the economy is embedded in society; further down the ladder of abstraction, any market relationship is embedded in a specific social configuration. A few considerations may clarify the range of applicability of social capital. (1) Social capital is particularistic. To networks there are boundaries and boundaries are exclusionary. 'Neighborhoods ... are a source of trust and neighborhoods are a source of distrust. They promote trust of those you know and distrust of those you do not, those not in the neighborhood or outside the networks' [*Levi, 1996: 51*]. The other side of embeddedness is exclusion; the other side of trust is risk. Accordingly, social capital may be a strategy of risk management. (2) Social exclusion and closure facilitate trust and co-operation by ensuring the predictability of relations and preventing the leakage of resources. (3) Concentrating social capital has long been a fundamental strategy of power, witness the circles of privilege of aristocracies, 'old boy' networks, clubs, inner circles, secret societies, lodges, sects, and crime networks. It has also been a strategy of subversion, insurgence, revolution, or conquest of state power, witness the Jacobins, Carbonari and the cells in international communism. Women's networks have cultivated sisterhood and autonomy. Common features include boundary-establishing rituals of initiation that serve to concentrate social capital, create bonds of obligation, establish a circle of trust and a common frame of understanding. (4) Co-operation can also be a competition strategy. Examples range from alliance policies, nonaggression pacts or peace treaties to firm mergers, all of which seek to reduce risk.

As Coleman [*1988: 118*] notes, 'most forms of social capital are created or destroyed as by-products of other activities'. The question is what difference policy can make, in other words, can social capital or civic participatory culture be nurtured, fostered, or harnessed as part of social development policies? In addition, to search for enabling features of social capital one must look not merely at internal relations within groups but at relations *among* groups. Under what conditions do widening circles of social capital arise?

On the premise that embeddedness involves inclusionary and exclusionary elements, the work on 'ethnic economies' may serve as an example [*Light and Karageorgis, 1994; Waldinger et al., 1990*]; the informal economy may also be a field of inquiry [*Portes, 1994*]. An interesting query would be not merely ethnic economies but *inter-ethnic economies*. In other words, the development or generation of trust *across* ethnic boundaries. For instance, the Chinese diaspora in the Pacific Rim countries involves not merely ethnic enclave economies but a wide range of collaboration with locals, such as joint ventures [*Seagrave, 1996*]. The attitude taken by governments in relation to these forms of cooperation can make a huge difference. By and large the New Order government of Suharto has utilised the Chinese business community as a classic 'trading minority', 'the Jews of the East', keeping them politically dependent, with limited political rights, while nurturing relations with a small coterie of tycoons [*Irwan, 1996*]; whereas the Malaysian government through its New Economic Policy (1970–90) has been able to strike an interethnic deal.

It follows that a policy of *democratisation*, rather than polarisation, of interethnic relations can contribute to economic achievement. This may be an instance with wider implications. Social development in this sense refers to policies promoting social trust *among* and *across* diverse communities – classes, status groups, minorities and so on. It may also refer to the creation of social infrastructure such as housing, schools, clinics, water supply; or asset development among low-income groups to encourage savings among the poor, which will foster social investments [*Midgley, 1995: 160*]. Government may play a facilitative role, in the form of managed pluralism. Synergies between regional, urban and local economic development are another relevant approach. The principle of co-operation also applies to relations among firms and between firms and subcontractors (see Dore [*1994*] on goodwill in Japan).

An extensive literature documents intersectoral co-operation and synergies in the context of community or local economic development (CED, LED); but this approach may also have international, macro-regional and global implications [*Thrift and Amin, 1995; Kuttner, 1991; Gerschenkron, 1992*]. Worth considering for instance is transnational social policy as an emerging theme [*de Swaan, 1994*]. A further proposition is that of a World Social Development Organisation to effect economic and social policy jointly on a world scale [*Petrella, 1995: 22*]. These propositions may be enriched by examining transnational social capital in the informal sector [*Portes, 1996*] and the formal sphere [*Strange, 1996*].

## CONCLUSION

> 'Economic growth does not cause an increase in the quality of life, but increase in quality of life does lead to economic growth' (Misanur Rahman Shelley, Center for the Study of the Global South, 1994, p.62).

Structural adjustment programmes and social safety nets make up a convenient combination; so do the 'Washington consensus' and the Copenhagen summit. In this configuration, social development is a matter of tidying up after the market. A polarising mode of economic growth, followed up by social impact studies to assess its pauperising impact and poverty alleviation measures to compensate for the immiserisation effect. This is the repair or damage control mode of social development. Upon closer consideration it is not so much social development, but rather political risk management and social fixing. Along the way, however, social inequality entails not merely a moral cost and political consequences: 'there is a point at which social injustice undermines economic efficiency' [*Center for the Study of the Global South, 1994: 15*].

In development theory a distinction runs between development as planned change or engineering, and development as immanent change, a process from within [*Cowen and Shenton, 1996*]. Modernisation theory followed a logic of development from above and outside. Structural adjustment follows in the same footsteps. Modernisation policies in the past and the current application of liberal productivism to developing countries first *destroys* existing social capital for the sake of achieving economic growth, and then by means of social policy seeks to *rebuild* social tissue. En route there is obviously a lot of slippage, displacement, rearticulation, and realignment of power relations. Pursuing Darwinist economics and then sending in Florence Nightingale to tidy up the damage is a cumbersome and economically counterproductive approach to development.

The point of this study is to take social development beyond the poverty alleviation approach toward a substantive and pro-active approach. The second objective is to go beyond the human capital approach of human development. A productivist approach to social development involves not merely investing in education, health, housing – the standard fare of human capital approaches – but also accommodating or investing in social networking across communities and groups and designing enabling institutional environments; in other words, a social capital or participatory civic society approach. As a supply-side argument (that is, enhancing productivity and output, rather than promoting consumption), this addresses the criticism of Keynesian demand stimulus policies on the part of the supply-siders of the 1980s. What it does not address is the problem of technological change and jobless growth.

On several grounds and in multiple fashions – human capital, social capital, democratisation – social development can contribute to overall economic achievement. In the words of Amin and Thrift [*1995: 21*], 'the argument within socio-economics that there can be a close connection between democracy and economic success is to be welcomed in our market-driven age'. If the market dominates it might as well serve socially useful purposes.

The neo-classical trickle-down argument cannot be made in generic terms because outcomes vary according to political and social circumstances. For the same reason, neither can equity-growth nor *trickle-up* arguments be made in general terms, for as such they would have very limited purchase. A social productivist approach might require an interventionist, developmental state,[9] but this may be too heavy-handed an approach. A more modest approach is managed pluralism [*Midgley, 1995*]. Intersectoral synergies among local government, NGOs and people's organisations, and firms are another field of cooperation [*Brown and Ashman, 1996; Wignaraja, 1992*].

Managed pluralism involves political regulation. Merging social and market concerns also involves the development of collective bargaining systems. This may be difficult to achieve in segmented societies. Ethnic segmentation is a case in point; caste and class antagonism is another obstacle. A civic culture that strongly privileges individualism, as in North American free enterprise culture, may be more conducive to a casino mentality than to socially inclusive political settlements. Even so, one application of this kind of approach would be to review affirmative action policies in the United States and reservations policies in India [*Nederveen Pieterse, forthcoming*]. For these legacies need not to be taken as destinies. The point of a social development approach is not to provide a menu but to suggest a direction of analysis and policy. Social development, redefined in a wide sense, can serve as an orientation for a new social contract and as such become a new assembly point for development.

## NOTES

1. In considering infant mortality rates, Drèze and Sen [*1989*] distinguish two patterns: growth-mediated security, in which the crucial factor in lowering infant mortality rates has been growth and in particular employment (for example, in Hong Kong, Singapore, South Korea) and support-led security in which infant mortality rates have come down although growth rates have been low (in Chile, Costa Rica, Jamaica, Cuba during the 1970s). The latter countries have since changed course or been overtaken by events: Chile embarked on a different course under the Pinochet regime; Costa Rica and Jamaica have implemented macroeconomic reforms since the 1980s; Cuba has a stagnant economy.
2. In view of the status of the Kerala model [*Robin, 1992*], a little more information may be in order. 'The open unemployment rate is around three times the national average. Kerala has earned the dubious distinction of being the only state in India whose real social expenditure has decreased during 1985–86/1991–92 period, compared to the decade 1974–75/1984–85' [*Isaac and Tharakan, 1995: 1996*].
3. For instance, Indonesia's report to the summit is entirely framed by the 'Presidential Instruction No. 5/1993 regarding the Intensification of Efforts to Alleviate Poverty', the so-called IDT Program (National Development Planning Agency and Ministry of Home Affairs, 1994). By contrast, the parallel meeting organised by NGOs followed different tracks. An example is the Philippine Rural Reconstruction Movement's (1994) 'The Way of Power: Development in the Hands of the People', which develops a civil society and grassroots-centred Sustainable Rural District Programme, in other words, a social action and participatory policy approach. Several submissions combine social action and policy approaches, from below and above, such as Møller and Rasmussen [*1995*]. UNRISD [*1995*] reviews several approaches, from poverty alleviation to participatory social policy and notions such as promoting global citizsenship.
4. The components of the Adelman-Morris index of social development are: sise of the traditional agricultural sector; extent of dualism; extent of urbanisation; character of basic social organisation; importance of indigenous middle class; extent of social mobility; extent of literacy; extent of mass communication; crude fertility rate; degree of modernisation of outlook [*Temple and Johnson, 1996: 10*].
5. Cultural bias may be another limitation to HD. Griffin and McKinley [*1994*] seek to accommodate this by making HD responsive to cultural difference and disaggregating HDI according to ethnic groups within a society. Griffin [*1996*] takes this argument a step further by considering cultural difference as an engine of economic growth.
6. Paul Streeten in ul Haq [*1995: xi*] mentions the conflict between human resource developers (who emphasise HD as a means to growth) and humanitarians (who view it as an end and who are also concerned with the unproductive and unemployable).
7. I will address this in another paper under the heading of 'the interaction of modernities'.
8. This occasion only allows a brief engagement. I have learned much from supervising two outstanding MA theses at the Institute of Social Studies in 1996: Melania Portilla Rodriguez, 'Social Capital in Developing Societies: Reconsidering the Links between Civil Agency Economy and the State in the Development Process' and Sergio Lenci, 'Social Capital? From Pizza Connection to Collective Action: An Inquiry into Power, Culture and Civil Society'.
9. Or, an 'intelligent' or educator state that is ahead of civil society, such as France and Singapore; a principle that is not part of the Anglo-American tradition which leans towards the minimal state.

## REFERENCES

Adelman, I. and C.T. Morris, 1967, *Society, Politics and Economic Development*, Baltimore, MD: Johns Hopkins University Press.

Amin, A., 1995, 'Beyond Associative Democracy', unpublished paper.

Amin, A. (ed.), 1994, *Post-Fordism: A Reader*, Oxford: Blackwell.

Amin, A. and N. Thrift, 1993, 'Globalisation, Institutional Thickness and Local Prospects', *Revue d'Economie Régionale et Urbaine*, Vol.3, pp.405–27.

Amin, A. and N. Thrift, 1995, 'Territoriality in the Global Political Economy', unpublished paper.
Berman, M., 1988, *All That is Solid Melts into Air*, New York: Penguin.
Booth, D. (ed.), 1994, *Rethinking Social Development*, Harlow: Longman.
Bourdieu, P., 1976, 'Les Modes de Domination', *Actes de la Recherche en Sciences Sociale*, Vol.2, Nos.2–3, pp.122–32.
Boyer, R. and D. Drache (eds.), 1996, *States Against Markets: The Limits of Globalisation*, London: Routledge.
Brown, D.L. and D. Ashman, 1996, 'Participation, Social Capital, and Intersectoral Problem-Solving: African and Asian Cases', Boston, MA: Institute for Development Research Report, 12 (2).
Buvinic, M., Gwyn, C. and L.M. Bates, 1996, *Investing in Women: Progress and Prospects for the World Bank*, Washington, DC: Overseas Development Council.
Center for the Study of the Global South, 1994, *Social Summit, Copenhagen: Expectations of the Global South*, Washington, DC: American University, School of International Service.
Chenery, H. *et al.*, 1974, *Redistribution with Growth*, Oxford: Oxford University Press.
Coleman, J.S., 1988, 'Social Capital in the Creation of Human Capital', *American Journal of Sociology*, Vol.94, pp.95–120.
Cowen, M.P. and R.W. Shenton, 1996, *Doctrines of Development*, London: Routledge.
Daly, H.E. and J.B. Cobb Jr., 1994, *For the Common Good*, 2nd Edition, Boston, MA: Beacon Press.
Dasgupta, P., 1988, 'Trust as a Commodity', in D. Gambetta (ed.), *Trust: Making and Breaking Cooperative Relations*, Oxford: Blackwell, pp.49-72.
Davis, A., 1991, 'Hazardous Lives, Social Work in the 1980s: A View from the Left', in M. Loney *et al.* (eds.), *The State or the Market: Politics and Welfare in Contemporary Britain*, Second Edition, London: Sage, pp.83–93.
Dore, R., 1994, 'Goodwill and the Spirit of Market Capitalism', in M. Granovetter and J. Swedberg (eds.), *The Sociology of Economic Life*, pp.159–80.
Drèze, J. and A. Sen, 1989, *Hunger and Public Action*, Oxford: Clarendon Press.
DSE, 1994, *Social Security in Africa: Old Age, Accident and Unemployment*, Berlin: Deutsche Stiftung für Internationale Entwicklung.
Ekins, P., 1992, *A New World Order: Grassroots Movements for Global Change*, London: Routledge.
Esping-Andersen, G., 1994, 'Welfare States and the Economy', in N.J. Smelser and R. Schwedberg (eds.), *The Handbook of Economic Sociology*, Princeton, NJ: Princeton University Press, pp.711–31.
Fei, J., Ranis, G. and S. Kuo, 1979, *Growth with Equity: The Taiwan Case*, Oxford: Oxford University Press.
Fukuyama, F., 1995, 'Social Capital and the Global Economy', *Foreign Affairs*, Vol.74, No.5, pp.89–103.
Galbraith, J.K., 1996, *The Good Society*, Boston, MA: Houghton Mifflin.
Gao, Z., 1995, 'Market Economy and Social Development', Beijing/Copenhagen: World Summit for Social Development.
Gasper, D., forthcoming, 'The Capabilities Approach and Development Ethics', *Journal of International Development.*
Gerschenkron, A., 1992, 'Economic Backwardness in Historical Perspective', in Granovetter and Swedberg (eds.), [*1992: 111–30*] (originally published 1952).
Gomez, E.T., 1994, *Political Business: Corporate Involvement of Malaysian Political Parties*, Townsville: James Cook University of North Queensland.
Granovetter, M., 1992, 'Economic Institutions as Social Constructions', *Acta Sociologica*, Vol.35, pp.3–11.
Granovetter, M. and R. Swedberg (eds.), 1992, *The Sociology of Economic Life*, Boulder, CO: Westview.
Griffin, K., 1996, 'Culture, Human Development and Economic Growth', Working Paper in Economics 96–17, University of California, Riverside.
Griffin, K. and T. McKinley, 1994, *Implementing a Human Development Strategy*, London: Macmillan.
Hamilton, G.G. and N. Woolsey Biggart, 1992, 'Market, Culture and Authority: A Comparative Analysis of Management and Organisation in the Far East', in Granovetter and Swedberg (eds.), [*1992: 181–223*].

Hanloe, M., Pickvance, C.G. and J. Urry (eds.), 1990, *Place, Policy and Politics: Do Localities Matter?*, London: Unwin Hyman.

Haq, M. ul, 1995, *Reflections on Human Development*, New York: Oxford University Press.

Harrison, B., 1992, 'Industrial Districts: Old Wine in New Bottles?', *Regional Studies*, Vol.26, No.5, pp.469–83.

Hill M. and L. Kwen Fee, 1995, *The Politics of Nation Building and Citisenship in Singapore*, London: Routledge.

Hirst, P.Q., 1993, *Associative Democracy*, Cambridge: Polity.

Hirtz, F., 1995, *Managing Insecurity: State Social Policy and Family Networks in the Rural Philippines*, Saarbrücken: Verlag für Entwicklungspolitik.

Hutton, W., 1995, *The State We're In*, London: Jonathan Cape.

Inter-American Development Bank, 1995, *Social Dimensions in the Agenda of the IDB*, Copenhagen.

Irwan, A., 1996, 'Rent and Ethnic Chinese Regional Business Networks: Indonesia's Puzzling High Economic Growth', unpublished paper, Kuala Lumpur.

Isaac T.M., Th. and M. Tharakan P.K., 1995, 'Kerala: Towards a New Agenda', *Economic and Political Weekly*, 5–12 Aug., pp.1993–2004.

Iwasaki, T., Mori, T. and H. Yamaguchi (eds.), 1992, *Development Strategies for the 21st Century*, Tokyo: Institute of Developing Economies.

Jessop, B., 1994, 'Post-Fordism and the State', in Amin (ed.), [*1994: 251–79*].

Jolly, R., 1986, 'Adjustment with a Human Face', in K. Haq and U. Kidar (eds.), *Human Development: The Neglected Dimension*, Islamabad: North South Roundtable, pp.386–400.

Jomo, K. S. (ed.), 1995, *Privatising Malaysia: Rents, Rhetoric, Realities*, Boulder, CO: Westview.

Kuttner, R., 1991, *The End of Laissez-Faire: National Purpose and the Global Economy after the Cold War*, New York: Alfred Knopf.

Lash, S. and J. Urry, 1994, *Economies of Signs and Space*, London: Sage.

Leipziger, D.M. and V. Thomas, 1995, *The Lessons of East Asia: An Overview of Country Experience*, Washington, DC: World Bank.

Levi, M., 1996, 'Social and Unsocial Capital: A Review Essay of Robert Putnam's Making Democracy Work', *Politics and Society*, Vol.24, No.1, pp.45–54.

Light, I. and S. Karageorgis, 1994, 'The Ethnic Economy', in Smelser and Swedberg (eds.), [*1994: 647–71*].

Midgley, J., 1995, *Social Development: The Developmental Perspective in Social Welfare*, London: Sage.

Mishra, R., 1996, 'The Welfare of Nations', in R. Boyer and D. Drache (eds.), *States Against Markets: The Limits of Globalisation*, London: Routledge, pp.316–33.

Moll, P., Nattrass, N. and L. Loots (eds.), 1991, *Redistribution: How Can it Work in South Africa?*, Cape Town: David Philip.

Møller, K. and E. Rasmussen (eds.), 1995, *Partnership for New Social Development: UN World Summit for Social Development*, Copenhagen: Mandag Morgen Strategisk Forum.

Myrdal, G., 1968, *Asian Drama: An Inquiry into the Poverty of Nations*, New York: Twentieth Century Fund.

Nederveen Pieterse, J., 1996, 'My Paradigm or Yours? Alternative Development, Post-development, Reflexive Development', *ISS Working Paper No.229*, The Hague.

Nederveen Pieterse, J., forthcoming, 'Racism and Social Development: Affirmative Action in the United States and India', in *Political, Social and Economic Racism*, Thessaloniki: Aristotle University .

Ohno, I., 1996, *Beyond the 'East Asian Miracle': An Asian View*, New York: UNDP, Office of Development Studies.

Okun, A., 1975, *Equality and Efficiency: The Big Trade-off*, Washington, DC: Brookings Institution.

Ottati, G. dei, 1994, 'Trust, Interlinking Transactions and Credit in the Industrial District', *Cambridge Journal of Economics*, Vol.18, No.6, pp.529–46.

Petrella, R., 1995, 'Europe Between Competitive Innovation and a New Social Contract', *International Social Science Journal*, Vol.47, No.1, issue 143, pp.11–23.

Portes, A., 1994, 'The Informal Economy and its Paradoxes', in Smelser and Swedberg (eds.), [*1994: 426–50*].

Portes, A., 1996, 'Transnational Communities: Their Emergence and Significance in the Contemporary World-system', in R. P. Korzeniewicz and W. C. Smith (eds.), *Latin America in the World Economy*, Westport ,CT: Greenwood Press, pp.151–68.

Putnam, R.D., 1993, *Making Democracy Work: Civic Traditions in Modern Italy*, Princeton, NJ: Princeton University Press.

Robin, J., 1992, *Women and Well-being: How Kerala Became a Model*, Basingstoke: Macmillan.

Rodan, G., 1989, *The Political Economy of Singapore's Industrialisation*, Kuala Lumpur: Forum.

Sabetti, F., 1996, 'Path Dependency and Civic Culture: Some Lessons from Italy about Interpreting Social Experiments', *Politics and Society*, Vol.24, No.1.

Seagrave, S., 1996, *Lords of the Rim*, London: Corgi Books.

Sen, A., 1985, *Commodities and Capabilities*, Oxford: Oxford University Press.

Sheffield Group, The (eds.), 1989, *The Social Economy and the Democratic State*, London: Lawrence & Wishart.

Singer, H.W., 1989, 'When Pursuit of Surplus Ends', *India International Centre Quarterly*, Spring.

Singer, H.W., 1996, 'How Relevant is Keynesianism Today for Understanding Problems of Development?', paper presented to 8th EADI conference, Vienna, Sept.

Smelser, N.J. and R. Swedberg (eds.), 1994, *The Handbook of Economic Sociology*, Princeton, NJ: Princeton University Press.

Stewart, F., 1996, 'Groups for Good or Ill', *Oxford Development Studies*, Vol.24, No.1, pp.9–25.

Straaten, F. van, 1996, 'Sociaal Paradijs Kerala Vergat zijn Economie', *NRC-Handelsblad*, 24 Aug.

Strange, S., 1996, *The Retreat of the State*, Cambridge: Cambridge University Press.

Swaan, A. de (ed.), 1994, *Social Policy Beyond Borders*, Amsterdam: Amsterdam University Press.

Taylor, L. and U. Pieper, 1996, 'Reconciling Economic Reform and Sustainable Human Development: Social Consequences of Neo-liberalism', *Office of Development Studies Discussion Paper*, UNDP, New York.

Temple, J. and P. Johnson, 1996, 'Social Capability and Economic Development', unpublished paper.

Thrift, N. and A. Amin, 1995, *Holding Down the Global*, Oxford: Oxford University Press.

UNRISD, 1995, *After the Social Summit: Implementing the Programme of Action*, Geneva: UN Research Institute for Social Development.

Wade, R., 1990, *Governing the Market: Economic Theory and the Role of Government Intervention in East Asian Industrialisation*, Princeton, NJ: Princeton University Press.

Wade, R., 1996, 'Japan, the World Bank and the Art of Paradigm Maintenance: The East Asian Miracle in Political Perspective', *New Left Review*, No.217, pp.3–36.

Waldinger, R. *et al.*, 1990, *Ethnic Entrepreneurs: Immigrant Business in Industrial Societies*, Newbury Park: Sage.

Weiss, L., 1996, 'Sources of the East Asian Advantage: An Institutional Analysis', in R. Robison (ed.), *Pathways to Asia: The Politics of Engagement*, St Leonard's: Allen & Unwin, pp.171–201.

Wignaraja, P., 1992, 'People's Participation: Reconciling Growth with Equity', in P. Ekins and M. Max-Neef (eds.), *Real-life Economics: Understanding Wealth Creation*, London: Routledge, pp.392–401.

World Bank, 1995, *Advancing Social Development*, Washington, DC.

# The Decentralisation Discourse: Post-Fordist Paradigm or Neo-liberal Cul-de-Sac?

FRANS J. SCHUURMAN

*Since the end of the 1980s there has been rapidly increasing global interest in the topics of decentralisation and local government. This interest is present among policy-makers, political parties, international financial organisations such as the World Bank and IMF, Northern NGOs engaged in development aid, grassroots organisations, and, of course, social scientists. The decentralisation euphoria is not limited to newly democratised countries in the South but is also present in the urban-industrial North. In many Latin American countries and in Africa decentralisation seems a very popular policy tool. The question addressed in this contribution is whether decentralisation and local government should be regarded as part of a progressive political project benefiting the poor in the Third World, or as part of a globalised neo-liberal project to disempower progressive elements in civil society and thereby remove the remaining obstacles to the global presence of capitalism. The discussion focuses on the Third World in general, with specific examples from Latin America.*

Every development decade has its preferred concepts which both reflect the *Zeitgeist*, and contribute to its construction. However, it is usually only with the benefit of hindsight that we can reconstruct the dialectical relationship between social science concepts and their historical context.

With respect to international development decades, many different concepts, theories and policies and have come and gone. In the 1980s, the preferred concepts were environment, gender and sustainability. Toward the end of that decade, globalisation, democratisation and civil society began to emerge in development discourse. These concepts are now so commonly accepted that one wonders how we could ever have managed without them. In this study I focus upon decentralisation, a concept which analytically and

Frans J. Schuurman, Third World Centre, University of Nijmegen, The Netherlands.

pragmatically ties together the main conceptual winners of the present development decade. For the purpose of my argument, I draw on the closely related topics of local government, local democracy, municipal democracy, devolution and decentralisation as forming the decentralisation discourse.

Decentralisation as a development tool is nothing new in itself. In the 1960s, many five-year Development Plans in Third World countries hinged on the establishment of regional growth poles, and the deconcentration of vital central ministries. What is new is that interest in decentralisation has become so widespread and acquired many more ideological connotations than before. An interest in decentralisation can be seen in such different circles as policy-makers, political parties, international financial organisations such as the World Bank and the IMF, NGOs in both North and South which are engaged in development aid, grassroots organisations, and, of course, social scientists. The decentralisation discourse is not limited to newly democratised countries in the South, but has a strong presence in the urban-industrial North.

Decentralisation discourse seems to have taken on truly global dimensions, especially in Latin America and Africa where decentralisation enjoys warm support across the political spectrum. Ongoing projects in these countries find the chances of financial and technical support from multi- and bilateral development aid agencies to be higher when decentralisation is involved; and, more strongly, decentralisation is sometimes a prerequisite for aid.

The question I would like to address here, however, concerns whether the global project of decentralisation will be of positive benefit to the underprivileged, marginalised and excluded – in short the poor – in the Third World in general, and in Latin America specifically. Is decentralisation (in the form of municipal democracy or local government) a progressive political project which emancipates the poor in the Third World, or is it merely a globalised neoliberal sham which disempowers the poor by giving free rein to global capitalism? I cannot go beyond pointing to some current tendencies, drawing some lessons from the past, and discussing their theoretical and politico-ideological nature. Rather than formulating a definite answer, I shall set out my doubts concerning the emancipatory potential of decentralisation.

As decentralisation discourse is a near global phenomenon, we must analyse some vital elements of what is known as the globalisation process. I will focus on those economic, political, and cultural aspects of globalisation which are important for understanding decentralisation discourse. The first section of this article concentrates on economic globalisation, structural adjustment and neoliberalism. Attention is then be paid to the 'transition to democracy' discourse and its emphasis on good governance as components of political globalisation. A final section on cultural globalisation discusses postmodernism and the issue of localised identity.

The sections have a similar structure. First, I set out the alignment of processes and discourses which have contributed to the globalised decentralisation euphoria. Then I make some critical points about each of these processes/discourses. The frame of reference for my critique is relatively simple – some might say simplistic. In the era of modern capitalism, emancipatory struggles have always resulted in renewed social contracts at the level of the nation-state. Now, I recognise very clearly that the nation-state has not only acted as the guarantor of social contracts but has at the same time constituted the major aggressor in the era of modern capitalism. Accordingly, I do not want to give the impression that I have a blind faith in the fundamental goodness of the nation-state and its desire to take care of its citizens. Still, I severely doubt whether the Third World poor can emancipate themselves without referring to the nation-state as a political, ideological and juridical framework. I do not see globalisation or localisation as leading in the foreseeable future to more benevolent institutionalised political frameworks for emancipatory struggles. There are no signs at all of the development of global or local social contracts. On the contrary, there seems to be a major fin-de-siècle crisis in global moral consciousness which surprisingly remains undetected by adherents of the decentralisation discourse. I do not believe that the local or the global provides a more suitable political arena for emancipatory collective action. My critique is specifically directed towards the rhetoric that decentralisation is a wholesome process of 'hollowing out the state'.

## ECONOMIC GLOBALISATION, STRUCTURAL ADJUSTMENT AND NEO-LIBERALISM

### *The Coalition in Favour of Decentralisation*

The concept of globalisation became popular during the 1980s and even more so in the 1990s. There are two different interpretations of this concept. The first interpretation refers to what has been called the McDonaldisation of the world. Here, globalisation means homogenisation, a standardisation of images, products, production techniques, the meaning of life and so on. There is seen to be a direct link between the global providers of these goods and the individual consumer. The nation-state, as an intervening filter between the global and the local, is considered to belong to a past era.

The second interpretation of globalisation sees a much more dialectical relationship between the global and the local. Naisbitt [*1994: 5*] refers to a global paradox: the bigger the world economy, the more powerful its smallest players.

> Big companies like AT&T, Coca Cola and British Petroleum are deconstructing themselves into autonomous units. The result is radical

> downsizing. Companies have to dismantle bureaucracies to survive. Economies of scale give way to speed, market flexibility and synergy. [This leads to] ... a collection of local businesses with intense global coordination [*Naisbitt, 1994: 7*]

And, 'The new era is an era of self-rule for peoples around the world, all connected with each other, a network of PCs' [*ibid.: 41*].

Sometimes the term *glocalisation* is used to indicate the dialectical interplay between the global and the local:

> Over the last decade or so the relative dominance of the nation state as a scale level has changed to give way to new configurations in which both the local/regional and the transnational/global scale have risen to prominence. Global corporations, global financial movements and global politics play deciding roles in the structuring of daily life, while simultaneously more attention is paid to local and regional responses and restructuring processes. There is, in other words, a double movement of globalisation on the one hand and devolution, decentralisation or localisation on the other [which has been termed] '*glocalisation*'. This concept also suggests that the local/global interplay of contemporary capitalist restructuring processes should be thought of as a single, combined process with two inherently related, albeit contradictory, movements and as a process which involves a *de facto* recomposition of the articulation of the geographical scales of economic and social life [*Swyngedouw, 1992: 40*].

Irrespective of whether globalisation is interpreted as a process of global (cultural) homogenisation or as a dialectical interplay between the global and the local, the role of the nation-state is seen as diminishing, or even vanishing to be replaced with notions of local government and decentralisation.

Structural Adjustment Programmes (SAPs), which were hoisted on heavily indebted Third World countries in the 1980s, provided a political-economic channel for disseminating decentralisation discourse to the Third World. The general characteristics of SAPs are well known and can be summarised as an emphasis on deregulation of central government activities, privatisation of state assets, curtailment of subsidies on some basic services, promotion of export-led industrialisation, and an opening up of the economy to international capital. Here, we see a clear example of the process of hollowing out the state. It is important to stress that this neoliberal logic is based upon the so-called end of the welfare state in the North and the ensuing policies of 'rolling back the state'. The Fordist regime of accumulation and the social regulation praxis which formed part and parcel of northern Fordism entered a crisis during the 1970s and brought an end to the welfare state in the North. Without making a detailed analysis of the circumstances in the South, the SAPs advocated a monetarist, neoliberal 'solution' which had been devised by the post-Keynesian economists to cure the economic crises in the North. Subsequently, 'rolling back the state' was adopted as the new policy guideline by those countries in the South which followed a SAP. This provided a favourable opportunity for decentralisation discourse to flourish.

### *A Critique*

To start with, it is important to realise that the neoliberal idea of limiting the role of the state and emphasising the free play of market forces originated from the urban-industrialised North whose Fordist model of accumulation underwent a global crisis during the 1970s. Let us reflect for a moment on the basic characteristics of Fordism as it arose after the Second World War because this sheds light on the role of the state in that period. French regulation theory provides us with the analytical tools to examine the relation between economy and politics during Fordism.

The basic assumption of regulation theory is that social regulation (social norms, mechanisms and institutions) helps capitalism to stabilise (albeit temporarily) its inherent contradictions in the sphere of economic accumulation. Social regulation, and thereby the role of the state, was vital under Fordism. The principle of the economic accumulation system was that rising productivity in the sector of mass production sustained rising incomes which in turn underpinned mass demand. This led to an autocentric system of accumulation and regulation. The role of the state was to institutionalise the processes of collective bargaining and the role of the trade unions, to subsidise social reproduction not covered by the rising incomes of the labourers, and to provide the physical infrastructure required by capital. The regime of accumulation and the system of social regulation jointly produced the phenomenon of the so-called welfare state, guided by Keynesian principles. Peck and Tickell [*1994b*] point out that there were a number of variations to the US-based Fordist model, such as *Flex-Fordism* in West-Germany, *Blocked Fordism* in Great Britain and *State Fordism* in France.

In addition to the role of the state in Fordism, it is important to point out that the mechanisms and components of regulation operated at the national level; the very reason why the Fordist accumulation regime showed increasing signs of crisis during the 1970s. Two of the most important factors which explain the Fordist crisis were the increasingly unregulated globalisation of the financial markets, and the internationalisation of production. These phenomena, which occurred at the same time, were to a certain extent related but each also had a major dynamic of its own. The international money economy became increasingly disassociated from economic production (something which Arjun Appadurai [*1990*] calls the *disjunction of scapes*).

The abolition of the gold standard in 1971 and the subsequent free floating exchange rates of national currencies against the dollar led to a rapid growth of the global financial market, especially in what is called derivatives (options, covering of risks and so on). Central banks increasingly lost control over their own currencies and the financial system truly globalised; anyone with access to a telephone could join in the global financial game.

The internationalisation of production broke the *virtuous circle of Fordism* in which the rise in productivity and the rise in labour income had secured mass demand. Wages were subsequently seen as a barrier for international competition instead of the foundation for a sustained national demand for wage goods. Real wages began to decline and as a consequence consumer-demand fragmented. The fragmentation of the pattern of demand was also a result of the increasing influence of television commercials, the revolution in micro-electronic consumer gadgets, etc. In a continuous display of postmodern creativity, capitalist entrepreneurs detect and create the smallest niches in the consumer market. Taken together these processes led to the end of the welfare state and the beginning of a new era known as Post-Fordism or After-Fordism (a neologism preferred by those, such as Peck and Tickell [*1994a; 1994b*], who doubt the stability of the Post-Fordist logic).

The main characteristics of Post-Fordism are flexible production, a flexible workforce, differentiation of the production of goods and services, technological innovation as the guiding principle of production, rising incomes for a limited group of skilled workers, and a rolling back of the Fordist regulatory powers of the state. As economy and finance globalised, those regulatory powers of the state which were limited to the national level were supposedly outdated. Neoliberalists saw Post-Fordism as an ideological ally in their efforts to roll back the state and make economic production and financial markets self-regulating. Accordingly, social policy was subordinated to the needs of the labour market, domestic full employment was sacrificed, and redistributive welfarism took second place to a productivist reordering of social policy [*Jessop, 1994*]. This new neo-liberal paradigm with a high dose of monetarism was inserted into the global flow of ideas, ideologies and images, and subsequently entered Third World countries in the form of Structural Adjustment Programmes.

The above leads to the conclusion that the notion of 'hollowing out the state' is a Northern 'invention' to solve the Fordist crisis and subsequently launched globally as the paradigm for the remainder of this century and into the next.

During the time that Fordism characterised the economy and society of the North, the countries in the South were defined as *Peripheral Fordist* (Mexico, Brazil), *Racial Fordist* (South Africa), *Primitive Taylorist* (Malaysia, Bangladesh and the Philippines) and *Hybrid Fordist* (Japan) [*Peck and Tickell,*

*1994b*]. Peripheral Fordism, for example, was characterised by local assembly plants exporting Fordist goods, heavy indebtedness, authoritarian state structures faced with movements for democracy, and (statist) attempts to emulate the Fordist accumulation system in the absence of corresponding modes of social regulation [*ibid.*]. The point to be made here is that the various forms of Peripheral Fordism in the South were not based on welfare state principles and the state played a very different role there than it did in the North during the golden age of Fordism (1950–70). This leads to the conclusion that 'rolling back' the state in an urban-industrialised Northern country which has gone through a Fordist accumulation phase is totally different from rolling back the state in a country which has never known Fordism. It is premature to hollow out the state in Third World countries just because current Post-Fordist neoliberal logic upholds this recipe for the North. If decentralisation as a regulatory principle of a Post-Fordist regime of accumulation were to be thrust upon the Third World, the following picture would emerge.

These countries, which never experienced the virtuous circle of Fordism or a period of welfarism, have now to jump over the Fordist phase, immediately enter the Post-Fordist accumulation logic and use decentralisation as the concomitant regulatory fix. It is not my intention to fall back on a kind of unilinear, evolutionary thinking in which Third World countries go from Fordism, to crisis and then take the route of Post-Fordism. That would be an absurd point of view. Nevertheless, the above sketch of Third World countries going from Peripheral Fordism straight into Post-Fordism is equally absurd, not because the Fordist phase is missing, but because in a strange kind of way Peripheral Fordism resembles Post-Fordism. Given this, there is little reason to suppose that Post-Fordism will mean anything different to the Third World then Peripheral Fordism did.

What resemblance can there be between Peripheral Fordism and Post-Fordism? First, neither involves the state in a welfarist, distributionist demand-side oriented regulatory logic; although the role of the state as an economic actor is much greater in Peripheral Fordism than in Post-Fordism. Second, both are characterised by a highly fragmented labour market. Third, in both economic activity is polarised between a sector producing for the national market and one producing for export. Fourth, in both wages are considered as an obstacle to stable accumulation. Fifth, both are characterised by increasing social polarisation. The OECD's most recent report, for example, clearly points out the growing income disparity within the European member countries; the polarising effects of Peripheral Fordism are a well researched phenomenon. Accordingly, from a more abstract regulatory logic, there is no case for decentralisation.

Let us add a less abstract argument by looking at the link between economic globalisation, decentralisation and local economies in the Third

World. It is increasingly doubtful whether Post-Fordism really is that global, whether economic (and financial) globalisation really exists. Irrespective of whether economic globalisation exists, it is also quite doubtful whether decentralisation will lead to anything significantly positive for marginal local economies in the Third World. In the case of economic globalisation, with a high degree of spatial mobility of economic capital, there is no reason to suppose that international capital will find marginal local economies remotely attractive. Should economic globalisation prove to be non-existent then the question of whether poor Third World localities can attract foreign investments is irrelevant. In neither scenario is there a case for decentralisation in which social regulation (formerly carried out at national level) is fragmented into a conglomerate of local governments and local economies.

Let us briefly look more closely at the following questions. (1) Are Post-Fordist dynamics at the international level of economic production and financial markets really that global? (2) Even where a case is made for economic globalisation, are we perhaps looking at a dynamic which could be characterised as deterritorialising (and as such counters the idea of decentralisation)? (3) Can poor local economies or local governments counteract the deterritorialising tendency in globalisation?

An increasing number of publications warn that globalisation might turn out to be a myth [*Ruigrok and van Tulder, 1995*]. The extent of the global and flexible character of the international economy is increasingly doubted. Many investments are in the sort of capital goods which are not easily transferable from one place to another. It seems that the footloose nature of international capital has been exaggerated by globalisation discourse. Gordon [*1989*], for example, points to a declining rather than an increasing spatial mobility of productive capital. The international economy can be more aptly described as *triadisation* (USA, Europe and Japan) than as globalisation. But let us suppose that there is indeed something called globalisation in which images, ideas, money, constantly and feverishly float around the globe, landing here and there to influence, indoctrinate, extract surplus value after a short production period, participate briefly in the stock market etc. We are talking then of globalisation in terms of *flows* [*Castells, 1985*]. These flows are developing a telesphere/cybersphere of artificial spaces created by streams of data, audio and video [*Luke, 1994: 619*], and money I would add. According to Luke these flows are 'disjunctive, fragmenting, anarchical and disordered'. Can we expect local governments of marginal regional or local economies in the Third World to tap into these flows when their nation-states have failed to do so for decades? It is possible, I suppose, but not likely. Besides, the jungle-law of globalisation makes this 'tapping into flows' a zero-sum game; success in one place means failure somewhere else [*Peck and Tickell, 1994a*].

In conclusion, there is little reason to assume that participation in the global Post-Fordist rat race and the adoption of decentralisation as its regulatory fix, will solve the problems of the majority of the Third World poor.

## POLITICAL GLOBALISATION, THE TRANSITION TO DEMOCRACY AND GOOD GOVERNANCE

### *The Coalition in Favour of Decentralisation*

The global transition to democracy, which started in the 1980s, has two variants. The first variant relates to the ending of military dictatorships, especially in Latin America, during the 1980s. The double-edged political pressure arising from SAPs on the one hand, and increasing opposition from social movements led to a process of (re)democratisation in these dictatorial countries. The actual transition to democracy occurred in various ways; in Latin America the *transición pactada* (such as in Chile) was the most common. According to the terms of this pact, the ruling military and the political opposition agree to safeguard the military against post-transition trials. The second variant relates to former dictatorships in Africa which opened up to democracy following the end of the Cold War in 1989. African dictators were suddenly confronted with declining support from the USA or the former USSR because their usefulness as pawns in the geopolitical and ideological game of the Cold War came to an end. The globally circulated images of the execution of Rumanian tyrant, Ceauçescu, an intimate friend of many dictators, must have provided food for thought.

In both the Latin American and African variants of the transition to democracy the policy tool of decentralisation assumed important features although for different reasons. Many African countries which embarked upon the road towards political democracy, albeit with varying degrees of enthusiasm, are characterised by the absence of an historic nation-building process. After independence, Western colonialism was generally followed by long periods of political instability and/or dictatorial rule. This did nothing to enhance a feeling of national identity which is a *sine qua non* for national democratic rule. In these countries regional solidarity (either ethnically or clan-based) is often more pronounced than national identity. This gives rise to a situation where decentralisation is the only way to construct the transition to democracy. In other cases, it provides autocratic leaders with a handy concept to construct a democratic façade while at the same time retaining power. As decentralisation is a volatile concept, open to many interpretations, its seemingly dynamic discourse can be drawn on by central government to unite many opposing forces. This attitude of the central government often led to a situation in which responsibility was decentralised but not power.

The context of the Latin American transition to democracy is very different for historical reasons which are too numerous to mention here. However, one difference with the African situation is worth specifying. Although a process of nation-building did take place in Latin America – with the indigenous peoples as the usual victims – decentralisation discourse is still as popular there as in Africa. To explain this, one must bear in mind the position of the Left in Latin America and the position of social movements.

*The End of Socialism and the Position of the Latin American Left*

The transition to democracy and the end of the Cold War created a new situation not only for those in power but also for the political opposition and for organised sectors of civil society, such as social movements. Before addressing the relationship between social movements and decentralisation discourse, I shall first explain the situation of the Latin American Left at the end of the 1980s. In Latin American countries which returned to democracy during the 1980s, whether through a *transición pactada* or not, the constellation of political power did not favour a major role for progressive political parties. Where they formed part of a political coalition (as the socialists in Chile), they adjusted their political programmes to fit in with the centre-rightist majority. People wanted stability after so many years of military dictatorship and any radical-leftist discourse was frowned on. In addition, there is an even more astute reason for the declining role of the Left in Latin America. The dramatic end of *real-existing socialism* in Eastern-Europe meant a global decline in the political value of the socialist paradigm. The Latin American Left faced near paradigmatic paralysis by the end of the 1980s because they could not fall back upon the familiar socialist rhetoric. They soon realised, however, that decentralisation discourse – with all its accompanying progressive-sounding issues like municipal democracy and empowerment of civil society – provided the chance to reclaim a progressive paradigm devoid of discredited and antagonising socialist/communist overtones.

This paradigmatic change, however, is not without ideological problems for the Latin American Left whose socialist ideas were grounded (like true Marxists) on the pre-eminence of the role of the state and the struggle for state power [*Castañeda, 1993*]. However, building a new political strategy literally from the ground upwards is regarded with suspicion by many orthodox Leftists. The current popularity of Gramsci's writings among the Latin America Left is explained by the fact that Gramsci is one of the few Marxists who provides an ideologically-based legitimation for embracing decentralisation as the new progressive paradigm. Likewise, more recent writings of a Post-Marxist nature, which focus on radical democracy, [*Munck, 1993; Laclau and Mouffe, 1985*] also enable decentralisation as a concept to be incorporated without problems.

### *The Transition to Democracy and Social Movements*

Social movements in Latin America also played a role in bringing about the transition to democracy [*Munck, 1989*]. Accordingly, their general expectation was that new democratically chosen regimes would take their historic role into account. However, political opportunism won the day in many new Latin American democracies; older political parties reappeared on the scene and social movements were increasingly marginalised. The fact that these movements were too fragmented to enter into stable coalitions with political parties provided the latter with an excuse to neglect them.

What changed, however, was that in many countries free and democratic municipal elections were held. The impression conveyed to low-income groups, especially in the cities, was that if not at the national level, then perhaps at the local level their needs would be taken into account and democracy would yield results. Thus, decentralisation became the name of the new political game. Owing to fragmentation, social movements were not in a position to present an alternative in the form of a centralised political project. For these reasons grassroots organisations all over Latin America supported the decentralisation discourse.

### *A Critique*

The emergence of democracy in the urban-industrialised North was intricately linked to development of capitalism (the spread of capitalist production relations to all sectors of the economy, the formation of an industrial and mercantile bourgeoisie and a labour proletariat). By contrast, in most Third World countries, democracy is a relatively recent phenomenon and one which is rather disassociated from economic dynamics. As mentioned earlier, the transition to democracy in the Third World can be attributed basically to two circumstances, internal and external. The *internal* circumstances relate to the increasing loss of legitimacy enjoyed by various forms of non-democratic regimes. Mounting popular protests against human rights violations and economic crises seriously weakened dictatorships which subsequently removed themselves from the political arena (as in Argentina) or negotiated their withdrawal (as in Chile). The *external* pressures to democratise are related to the ideological effects of the end of the cold war, and to the introduction of Structural Adjustment Programmes which increasingly insisted on the democratisation of society in order to create a stable political environment for (international) capital investment. So, on both counts, the emergence of democracy in many underdeveloped countries from the 1980s onwards was not specifically related to a regime of economic accumulation which consolidated interest groups and resulted in political pluralism as occurred in the North. Rather, democracy was parachuted into many currently democratising Third World countries, and particularly into those where external pressures played a major role.

This parachuting in of democracy was accompanied by two other phenomena: the hollowing out of the state through a forced programme of deregulation and privatisation, and stagnating economic growth. The combination of these two phenomena made decentralisation appear as a way for many nation-states to give democracy some substance. However, democracy does not function in isolation from events in the local and national economy. Advancing local democracy within the framework of a decentralisation policy may work for a while. People can choose their local representatives, grassroots organisations may be stimulated to take part in newly devised (and institutionalised) participatory organisms, and an initial financial impetus arising out of the redistribution of a part of the state's resources to the municipalities will contribute to initial euphoria (as recently in Bolivia in the context of the *Ley de Participación Popular*). But if the local economy does not grow, initial enthusiasm will decline, local social polarisation will increase and people will lose their faith in this democratic experiment.

Nevertheless, Castañeda and even Lipietz are optimistic. Lipietz formulates *the alternative*, as he calls it, as follows:

> [the alternative] as a new model of progress takes over from the former democratic movement … its foundation would gather the oppressed, the abused and the exploited, in revolt against alienating social relations, bringing together, thus, women, workers adversely affected by economic restructuring or degrading technologies, the unemployed and precariously employed, the multicultural youth of the conurbations, indebted or non-industrialised peasants, and so on [*Lipietz, 1994: 346*].

Castañeda, in turn, is more interested in what decentralisation and local government can bring to the leftist parties in Latin America in their effort to regain a progressive political project. In his view, grassroots groups cannot 'preserve their virginity and achieve results' at the same time [*Castañeda, 1993: 364*]. In forging a link between social movements and the Latin American left, the leftist parties should take the initiative as social movements are seen as too unstable to play a leading role. Nevertheless, Castañeda in the end sees the purpose of the Latin American Left as being the development of the welfare state through profound tax reforms, massive debt relief, major cuts in military spending and a nationally devised strategy for export-led, environmentally sustainable industrial growth [*ibid.: 451*]. These are all policy tools of a nation-state and not of a local government. However, Castañeda advises the Latin American Left to pursue a bottom-up strategy, by using municipal democracy as a platform to reconquer the national political scene.

A brief look at the current effects of decentralisation policy in Chile is illustrative. Serious decentralisation in Chile started under the Pinochet-dictatorship and was continued (in a democratised form though) in 1990 first under President Aylwin and now under President Frei. Some effects of this *municipalización* (the institutionalisation of local government) can already be clearly seen.

First, many poor municipalities remain very dependent on redistributed national funds. They have not succeeded in developing an autonomous tax base which would allow greater financial independence from central budgets for the simple reason that they were not attractive enough to economic investors.

Second, the way in which redistribution of central budgets occurs fails to break the vicious circle of poverty in these poor municipalities. Education provides a good example. The budget which primary schools receive is related to the number of pupils. Seasonal drop-out rates are significantly higher in low-income areas, in part because of higher health problems among low-income children, especially in winter. Higher drop out rates mean that schools in low-income areas tend to become underfinanced. Being unable to pay decent salaries, they start to lose good teachers, the teaching quality of the school drops and those parents who can afford it send their children to other schools. Consequently, the drop-out rate increases and the school again loses out on state subsidy. It seems that Gunnar Myrdal's theory of *circular and cumulative causation* is as applicable to the 1990s as it was to the 1950s when Myrdal presented his theory.

Third, although the role of social movements within municipalities has been substantially reduced, this has not lessened their fragmentation. Ironically, the existence of General Pinochet as a common enemy in the years 1973-1990 did more to unite the Chilean people than the transition the democracy. After the return to democracy in 1990, the Chilean political parties resumed their co-optive attitudes to social movements. As such, civil society became thoroughly politicised once again and participation in political decision-making was only possible through party channels. In addition, social movements lost their former *élan* and increasingly 'technified'. The same is true of non-governmental organisations.

Fourth, poor communities in particular lack a professionalised bureaucracy which hampers efficient planning. As in the example above of education, a negative spiral comes into play. When poor communities cannot afford to pay good professionals, their project proposals tend to be turned down by central government ministries. Consequently, their budgets diminish, making it even more difficult for them to attract good quality professionals.

Fifth, within the decentralisation framework, popular participation in local government does not function. Local councils (especially in the larger cities) are hopelessly fragmented. The number of social categories (sports clubs, NGOs, employers) which participate in the popular council is simply too large and heterogeneous. In addition, local government officials and politicians do not take the popular councils seriously.

Sixth, political parties still seem more interested in national than local politics, unless this concerns high-income communities in the capital city. Parties do not take local politics seriously, much to the detriment of local government. Party representatives in local government tend to regard it as a stepping stone to becoming a *diputado* or *senador*.

As a result of the above factors, inequalities in welfare between communities have not diminished. Decentralisation in itself is no guarantee that things will improve for the poor. Where national political interest is focused on neoliberalism and on an export-led development disembedded from a welfarist state policy, then decentralisation is powerless to prevent spatial inequalities from persisting or even increasing. Political participation at local government level will only reflect the fragmentation of civil society and the neofeudal attitude of political parties *vis-à-vis* social movements.

Mohanty [*1995: 1435*] questions the emancipatory potential of decentralisation as follows:

> 'Empowerment', 'civil society' and 'democratisation' form the new package of liberalisation discourse which on their face value respond to the long-standing demands of struggling groups. In practice, however, each of them has been given a restricted meaning and has been oriented to serve the present global drive of western capitalism.

## CULTURAL GLOBALISATION, POSTMODERNISM AND IDENTITY

### *The Coalition in Favour of Decentralisation*

While the above was going on in the political-economic sphere, the (modernist) foundation of the academic world has also been rocked by the onslaught of postmodern thinking. There are at least two lines of reasoning which establish, perhaps indirectly, a link between cultural globalisation, postmodernism and the popularity of the decentralisation project. The first is that postmodern discourse, like decentralisation discourse emphasises *the particular*, in contradistinction to the modernist emphasis on *the universal*. The *Other*, to use the postmodern term, has increasingly come under the global spotlight along with the hitherto untold stories of the excluded in the Third World. The local, then, is the spatial frame of reference for the Other in the Third World to tell his or her story. As such postmodernism unwittingly supported a decentralisation discourse.

The second link comes from those postmodernists (a minority) who are interested in giving the Other a political as well as a cultural voice. In this case, decentralisation provides a suitable local political context in which the Other can effectively organise and confront the political powerholders. The newly-emerging school of Communitarians – with Amitai Etzioni as its foremost adherent, and Alain Lipietz as its most unlikely ally – is making headway in postmodernist circles which favour decentralisation. The Communitarians regard the community as vital for the well-being of the individual. The triumph of liberalism erodes solidarity with negative consequences, especially for the weak. In their view liberalism, through its overexploitation of natural resources, will result in neo-feudal patronage systems (such as the Somalian war-clans) in some parts of the world and in an autocratic Brave New World-tyranny in other parts. The only way to counteract this dark future scenario is to reinstate the *Gemeinschaft* in which solidarity, authenticity and autonomy form the basic ingredients of community-life. Decentralisation would create the institutional political framework to affirm local identity and autonomy.

*A Critique*

The Communitarian rhetoric sounds idyllic but in my view it will lead to political fragmentation and, far worse, to a privatisation of public space in which solidarity with Others will be even further from sight than before. As mentioned above, Communitarians themselves fear that liberalism will in the end lead to a sort of Mad Max scenario in which urban fortresses are surrounded by resource-starved mutants. They may be right, but it is the Communitarian-like reality of the *gated communities* in the United States which brings to mind those Mad Max scenes. These private neighbourhoods, surrounded by electronic fences and guarded by armed guards, enjoy a fast growing popularity. Solidarity with Others outside the community, or plain and simple humanism, is sacrificed in order to increase the feeling of security of those in these high-income ghettos. The *over the wall crowd* is tolerated but nothing more. The regulations (the so-called CC&R's: Covenants, Conditions and Restrictions) within these gated communities are very strict, not unlike the dreaded neo-feudal patronage system. This postmodern-inspired interest in decentralisation implies that the stories of the Others must be limited to the local scene so as not to develop into an undesirable Grand Narrative.

Thus, fragmentation and an absence of global solidarity with the plight of Others, is an inherent consequence of the postmodern emphasis on the particular rather than the universal. This is a rather paradoxical result given the original postmodernist interest in the Other. If not united by a political project, the Others tend to fragmentation; a not undesirable result as far as the interests of (international) capital are concerned. The recent referendum on separate status held in the Canadian province of Québéc is a good illustration of a number of points. Organised by francophone separatist political leaders, their decentralisation rhetoric stressed the different identity of the francophone majority. At the same time, however, this discourse disguised a political manoeuvre aimed at evading the local implementation of neo-liberal austerity measures thrust upon all Canadian provinces by the central government in Ottawa. The question which concerns us here is whether a separatist discourse (an extreme form of decentralisation) stressing cultural identity is inherently progressive and positive for the poorer segments of the Québécois. In my view there is nothing inherently progressive in a separatist discourse on the basis of being a *société distincte*. Fragmented identities have always worked in the interest of capitalism as long as surplus value could be extracted.

To conclude this section, there seem to be no grounds to assume that the negative effects of universal, global capitalism can be counteracted by strengthening localist, culturalist, and particularistic values within a project of decentralisation.

## CONCLUSION

A surprisingly heterogeneous group of actors is in favour of decentralisation: international financial organisations, central governments (in North and South alike), the political left, grassroots organisations, non-governmental organisations, post-Marxists and postmodernist social scientists. It comes as no surprise that decentralisation is likely to become *the* policy tool for the rest of the 1990s and well into the next century. I have pointed to a number of theoretical and empirical reflections which question this decentralisation euphoria. These centre around the issue of whether 'hollowing out' or 'rolling back' the state in Third World countries is such a good idea.

In addition to my critical assessment I would like to quote David Harvey who in no uncertain terms condemns decentralisation as a reactionary project because it furthers local fragmentation. In reference to the 'place-specific myths of Nazism in opposition to the rational utilitarianism of Enlightenment', Harvey warns against 'a whole set of political, cultural, and spatial practices that sought to reinforce local community solidarity and tradition in the face of the universalism and globalism of money power, commodification, and capital circulation' [*Harvey, 1989: 277*]. According to Harvey, this perspective is especially likely under conditions of time-space compression.

> We thus approach the central paradox: the less important the spatial barriers, the greater the sensitivity of capital to the variations of place within space, and the greater the incentive for places to be differentiated in ways attractive to capital. The result has been the production of fragmentation, insecurity, and ephemeral uneven development within a

> highly unified global space economy of capital flows. The historic tension within capitalism between centralisation and decentralisation is now being worked out in new ways [*Harvey 1989: 296*].

Harvey's remarks are in line with the idea that decentralisation furthers an international zero-sum-game between localities of which the poor will be the victim. As long as current instability of the international economic and financial system lasts, as long as the decentralisation discourse contributes to hollowing out the state, and as long as there is no institutionalised social contract at the global and/or local level, it is rather premature to parade decentralisation as the Post-Fordist paradigm. Decentralisation could well turn out to be a neoliberal cul-de-sac for the poor in the Third World.

## REFERENCES

Appadurai, A., 1990, 'Disjuncture and Difference in the Global Cultural Economy', in M. Featherstone (ed.), *Global Culture. Nationalism, Globalisation and Modernity*, London: Sage, pp.295–311.

Castañeda, J., 1993, *Utopia Unarmed, The Latin American Left after the Cold War*, New York: Alfred A. Knopf.

Castells, M. (ed.), 1985, *High Technology, Space, and Society*, London: Sage.

Gordon, D., 1989, 'The Global Economy: New Edifice or Crumbling Foundations?', *New Left Review*, No.178, pp.24–64.

Harvey, D., 1989, *The Condition of Postmodernity*, Oxford: Blackwell.

Jessop, B., 1994, 'Post-Fordism and the State', in A. Amin (ed.), *Post-Fordism*, Oxford: Blackwell, pp.251–80.

Laclau, E. and C. Mouffe, 1985, *Hegemony and Socialist Strategy: Towards a Radical Democratic Politics*, London: Verso.

Lipietz, A., 1994, 'Post-Fordism and Democracy', in A. Amin (ed.), *Post-Fordism*, Oxford: Blackwell, pp.338–59.

Luke, T., 1994, 'Placing Power/Siting Space: The Politics of Global and Local in the New World Order', *Environment and Planning*, No.12, pp.613–28.

Mohanty, M., 1995, 'On the Concept of "Empowerment"', *Economic and Political Weekly*, 17 June, pp.1434–36.

Munck, R., 1989, *Latin America, The Transition to Democracy*, London: Zed Books.

Munck, R., 1993, 'Political Programmes and Development: The Transformative Potential of Social Democracy', in F. Schuurman (ed.), *Beyond the Impasse, New Directions in Development Theory*, London: Zed Books, pp.113–23.

Naisbitt, J., 1994, *Global Paradox*, New York: Avon Books.

Peck, J. and A. Tickell, 1994a, 'Jungle Law Breaks Out: Neoliberalism and Global-Local Disorder', *Area*, Vol.26, No.4, pp.317–26.

Peck, J. and A. Tickell, 1994b, 'Searching for a New Institutional Fix: The After-Fordist Crisis and the Global-Local Disorder', in A. Amin (ed.), *Post-Fordism*, Oxford: Blackwell, pp.280–316.

Ruigrok, W. and R. van Tulder, 1995, *The Logic of International Restructuring: The Management of Dependencies in Rival Industrial Complexes*, London: Routledge.

Swyngedouw, E., 1992, 'The Mammon Quest, "Glocalisation", Interspatial Competition and the Monetary Order: The Construction of New Scales', in M. Dunford and G. Kafkalas (eds.), *Cities and Regions in the New Europe, The Global–Local Interplay and Spatial Development Strategies*, London: Belhaven Press, pp.39–67.

# Opportunities and Insecurities: Globalisation, Localities and the Struggle for Urban Land in Manila

ERHARD BERNER

*Globalisation is a contradictory process: integration on a global scale is connected to processes of fragmentation within world cities. The juxtaposition of global and local, rich and poor, skyscrapers and squatter shacks is characteristic of Manila as of every other metropolis. Based on an empirical study of squatter areas, the research found that everyday life in the locality is the major basis for the emergence of organised groups. Local associations form alliances with NGOs, mobilise the support of the media and church, and force politicians and land developers to take their existence into consideration. The paramount goal of squatter organisations is habitat defence and security of tenure. Despite many setbacks, they have made considerable progress in recent years.*

## GLOBALISATION AND COMPETITION FOR SPACE IN THE METROPOLIS

Although globalisation is, by definition, a process of world-wide integration its distribution is uneven, giving rise to a concentration of power and control and, thus, to the rise of centres. The advent of a world economy is, literally, *taking place* in major cities or metropolises. 'Cities serve as the nexus of the global society' [*Knight and Gappert, 1989: 12*]. A limited number of 'world cities' reap the lion's share of the economic benefits of globalisation [*Sassen, 1991*], but competition is becoming wider and fiercer. While world-wide networks are becoming close-meshed, the number of nodes is growing. Established centres like New York, London and Tokyo are facing the challenge of aspiring metropolises like Singapore and Kuala Lumpur for (at least regional) supremacy.

---

Erhard Berner, Senior Research Fellow and Lecturer, Sociology of Development Research Centre, University of Bielefeld, Germany. This study is based on a research project financed by the Deutsche Forschungsgemeinschaft; for a more detailed discussion, see Berner [*1997*].

Not all the effects of globalisation are beneficial to cities, however. In this contribution I take the case of Manila to demonstrate that globalisation is a contradictory process. Intensified integration on the global scale is connected to processes of fragmentation and disintegration. The city as a whole does not form part of the global society but only certain strongholds and citadels within it. In these strongholds, the global information economy with its advanced technology and transnational corporate culture reigns supreme and dominates the physical as well as the social image of the metropolis. Professionals and managers are seen as the protagonists of the global society. This image, however, involves 'the eviction of a whole array of activities and types of workers from the account about the process of globalisation which . . . are as much a part of it as is international finance' [*Sassen, 1994: 9*]. Historically, every city was dependent on its hinterland; today, the global economy of a metropolis is based on and articulated with non-corporate, local sectors which are regarded as backward and marginal.

The rapid expansion of these sectors can be observed in all metropolises, and it is essentially a result of the demands of the global society itself. The world city is marked by dynamics which lead to extensive building activity. Established business centres grow, new ones emerge and assume importance and the demand for office towers, high-rise apartment buildings, hotels, expensive residential quarters, shopping malls and recreation centres increases. All these buildings have to be supplied with infrastructure, roads, mass transportation and communication lines, cleaned, maintained and guarded. Even in the centres of the world economy, professionals are clearly outnumbered by construction workers, cleaners, waiters, janitors, clerks, security personnel, drivers, domestic helpers and providers of all kinds of petty services and trade. To remain competitive in what has become a global division of labour, a metropolis has to maintain an adequate supply of these services at a low price.

The aggravation of conflicts in the city is the result of a fundamental contradiction which we have called the 'metropolitan dilemma' [*Berner and Korff, 1995*]. The economic dynamics of a globalising metropolis jeopardises the precondition of its own competitiveness, namely the supply of cheap labour. On the one hand, urban land becomes scarce as demand is rapidly increasing; on the other, a growing number of people, many of them migrants attracted by the new economic opportunities, cannot pay the market price for housing. Predatory competition is ruling the land market. The escalating price of real estate and the accompanying economic restructuring of the city lead to huge movements of people, many of them forcibly evicted. Economic recuperation in the Philippines during recent years has meant that foreign investment in real estate, particularly Japanese and Taiwanese, has fuelled land speculation and contributed to skyrocketing prices in Metro Manila.[1]

For large parts of the urban labour force, access to housing and, thus, to the city and its opportunities is fundamentally insecure. A clarification is in order here. In Manila and other large cities, the so-called 'urban poor' (people living in slums and illegal settlements[2]) include not only the un- and underemployed and members of the informal sector but also major segments of the middle classes such as policemen, teachers, nurses, office clerks, sales personnel. In Manila, a schoolteacher's salary is not enough to rent a simple apartment in the city; to buy a 100 $m^2$ lot (not to mention a house) in a middle-class residential area costs more than schoolteachers earn during the whole of their working lives. Moving to the urban fringe is not a viable strategy either. For those who work long hours for a low income, any increase in time and money needed for transportation is unmanageable. All these groups need to 'stay where the action is' [*Guerrero, 1977*] to remain competitive in the contested market of low and medium skilled labour. The market mechanism does not allow them access to the centres of the city which are also the centres of employment. At the same time, state efforts to solve the problem through socialised housing have remained largely ineffective and have failed to benefit the alleged target group, namely the urban poor.[3]

The result is widespread squatting. Illegal settlements on public or private land presently account for the homes of more than half of Metro Manila's population. Their role is fundamental rather than marginal. The globalised metropolitan economy is heavily subsidised by the existence of squatter colonies, and cannot function – let alone be competitive – without this subsidy. Evictions and demolitions are regular occurrences in Manila. Nevertheless some slums and squatter settlements, many of them in central locations, have frustrated all attempts to upgrade or destroy them for 30 years or more. The result is a cityscape marked by sharp contrasts. Within sight of the modern, polyglot centres with their skyscrapers, parks and splendid boulevards lie small and cramped shanty towns. The immediate juxtaposition of global and local, of rich and poor, of palaces and shanties is characteristic of every metropolis and caused in part by globalisation itself. Centre and periphery are no longer located far apart in different world regions, but confront each other directly in the world cities [*Davis, 1990; Korff, 1993*].

In the course of globalisation, coexistence has given way to open and intensifying conflicts, occurring in London, Paris and Los Angeles as well as in Manila, Bangkok, Rio de Janeiro and Mexico City. There is, of course, nothing new about contrast and diversity; these have always formed part of the city [*Wirth, 1938*]. What is new is the *apartheid* of contrasting elements, their segregation and mutual exclusion. In the 1950s and 1960s, Manila's elites were still present in the poorer districts [*Joaquin, 1977: 173; Feria, 1984: 106–8*]. This is no longer the case. Whilst the Berlin wall has fallen, the iron curtain protecting the quarters of the wealthy from the majority of the population has become more impenetrable. Since the 1970s a process of local fragmentation has taken place; an exhaustive emergence of enclaves and a de-differentiation of the city's population owing to the social and economic differentiation of urban space. Imagined differences between classes and cultures have become social and spatial boundaries which divide the city into different territories.

The functional necessity of self-help housing precludes any comprehensive solution of the 'squatter problem' but it does not ease the pressure on squatter settlements, a pressure which is intensified by the globalisation process. Land in strategic locations has become a crucial power resource, so that ultimately the powerless are evicted and lose their access to the metropolis. The fact that many slums and squatter areas persist close to city centres and strongholds of globalisation therefore needs to be explained. What are the sources of power that enable the poor to defend their pieces of precious land against global players and other strong competitors? Based on my empirical study of several squatter areas in Metro Manila, I will show that it is the local context itself which provides a basis of organisation and, thereby, of empowerment and habitat defence.

## STRUGGLING FOR SECURITY: GROUP BUILDING IN THE LOCALITY

The relative economic security of the city is a major incentive for migrants from the countryside. The multitude of jobs and business opportunities in the globalising metropolis enables diversification, reducing the risk of a livelihood crisis if one family member's income runs dry. Most squatter households participate in the local 'shadow economy'. Subsistence production helps to reduce expenditure, and trade and petty commodity production provide additional cash income.[4] The general strategy is *isang kahig, isang tuka* (literally, one scratch here, one pick there) or having several sources of subsistence. Even those who are lucky enough to have regular employment as factory workers, workmen, drivers or office employees often earn less than the official minimum wage. Apart from larger-scale entrepreneurs and slumlords, the only families who earn a comfortable living from a single source are *saudis* (the general term for overseas workers) and seamen. To improve their living conditions, most people tap as many sources of livelihood as possible, demonstrating an immense creativity which can only be hinted at here.

According to Friedmann and Salguero [*1988*], the 'barrio economy' is not only a means of subsistence but a 'moral economy' which provides a network of social relations and increased capacity for action. Its function is not so much the maximisation of cash income as a gain in social security. If a household faces a temporary subsistence crisis, it can expect assistance from other members of the network. Evers [*1989*] makes clear that 'sharing of poverty' is a general phenomenon among the urban poor. 'Low-income groups with a low but stable income may still be poor, but as long as their survival is not threatened, they would not regard their situation as desperate ... Strategies for the allocation of their major asset, labour power, seem to be mainly directed at reducing ... insecurity' [*ibid.: 164–5*]. The opportunities of the city are not there for the taking, however.

> A precondition for subsisting in an urban environment is access to the use of urban land to build a house, to put up a hut, or at least to find a temporary space for sleeping, eating and defecating. Property rights regulate this access to urban land and thereby the chance to subsist, or at least to be physically present. From this point of view access to urban land becomes the most basic human need in an urban area [*Evers, 1984: 481*].

For the squatters, renters and sidewalk dwellers who are the majority of Manila's population, eviction is a permanent threat and insecurity of tenure the most severe problem. Precarious legal status and the lack of basic infrastructure are obvious reasons to build up organisations in slums, squatter settlements and low-income quarters. Although the problems faced are shared by all members of a local community, they are not necessarily perceived as common interests which require collective action. If individual strategies fail, people may rely on clans, cliques or patron–client relations rather than on forming organised groups.

Nelson [*1979*] points out that group building and collective action among the poor are highly conditional and precarious processes. Where, when and if locally based groups come to form a larger movement are empirical questions which cannot be answered a priori. Formulating hypotheses about the emergence of groups among squatters and slum dwellers involves emphasising the territorial quality of their struggles and, specifically, conceptualising their local basis. Friedman and Salguero [*1988*] in their 'Framework and Agenda for Research' state that urban movements are actually 'barrio movements', composed of a multitude of territorial communities which are the fundamental basis of group building. 'Poor people gain greater access to the bases for social (not yet political) power primarily by joining in collective, community-based efforts of struggling for survival in difficult times' [*Friedmann and Salguero, 1988: 8*].

It is my hypothesis that the local context – or in my terms the 'locality' – provides multiple relations and interdependencies which can form the basis of group building and collective action. My concept of the locality as a socially defined spatial entity comes close to the Latin American term *barrio* as elaborated by Friedmann and Salguero.

> The barrio constitutes the space for the production and reproduction of ... life, because it is here, in the immediacy of their everyday social relations, that households are able to increase their capacity for action by gaining improved access to social power ... As the habitat of the vast majority of the popular sectors, barrios typically have a name, a sense of their own identity, a history still fresh in the memory of its older inhabitants, dense social networks, a formal or informal structure of governance, and other attributes of a spatially defined political community [*Friedmann and Salguero, 1988: 11*].

If it is difficult to conceptualise 'the city' as a unit of analysis [*Giddens, 1979: 148; Saunders, 1981, 1985*] it seems impossible to define 'the locality'. Beauregard [*1988*] correctly points out that locality research suffers from a fundamental arbitrariness. The researcher is informed by common sense rather than theory when deciding how to draw up a survey 'barrio', 'community' or 'locality'; it may encompass a small neighbourhood of 50 families, or part of the city with over 10,000 inhabitants. Adopting administrative units as 'objective' points of reference is not a satisfactory solution either as their boundaries are no less arbitrary. Under authoritarian regimes, they are often delineated in order to enhance control and may even divide existing territorial communities. The social relevance of a place and the existence of 'local communities' are fluid subjects. More than 20 years ago, Clark [*1973*] criticised conventional definitions of community for assuming a sense of solidarity, rather than investigating the actual significance of community for members. Following Clark, research does not begin with localities but with interest groups which may define localities. Locality theory has seemingly failed to learn this lesson, leaving it prone to criticism regarding its inadequate conceptual scheme [*Taylor, 1975; Beauregard, 1988; Duncan and Savage, 1989*].

Taking Elias's [*1965*] concept of social cohesion as a starting point, I define localities as socially 'created' and demarcated spatial entities. In the process of locality building the loosely structured context of neighbourhood and familiarity is transformed into a territory which, in turn, becomes the point of reference of communal identity. Although the boundaries of the territories often coincide with streets, rivers and the like, they have to be continuously reinforced by social action. It is plausible to assume that individuals cannot perform this task if they are neither financially resourceful nor politically powerful. We therefore have to look for collective actors or *groups*, and organisations are a good indicator of the existence of groups pursuing communal interests. If localities are regarded as significant by their residents I expect them to develop a more or less formal organisational structure. In other words, only if a place is the basis as well as the subject of organised (regular and reliable) social action can we sensibly call it a locality.

The findings of my quantitative and qualitative survey in Manila can be summarised as follows. The dense web of both personal and functional relations and dependencies gives rise to mutual trust and, consequently, to relatively stable and durable alliances. In a protracted process of social integration, residents develop we-consciousness and think of themselves as a group. If the fluctuation of residents is not too high, most newcomers are integrated quite quickly. Many networks, based in the locality and formalised in *compadrazgo* (ritual kinship) relations, are connected to a limited number of, often long-established and wealthy, households. These are, for instance, slumlords who rent out several houses and rooms; persons and families who control vital resources such as deep wells and electricity connections; those with links to politicians, administrators and employers outside the locality; entrepreneurs who provide jobs for a number of residents; and traders who can grant credit. Quite frequently one family controls two or more of these resources and thus has considerable power; their position, however, remains dependent on respect and trust within the local community. As will be seen, these 'cores' of the locality play a crucial role in the formation of organised groups which are capable of collective action and conflict.

Surprisingly, ethnicity or common origin do not play a major role in group building. To my knowledge, there are hardly any residential areas in Metro Manila that are ethnically homogeneous. Apart from cultural patterns prevalent in the Philippines, the insignificance of ethnic identities can be explained by the fact that most migrants in my sample can no longer be sensibly described as provincials and would themselves reject this label. Having lived in Metro Manila for decades, they have become urbanites in an intricate learning process [*Abu-Lughod, 1961; Hollnsteiner, 1972; Dewan, 1989*]. It is the locality which functions as the basic instance of socialisation in the urban environment; a local identity is the basis, and the crucial precondition, of an urban identity.

## COLLECTIVE AGENCY AND EMPOWERMENT: LOCAL ORGANISATIONS

A locality as a socially meaningful spatial entity is defined by groups which have been formed in a settlement. Agency, stability and legitimacy of these groups are based on organisations which claim to represent the whole community. Local associations are, thus, a crucial point in this analysis. In line with an argument made by Poethig [*1972*], I see a close relation between squatters' capacity to organise and their integration into, and ability to act in, the urban environment.

> To live in the city, a person takes part in its organisations ... the casualties of city life are those who are not tied to it organisationally. Organisation becomes an essential factor in the participation of the poor in urban society ... participation in their social, ethnic, or regional associations begins to provide the poor with a sense of belonging to the city [*Poethig, 1972: 42*].

Based on the results of my research, this statement can be elaborated. In a laborious process of local integration, ethnic and regional alignments lose much of their relevance and are superimposed by the emergence of local solidarity. The necessary basis for a 'sense of belonging to the city' is a sense of belonging to a place, namely the locality. As squatters and slum dwellers are effectively excluded from direct participation in politics and urban decision-making, they have to organise themselves to achieve some bargaining power. My own findings as well as other literature [*Nelson, 1979; Schuurman, 1989; van Naerssen, 1989*] show that locally based associations can be stable, durable and effective without defining themselves as anti-systemic 'movements'.

In her comparison of 'Politics and the Urban Poor in Developing Nations', Nelson [*1979: 252–5*] makes a very useful distinction between the 'incentives' and the 'capacity' to build and maintain organisations, both of which are necessary conditions in their own right. Both incentives and capacity are dependent on the specific characteristics and the present situation of a locality and on the abilities, commitment and social creativity of its residents.

A common interest can become an incentive if it is perceived as such and regarded as important.

> At least a substantial core of residents must feel that some aspect of neighbourhood life creates a high-priority problem for them – a problem important enough so that they are willing to devote time, energy, and usually some money to its solution. The most dramatic instance of a high-priority, shared problem is the threat of eradication [*Nelson, 1979: 255*].

As the localities discussed here are squatter settlements, this threat is always present, if only latently. Another rationale is the improvement of services and facilities which leave much to be desired in Manila squatter areas.

Like Elias, Nelson sees social cohesion based on shared history as the fundamental precondition for the capacity to organise. Urry [*1985*], in his reflections on the role of space in social relations, shows that even class-based collective action is dependent on a 'high rate of participation and of organised action within a range of spatial specific yet overlapping collectivities. Potential collective agents are thus involved in a face-to-face contact within dense, multiplex relations where there is a high certainty of the participation of others' [*Urry, 1985: 43*]. The networks of personal, social and economic interaction and interdependencies which characterise a locality, although not based on common ethnic origin or social position, can become a firm basis for organisation building and collective action.

In my survey I found a wide variety of organisations, some loosely structured or dormant, others very active and successful. In most Manila squatter areas there is one primary association which claims to pursue communal interests and to represent all residents [*Aldrich, 1985*]. Each of these organisations has a formal structure, with a president, a vice-president and a set of board members and officers, including secretary, treasurer, sergeant-at-arms, and public relations officer. Most activists are women over forty who, relieved of the duties of childrearing, devote much of their time and energy to the community. Many associations, and especially those which have entered negotiations with landowners and/or the administration, are officially registered.

The internal structure of local organisation is far from being egalitarian, just as social relations between residents are highly differentiated. Local networks are not evenly distributed but concentrated in relatively few 'nodes'. Those people and families who play a crucial role in the social and economic life of the community also take the initiative when it comes to organisation building, and almost always assume the leadership. Their function as 'cores' of the locality is transferred to the association and thereby institutionalised and legitimised at the same time. This outcome is confirmed by quantitative analysis. Association officers have lived in the locality for a much longer time than others, command a higher family income, and have more intensive personal relations. Non-members, in contrast, are often newcomers, renters, or belong to the dire poor. In other words, non-participation in organisational activities is an indicator of social marginality. For the association itself, the question of trust is crucial. People have to be confident that the activists will articulate the needs of the whole locality and not only care about themselves.

The organisations I studied play a strong role in the local power structure, particularly by controlling access to the political system and other external resources. Local politicians as well as activists from non-government organisations (NGOs) address the association by offering services and claiming loyalty in return. Undoubtedly, officers use their key position to get occasional kickbacks. As compensation for their efforts in terms of time and money, a certain level of personal profit is even seen as acceptable so long as the association's role in representing all residents is not jeopardised [*Goss, 1990: 296–8*]. Apart from the – normally very modest – material gains, the position of officer is quite prestigious. Free-riding, which Olson [*1971*] identified as the crucial obstacle of purposeful voluntary organisations, is not a major problem.

For most residents in my research areas, the locality is the focus of everyday life, and the local organisation embodies their communal identity. People feel that they are 'established' in Elias' sense. They belong to the place, and the place belongs to them. By defining a territory that comprises all individual perceptions of neighbourhood, the association makes membership a synonym for local identity. Many respondents say that they are 'automatically' members by residing in the locality. Even outsiders identify association and local community, for instance by referring to the settlement Waterhole A as the 'Kapit-Bisig area'. Most organisations are named after their respective locality, often followed by 'Neighborhood Association' or 'Homeowners Association'.

My findings provide firm evidence for the hypothesis that successful associations are deeply rooted in the local community. The emergence of organised groups occurs in the face of crisis and grave common problems; it requires, however, the prior existence of multiple and reliable networks and alliances, whose development is a protracted process. A local identity and we-consciousness may develop only on the basis of a shared history. Attempts of NGOs to set up organisations in newer settlements bear little fruit even when faced with an acute external threat. 'These (organisations) are imposed rather than rooted', as one informant put it, and they cannot survive without continuing outside intervention. The clans and cliques refuse to cooperate out of a lack of trust and confidence.

Lack of security of tenure is the paramount problem which the associations react to. It is plausible to assume that local organisation would scarcely exist without an external threat. The results of my recent survey in a secondary city confirm this assumption. Even in the oldest slums of Cebu City, associations only formed in the late 1980s when the competition for land intensified in the course of rapid economic development and increasing foreign investment. In other words, organising was instigated in part by the thrust of globalisation. In Manila, Laquian [*1969*] noted more than 20 years ago that the defence of contested urban land was the major incentive for building local organisations.

> Because of the insecurity involved in squatting on government land, the people have been forced to set up and join existing associations. Interviews with many leaders, however, showed that in lobbying they did not see themselves fighting against something but rather as maintaining unity to achieve something. They want the land. By their long stay on the land, they feel that they have already earned the right to own it [*Laquian, 1969: 88–9*].

Local groups can acquire some bargaining power and become actors – not merely victims – in conflicts over the use of urban space. They are often highly organised, fulfilling the conditions of order, continuity, regularity, and internal consensual purpose that Wirth [*1938*] set out for social organisations but did not expect would exist at this level. Some associations are capable of increasing security in their localities, effectively hampering and resisting the plans of land developers, city governments and corporations; others fail and cease to exist.

## A PLACE TO LIVE: LOCALITIES AND THE SOCIAL VALUE OF URBAN LAND

The diversity of slums and squatter settlements in Metro Manila is immense, as is the multitude of situations amongst their residents. Far from being 'representative' of the whole picture, the research localities have been selected with a view to exploring this diversity. They have, therefore, little in common except two facts. They have survived in a principally hostile environment for 20 years or more; and they have developed a strong and durable organisational structure. The argument put forward here is that both facts are closely interrelated. By forming their own associations, slum dwellers articulate their interests as common and, thereby, become capable of collective action. They improve their bargaining position, form vertical links to potential allies, and put up considerable resistance to attempts to destroy the place they call their own.

In one study, the interrelation between functioning organisations and the capacity of resistance can be shown to be plausible. Only a comparison of victories and defeats in the struggle for urban land, and the role of local associations in the respective conflicts, could supply harder evidence. Little research has been done, however, on demolitions and the affected localities. A notable exception is a research project sponsored by the Asian Coalition for Housing Rights [*Murphy, 1993*]. Murphy's team drew up a list of all known demolition attempts in Manila between 1986 and 1991 and investigated 46 cases in detail. Owing to methodological problems – few of the victims were interviewed being scattered all over the city – the material is far from being conclusive. Nevertheless it illustrates that local associations often put up considerable resistance. Some successfully defended their community, others obtained an acceptable relocation site and/or financial compensation. Most, however, achieved nothing at all; local resistance against demolition attempts, however brave it may be, is limited. Even well-organised squatters are no match for heavily armed police squads or privately hired goons.

Studying demolitions, however, neglects the fact that many established squatter settlements have never been seriously threatened by eviction. Apart from direct resistance, localities and local organisations play a momentous role as their existence alters the land market and, thereby, the physical appearance and image of the city. It is common knowledge that land is significantly depreciated by squatter occupation as it is not readily available for the market.

The market value of land is a mere fiction in considerable parts of the city.[5] An owner who wants to use such land profitably or to sell it at a reasonable (or rather exorbitant) price has to establish control first. If a place is defended by a strong organisation, this process is both tedious and costly. A court order against the squatters has to be obtained and, much more troublesome, enforced. Politicians are doubtful allies as they can ill-afford to be perceived as anti-poor; after all, the poor form the large majority of their constituency. The Urban Development and Housing Act (UDHA) of 1992 has further enhanced the bargaining position of squatter organisations. It states that 'eviction or demolition as a practice shall be discouraged' (Article VII, Sec. 28) and enumerates those situations in which demolitions are still permissible; the mandatory provision of a relocation site adds to the costs of evicting squatters.

In recent years, attempts have been made to tackle the problems of mass housing by on-site development and land transfer schemes. The negotiations and conflicts in implementing these programmes enable the 'power game' over the use of urban space to be reconstructed. The 'actual' value of squatter land is a double compromise. First, residents have to agree among themselves what they are willing to pay for their land, and they can do this only if there is a functioning organisation. Second, the association has to negotiate the actual selling price with the landowner whose point of reference is the market value.[6] An agreement can only be reached if there is not too much discrepancy between the two sets of figures and is, therefore, impossible for localities on prime urban land. Transfer schemes have been quite successful in many parts of Metro Manila because they offer the chance of a compromise between contradictory logics of action. Owners can capitalise their land, albeit at reduced prices, without the largely incalculable costs and risks of demolition; squatters can obtain security and preserve their locality from the threat of eradication which has never been calculable for them.

My findings, however, indicate that such programmes exclude a substantial group of residents, among them the much-discussed 'poorest of the poor'. In other words, success in the struggle for land jeopardises the association's claim to represent all residents and leads to internal struggles. The outcome is a new and more marked de-differentiation. While the marginal segments of the population are expelled by their neighbours and forced to move on to find shelter in other squatter settlements, the former slums become middle class areas[7]; not by invasion or gentrification, but because most residents, or at least those who have the capacity to organise, are members of the middle classes anyway. The 'petty-bourgeois consciousness' of the so-called 'urban poor', which has been criticised by many observers [*T. Evers, 1985; Goss, 1990: 520*] is, thus, a reflection of social reality.

## CONCLUSIONS

Many observers, and city planners in particular, see slums and squatter areas as backward and marginal, pre-modern remnants of an incomplete development. Nothing could be further from reality. Slums and squatter settlements are not 'urban villages' in an ecological sense but part of the city's diversity and heterogeneity which is constitutive for urbanism and urbanity. The emergence of local territories is not merely a process occurring at the 'underside' of globalisation but a specific counterplay which alters the shape of the world city, Manila. A locality must be seen as a response to, and an attempt to cope with, the metropolitan environment in the course of a globalisation process which has changed the players and altered the arena. Many rank and file workers of transnational corporations live in informal settlements. 'Self-help housing', as squatting is euphemistically called, has proven to be more efficient in terms of space and costs than all attempts by the state and the private sector.[8] The latter's efforts are quite limited as the globalising metropolis offers much more profitable opportunities for land use than low-cost housing.

Human security is affected by globalisation in an ambivalent way. On the one hand, growing economic opportunities enable a strategy of diversification of income sources which reduces the risks of city life significantly. On the other hand, the fundamental precondition for making use of these opportunities – access to urban land – is precarious. The paramount goal of urban poor organisations is security of tenure. Despite many setbacks, they have made significant progress in recent years.

The occupation of precious urban land by squatter communities is the source of permanent conflict and confrontations, and the outcome of these conflicts cannot always be determined in advance. Large squatter settlements have persisted for more than 30 years just a stone's throw away from Manila's political and economic centres. Although the capacity to organise has proven to be a necessary basis for the poor's 'empowerment' and ability to resist eviction, they are still no match for international investors and land developers who compete for the limited space in the metropolis. The scope of the associations is strictly parochial, reactive and defensive; there is little supra-local communication, not to mention solidarity. Local organisations in Manila can find allies among NGOs, the media and, through the sheer number of their votes, among politicians. The quite progressive legislation and the funding of land transfer schemes demonstrate the impact of this alliance.

How should we assess the process of local fragmentation? Does it lead towards more urbanity and better living conditions in the metropolis Manila, or to marginalisation and *anomie*? The answer is ambivalent. Although far from being uniform 'quarters of misery', squatter settlements are certainly not idyllic, conflict-free spaces. Many of them are petty fiefdoms of slumlords or they are controlled by syndicates which profit from housing needs which are not served by the market. Internal relations are not only characterised by trust but also by inequality, exploitation and dependency. Local resistance is particularistic, disregarding the legal rights of others and may hamper even sensible development projects. On the other hand, localities establish effective mechanisms of pacification and violence control; conflicts are regularly settled without resorting to external institutions such as the police or administration. Moreover, the local context is an important means of adaptation and socialisation; it serves as a milieu where the migrants from the countryside become urbanites who are able to handle difference and diversity. In sum, localities are multifunctional entities which are part and parcel of the globalising metropolis.

## NOTES

1. 'Metro Manila' refers to the agglomeration of eight cities and nine municipalities which form the National Capital Region.
2. While 'squatter' is a legal concept, 'slum dweller' refers to the physical characteristics of the place of residence, and 'urban poor' to the income of residents. Philippine literature uses these terms interchangeably [*Murphy, 1993: v*]. This terminology reflects the crucial dividing line in the city between those who have legitimate and reasonably secure access to land, and those who have not. However, it obscures the fact that not all squatters are poor and not all their houses are shanties.
3. Singapore's successful housing policy demonstrates that this failure is not inevitable. Even if the Philippines were able to invest the same amount of money in public housing projects – which is unlikely in the near future – it would still lack the city state's ability to control the influx of migrants from the countryside.
4. I am aware of the problems of conceptualisation regarding the informal sector [*Elwert et al., 1983; Korff, 1988*]. According to Evers' [*1987*] pragmatic definition, the shadow economy consists of all economic transactions not controlled and enumerated by governments. This includes – but is not restricted to – all production within the locality as state control is virtually non-existent there.
5. 'Considerable' is, of course, a relative term. Even though much more than half of the metropolitan population are squatters, they occupy less than 10 per cent of Metro Manila's land area.
6. In the cases I observed, residents paid about 15 to 20 per cent of the market price of comparable idle land in the vicinity. Payment is financed by state institutions or NGOs and repaid in instalments over a period of 25 years. The resulting expenses are in most cases considerably lower than the rent for an apartment in the same locality.
7. This change is very visible. As they are no longer forced to keep their property mobile, the new landowners invest heavily in upgrading and extending their houses.
8. The illegal status of squatter settlements does not mean that residents do not pay for their use of urban land. 'There's no free squatting' [*Murphy, 1993: vii*]. The 'rights to squat' are bought and sold at substantial prices in an informal land market, and 'emic taxes' [*Schiel, 1987: 96*] are collected by semi-criminal syndicates and corrupt officials.

## REFERENCES


Abu-Lughod, J., 1961, 'Migrant Adjustment to City Life: The Egyptian Case', *American Journal of Sociology*, Vol.67, No.1, pp.22–32.

Aldrich, B. C., 1985, 'Habitat Defense in Southeast Asian Cities', *Southeast Asian Journal of Social Science*, Vol.13, No.1, pp.1–14.

Beauregard, R. A., 1988, 'In the Absence of Practice: The Locality Research Debate', *Antipode*, Vol.20, No.1, pp.52–9.

Berner, E., 1997, *Defending a Place to Live: Localities and the Struggle for Urban Land in Metropolitan Manila*, Quezon City: Ateneo de Manila University Press.

Berner, E. and R. Korff, 1995, 'Globalisation and Local Resistance: The Creation of Localities in Manila and Bangkok', *International Journal of Urban and Regional Research*, Vol.19, No.2, pp.208–22.

Clark, D.B., 1973, 'The Concept of Community: A Re-examination', *Sociological Review*, Vol.21, No.3, pp.397–416.

Davis, M., 1990, *City of Quartz: Excavating the Future in Los Angeles*, London: Verso.

Dewan, R., 1989, 'Deethnicisation: A Study of Language and Culture Change in the Sindhi Immigrant Community in Metro Manila', *Philippine Journal of Linguistics*, Vol.20, No.1, pp.19–27.

Duncan, S. and M. Savage, 1989, 'Space, Scale and Locality', *Antipode*, Vol.21, No.3, pp.179–206.

Elias, N. (with J.L. Scotson), 1965, *The Established and The Outsiders: A Sociological Enquiry into Community Problems*, London: Frank Cass.

Elwert, G., H.-D. Evers and W. Wilkens, 1983, 'Die Suche nach Sicherheit: Kombinierte Produktionsformen im sogenannten informellen Sektor', *Zeitschrift für Soziologie*, Vol.12, No.4, pp.281–96.

Evers, H.-D., 1984, 'Urban Landownership, Ethnicity and Class in Southeast Asian Cities', *International Journal of Urban and Regional Research*, Vol.8, No.4, pp.481–96.

Evers, H.-D., 1987, 'Schattenwirtschaft, Subsistenzproduktion und informeller Sektor: Wirtschaftliches Handel jenseits von Markt und Staat', in K. Heinemann (ed.), *Soziologie wirtschaftlichen Handelns*, Opladen: Westdeutscher Verlag, pp.353–66.

Evers, H.-D., 1989, 'Urban Poverty and Labour Supply Strategies in Jakarta', in G. Rodgers (ed.), *Urban Poverty and the Labour Market: Access to Jobs and Incomes in Asian and Latin American Cities*, Geneva: ILO, pp.145–72.

Evers, T., 1985, 'Identity: The Hidden Side of New Social Movements in Latin America', in D. Slater (ed.), *Social Movements and the State in Latin America*, Amsterdam: CEDLA, pp.43–72.

Feria, D.F., 1984, 'The Patriarchy and the Filipina as Writer', *Diliman Review*, Vol.32, No.5, pp.103–15.

Friedmann, J. and M. Salguero, 1988, 'The Barrio Economy and Collective Self-Empowerment in Latin America: A Framework and Agenda for Research', in M. P. Smith (ed.), *Power, Community and the City*, New Brunswick and Oxford: Transaction, pp.3–37.

Giddens, A., 1979, *Central Problems in Social Theory: Action, Structure and Contradiction in Social Analysis*, Berkeley, CA and London and Berkeley: University of California Press.

Goss, J.D., 1990, 'Production and Reproduction Among the Urban Poor of Metro Manila: Relations of Exploitation and Conditions of Existence', unpublished Ph.D thesis. University of Kentucky, Lexington.

Guerrero, S.H., 1977, 'Staying Where the Action is: Relocation Within the City', *Philippine Sociological Revue*, Vol.25, No.1, pp.51–5.

Hollnsteiner, M.R., 1972, 'Becoming an Urbanite: The Neighborhood as a Learning Environment', in D.J. Dwyer (ed.), *The City as a Centre of Change in Asia*, Hong Kong: Hong Kong University Press, pp.29–40.

Joaquin, N., 1977. *Doveglion and Other Cameos*, Manila: National Bookstore.

Knight, R.V. and G. Gappert, 1989, 'Preface', in R. V. Knight and G. Gappert (eds.), *Cities in a Global Society*, Newbury Park, London and New Delhi Sage, pp.11–13.

Korff, R., 1988, 'Informeller Sektor oder Marktwirtschaft? Märkte und Händler in Bangkok', *Zeitschrift für Soziologie*, Vol.17, No.4, pp.296–307.

Korff, R., 1993, 'Der Nord-Süd-Konflikt in den Städten', in B. Schäfers (ed.), *Lebensverhältnisse und soziale Konflikte im neuen Europa: Verhandlungen des 26. Deutsche Soziologentages in Düsseldorf*, Frankfurt and New York: Campus, pp.330–36.

Laquian, A.A., 1969, *Slums are for People: The Barrio Magsaysay Pilot Project*, Manila: UP College of Public Administration.

Murphy, D., 1993, *The Urban Poor: Land and Housing*, Bangkok: Asian Coalition for Housing Rights.

Naerssen, T. van, 1989, 'Continuity and Change in the Urban Poor Movement of Manila, the Philippines', in F.J. Schuurman and T. van Naerssen (eds.), *Urban Social Movements in the Third World*, London and New York: Routledge, pp.199–219.

Nelson, J.M., 1979, *Access to Power: Politics and the Urban Poor in Developing Nations*, Princeton, NJ: Princeton University Press.

Olson, M., 1971, *The Logic of Collective Action*, Cambridge, MA: Harvard University Press.

Poethig, R.P., 1972, 'Life Style of the Urban Poor and People's Organisations', *Solidarity*, Vol.VII, No.1, pp.37–43.

Sassen, S., 1991, *The Global City: New York, London, Tokyo*, Princeton, NJ: Princeton University Press.

Sassen, S., 1994, 'Identity in the Global City: Economic and Cultural Encasements', paper presented at the conference on 'The Geography of Identity', University of Michigan, 4–5 Feb.

Saunders, P., 1981, *Social Theory and the Urban Question*, London: Hutchinson.

Saunders, P., 1985, 'Space, the City and Urban Sociology', in D. Gregory and J. Urry (eds.), *Social Relations and Spatial Structures*, Basingstoke and London: Macmillan, pp.67–89.

Schiel, T., 1987, 'Suche nach Sicherheit und Sehnsucht nach Geborgenheit: "Dualwirtschaft" und "informeller Sektor" als Phänomen und Fiktion', *Zeitschrift für Soziologie*, Vol.16, No.2, pp.92–105.

Schuurman, F.J., 1989, 'Urban Social Movements: Between Regressive Utopia and Socialist Panacea', in F.J. Schuurman and T.V. Naerssen (eds.), *Urban Social Movements in the Third World*, London and New York: Routledge, pp.9–26.

Taylor, B.K., 1975, 'The Absence of a Sociological and Structural Problem Focus in Community Studies', *Archives Europeennes de Sociologie*, Vol.16, No.2, pp.296–309.

Urry, J., 1985, 'Social Relations, Space and Time', in D. Gregory and J. Urry (eds.), *Social Relations and Spatial Structures*, Basingstoke and London: Macmillan, pp.20–48.

Wirth, L., 1938, 'Urbanism as a Way of Life', *American Journal of Sociology*, Vol.44, No.1, pp.1–24.

# Institutional Contradictions in Rural Development

LARS ENGBERG-PEDERSEN

*Rural development is the scene of different groups interacting on the basis of conflicting interests and strategies. Contemporary analytical approaches emphasise that actors develop strategies on the basis of their own preferences, experiences and understandings, and with reference to the constraining institutions and structures. However, they tend to ignore the symbolic aspects of institutions which provide some order in an otherwise chaotic world. Based on a study of the introduction of representative councils in four villages in Burkina Faso, this contribution argues that these symbolic aspects are important elements for understanding the changing processes of collective decision-making. Thus, new ways of organising decision-making might involve contradictions with respect to the existing institutional order.*

Rural communities are often regarded as workable objects in need of development interventions by projects, NGOs, and the state. With respect to natural resource management in particular, it is commonly argued that existing farming practices are inadequate, even destructive, and should be changed. There are, however, reasons for scepticism as to how workable rural communities are. Vested interests connected to the existing social and material organisation of the communities are likely to prevent drastic changes, and so are local institutions understood as rules and shared meanings.

There are two sides to institutions. They support the distribution of rights and duties, political authority and economic opportunities. Accordingly, institutions affect actors' strategies and their ability to pursue them. But institutions also contribute to shaping people's understanding of social meaning and order. Actions acquire meaning and legitimacy when they comply with specific institutions. If new procedures are introduced and

---

Lars Engberg-Pedersen, Research Fellow, Centre for Development Research, Gl. Kongevej 5, 1610 Copenhagen V, Denmark (E-mail: lep@cdr.dk). The author would like to thank the villagers in Ninigui, Pogoro Silmi-Mossi, Tankiédougou and Nahirindon for their generous hospitality and willingness to spend hours answering questions. Neil Webster, Ole Therkildsen, Peter Gibbon and three anonymous referees also deserve much appreciation for helpful comments.

profound changes which shatter people's conceptions occur, these changes might be resisted or modified.

The analysis of the interaction between rural people and projects can be approached in different ways. Two well-established frameworks are the actor-oriented sociological approach and the rational choice approach. Their emphasis is different but both agree that actors' interests are a decisive factor in explaining the interaction. On the other hand, neither approach draws much attention to the symbolic aspects of institutions and the institutional contradictions which can arise when rural dwellers and projects interact. Accordingly, they neglect the fact that institutions contribute to people's understanding of their social environment, and that planned intervention from outside cannot transform local institutions in an unresisted, straightforward manner even if the intervention is welcomed locally.

This essay discusses the attempt to introduce representative village councils in charge of natural resource management in Burkina Faso. Since the mid-1980s a national programme for land management (*Programme National de Gestion des Terroirs*) has been tested and implemented in parts of the country [*GOB, 1989*]. The major aims of the programme are to separate animals from crops, to create an awareness of the scarcity of natural resources, to consolidate local efforts to conserve and improve resources, and to create clear procedures for resolving conflicts concerning land, crops, vegetation etc. Village councils, with representatives from all socio-economic groups, are seen as appropriate bodies for uniting resource users and achieving environmental goals.

The analysis is based on a case study of decision-making processes in four villages. The villages are situated in two provinces (Yatenga and Bougouriba) whose environmental conditions, social organisation and history differ substantially. The fieldwork consisted primarily of open-ended interviews with individuals and groups representing different socio-economic categories and with differing degrees of proximity to the centres of decision making. The interviews concentrated on issues which were being discussed and decided upon in the villages at the time. In this context, the introduction and function of the village councils were investigated.

The study begins with a brief account of different theoretical approaches and the points they emphasise in understanding rural development. The symbolic aspects of institutions are then introduced. The field setting is briefly described, followed by an analysis of the representative councils and the institutional contradictions involved. Finally, some implications of the study are discussed.

## CONTESTED DEVELOPMENT

The actor-oriented sociological approach emphasises the struggles taking place between actors with different interests. The rural scene is an arena where diverse actors compete for scarce resources and where interactions have unpredictable outcomes because of the particularity of the situation and the specific life-worlds of the actors [*Long and van der Ploeg, 1989; 1994; Olivier de Sardan, 1988; Berry, 1993*]. Rural development is, accordingly, a contested and inconclusive process.

A particularly important question concerns the fluid and multi-dimensional character of social processes. Institutions, values, goods and transactions are open to different interpretations and multiple meanings. Since actors' experiences, knowledge and concerns differ, they approach similar issues and situations in different ways. Thus, actors' interactions mould both individual and collective understandings of social processes, and the result is ever changing and infinite interpretations of economic goods and social institutions [*Berry, 1993; Long and Villarreal, 1993*].

In this situation of fluidity and ambiguity, the actors' 'room for manoeuvre' is a focal point [*Olivier de Sardan, 1988*]. Since power relations and socio-economic conditions restrain the range of actions that can be undertaken, the limits of potential initiatives need to be explored. These structural properties can enable as well as restrain action, in so far as they may produce appealing opportunities for particular actors, and they are sometimes viewed as the unintended consequence of numerous social interactions [*Long, 1989*]. However, the 'room for manoeuvre' is diffuse and can be transgressed by actors, since constraints can be challenged and interpreted in different ways [*Long and van der Ploeg, 1994*].

In this perspective, development interventions by NGOs, projects, or the state are analysed as an activity initiated by one actor and challenged by many others. Interventions are typically followed by resources, and therefore become the object of attention and confrontation. Rural dwellers seek to 'unpack' interventions by selecting and transforming the elements that suit their strategies [*Olivier de Sardan, 1988; Berry, 1993*]. There are, however, no clear dividing lines between the actors or the outcomes of these processes of interaction. Since all actors possess different experiences and life-worlds, interventions often consist of

> ... officials, project staff, and local authorities, in which the objectives of a project or program are neither achieved nor resisted in a consistent fashion, and its effects on rural economic performance are often contradictory or unclear [*Berry, 1993: 45*].

Moreover, the implementation of policies is seldom unaffected by the varied responses. Thus,

> … planned intervention is an ongoing transformational process that is constantly re-shaped by its own internal organisational and political dynamic and by the specific conditions it encounters or itself creates, including the responses and strategies of local and regional groups who may struggle to define and defend their own social spaces, cultural boundaries and positions within the wider power field [*Long, 1989: 241*].

These insights suggest that interventions are highly inconclusive and easily become the object of change instead of the agent of change. This should not be taken too literally; interventions are likely to provoke change but in an unpredictable way. Attention is directed towards the ambiguous interaction of individuals, groups and organisations. However, ambiguity and inconclusiveness are not all that characterise encounters in the context of planned intervention.

It follows from this brief discussion that the actor-oriented sociological approach is based on an understanding of the actor as fairly rational and as constantly trying to get the best out of existing opportunities. Although faced by constraints, rural actors evaluate these restrictions and devise strategies to by-pass them and exploit whatever opportunities they can. There is good reason to emphasise that rural dwellers are active, careful and strategic actors given the paternalistic and arrogant attitudes underlying many official development efforts. However, the perspective should be combined with an attention to the stability and continuity upheld by institutions which provide a degree of order in unstable and ever-changing environments.

Statements such as '[p]easants select among innovations coming from outside' [*Olivier de Sardan, 1988: 222*]; 'people … seek access to resources and opportunities through multiple channels, diversifying their memberships in political groups and other social networks, and shifting allegiances whenever the fortunes of one group [take] a turn for the worse' [*Berry, 1993: 53*]; and '[f]armers' projects … are actively managed as differential responses to the strategies and circumstances generated by others, which they modify, transform, adopt and/or counteract' [*Long and van der Ploeg, 1994: 74*], indicate a great deal of reflection and calculated decision-making on the part of the actors. Undoubtedly, this is the case in particular situations, but it seems exaggerated to attribute an independent and ever alert decision-making propensity to actors. Apart from the problems of understanding a complex world, actors are influenced by institutions at various levels, and their actions and strategies are not, accordingly, always the sole result of an autonomous reflective process.

## RATIONAL DEVELOPMENT

Another well-established framework for the analysis of rural development is the rational choice approach. Here, the basic focus is on individual behaviour within the incentives and constraints of their institutional and natural setting [*Wade, 1988; Ostrom, 1990; Bromley, 1992; Thomson, 1992; Ostrom, Schroeder and Wynne, 1993; White and Runge, 1994; 1995*]. Much work has been done on the management of collectively used natural resources (pastures, lakes, forests, etc.) and on the establishment and maintenance of common or public goods (irrigation systems, windbreaks, health clinics, etc.). The specific concern is to clarify the conditions for successful collaboration between individuals seeking to optimise the satisfaction of their preferences.

Within this approach, the individual is regarded as being of limited rationality, self-interested, and opportunistic [*Williamson, 1993*]. Individuals cannot live up to classical economic assumptions about perfect rationality since the environment is complex and uncertain, and individuals lack the necessary information-processing capacities. Hence, behaviour is seen as rational in intention, but limited in reality. Moreover, when selecting behaviour, individuals evaluate the costs and benefits of the going alternatives in order to optimise personal gain. Should such behaviour include cheating others, this is no obstacle to opportunism on the part of individuals [*Ostrom, Schroeder and Wynne, 1993: 44–46*].

On the basis of this understanding of individuals and their behaviour, the rational choice approach has focused on the nature of the goods and services in question, and on the institutions organising their provision and use. Goods and services possess physical attributes with clear implications for their exploitation [*Thomson, 1992: 9–14*]. For instance, the way in which an irrigation system is constructed has considerable implications for users, since being an 'upstream' consumer secures a safer supply than being a 'downstream' consumer. Similarly, the precise location of a piece of communal forest will affect its supervision for use. Thus, it is important to analyse the character of the particular good in question.

Institutions are primarily regarded as sets of rules, norms and sanctions guiding and restricting individual behaviour [*Ostrom, 1990: 51*]. 'Appropriate' institutions limit the pursuit of interests that harm other people, and they provide some clarity in an uncertain world by making the behaviour of others more predictable. However, 'perverse' institutions exist which channel efforts into counter-productive activities or impede pertinent initiatives [*North, 1990*]. It is, accordingly, crucial to investigate the institutional setting and relate it to the goods and services involved in rural development.

In the rational choice perspective, development interventions are analysed primarily with respect to their potential for establishing relevant institutions

[*Thomson, 1992*]. External intervention is believed to be important in situations where local institutions frustrate cooperation or divert efforts from what are considered to be necessary activities. Even though individuals recognise the usefulness of changing inappropriate institutions, they may continue using them as it is too costly from an individual standpoint to try to transform them. Therefore, external intervention is sometimes needed to reform local institutions, although a basic scepticism exists about the usefulness of publicly provided goods and services [*Ostrom, Schroeder and Wynne, 1993*].

When approaching the analysis of institutions in rural development in this way, institutions appear to exist as an objective reality external to the individual. Individuals consider the costs and benefits of complying with or resisting institutions which are interpreted similarly by everyone. Multiple meanings and diverse experiences do not influence social interaction, nor do institutions play a normative or cognitive part when individuals make up their minds about their activities. Thus, the rational choice approach to the understanding of institutions is narrow and mechanistic. Its basis in methodological individualism prevents it from recognising that individuals and groups draw more or less consciously on institutions when making sense of their social environment and how to act in it.

## THE SYMBOLISM OF INSTITUTIONS

Institutions must be conceptualised

> ... as simultaneously material and ideal, systems of signs and symbols, rational and transrational. Institutions are supraorganisational patterns of human activity by which individuals and organisations produce and reproduce their material subsistence and organise time and space. They are also symbolic systems, ways of ordering reality, and thereby rendering experience of time and space meaningful [*Friedland and Alford, 1991: 243*].

Accordingly, institutions should not be viewed as external constraints to actors who conceive strategies to manoeuvre between institutional limitations. By organising social life, institutions give meaning to action. Activities in correspondence with institutions are understandable to others, locating the actor in a particular symbolic order and thereby contributing to the actor's self-understanding as well.

However, institutions do not determine social processes; actors may consider institutional elements critically. When an actor chooses to engage in action which confronts or bypasses a specific institutional element, this can form part of self-understanding. So, in arguing that preferences and strategies are devised on the basis of existing sets of institutions, this does not imply that actors are cultural dopes incapable of reflecting on the institutional context.

One basis for action causing institutional change is institutional contradiction. As institutions relate to different domains of life, within any given social setting several partly incompatible institutions coexist. For instance, in many contemporary societies the institutional logic associated with the family includes a consideration of others' needs, while the one connected to the market stresses optimising personal gains from scarce resources [*ibid.: 248*]. When actors believe that both these institutions have a bearing on what is appropriate action in particular situations, the contradiction of their logics might generate action which initiates a process of institutional change.

Another instance of institutional contradiction can occur when social groups with very different historical backgrounds and ways of addressing particular problems interact. This is often the case in rural development, where resource-strong external actors intervene in local communities. The interventions frequently aim at changing widespread practices; a change which cannot take place without a concomitant change in the symbolic order. Thus, different institutions do not just co-exist in rural development; they are specifically brought into contradiction.

The term institutional dissonance has been used in a way similar to institutional contradiction. It refers to 'a disjuncture between institutional structures or rules that shape the ways people deal with one another or with the natural environment' [*Thomas-Slayter and Barbara, 1994: 1481*]. For instance, different sets of rules often determine access to land so that different people could be regarded as the rightful holder of a specific piece of land. Related to this idea is the proposition that different meanings are associated with the various sets of rules. Thus, eliminating or modifying a set of rules does not necessarily reduce the contradiction, since shared meanings cannot be suspended overnight. David Mosse touches on this point in the context of a project intervention to support tank irrigation in South India:

> As in earlier times, the tank institution was more than a system for efficient water management. Since asserting rights in paddy cultivation concerns not only production but also 'assertions about standing, belonging and community' ... , the project institution (the Society) became a means for renegotiating the meaning of 'community' locally (Mosse [*1995: 153*] quoting Spencer [*1990: 101*]).

Whether the intervention leads amongst others to a deliberate renegotiation of meaning, to unintended changes of shared understandings or to a reinforcement of existing perceptions is a question which can hardly be answered a priori.

We can now understand development interventions as more than attempts to correct institutions that supply 'perverse' incentives or arenas of social struggle where different actors manoeuvre to gain access to resources. They are also a more or less deliberate attempt to establish a particular symbolic order, and they interact with people whose strategies sometimes reflect substantially different institutional logics. Interventions seeking to change prevalent practices, therefore, have a symbolic aspect in addition to their more immediate material objectives and context.

In our analysis of the introduction of representative councils in villages in Burkina Faso, attention is drawn to the contradictions between existing forms of decision-making at village level and the institutional arrangements proposed by intervening projects. In particular, the study concentrates on elements which reflect contradictory ways of understanding what 'proper' decision-making is. This is evidently a diffuse subject, but the villagers unanimously showed a particular understanding of who they expect to deal with certain issues, when and how. The contradictions between this understanding and the organisation of the representative councils are spelled out below.

## FOUR VILLAGES IN BURKINA FASO

The land management programme in Burkina Faso was initiated in the context of deteriorating natural resources, presumably the result of declining rainfall, increasing population pressure on fertile land, the breakdown of resource management institutions and inappropriate cultivation practices and so on. The programme is intended to cover the whole country but, given the limited financial resources of the state, is currently limited to projects working in specific areas.

The overall purpose of the programme is to involve the local population in extensive management of the natural resources. Policy-makers acknowledge that it is impossible to secure resource improvement and carry out conservation activities without the active involvement of the resource users. The establishment of village councils in charge of the management of local natural resources is thereby regarded as a crucial element in environmental policies. The councils are seen as a focal point in the interaction between rural dwellers and external officials, and they are expected to coordinate local activities as well as solve conflicts between resource users.

The fieldwork for the present study was undertaken in 1993 and examined the creation of councils in four villages. The villages are located in two substantially different regions: Ninigui and Pogoro-Silmi-Mossi in Yatenga Province in the northwest and Tankiédougou and Nahirindon in Bougouriba Province in the southwest (see Map). All four villages are affected by projects financed by foreign donors working in the field of natural resource management.[1]

MAP

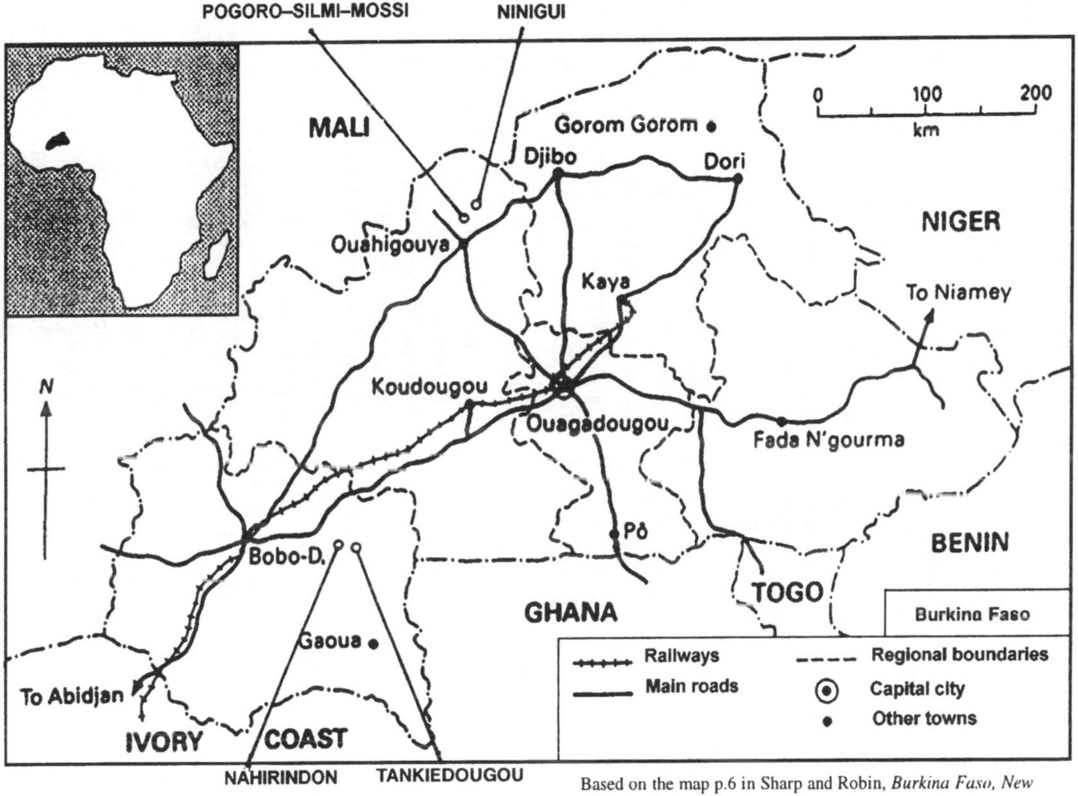


Based on the map p.6 in Sharp and Robin, *Burkina Faso, New Life to Sahel*, Oxfam, 1990.

The mean annual rainfall in Yatenga Province is 530mm [*Dugue, 1990*], but there are substantial differences between localities and from year to year. Comparing averages on a 30 year basis, the past 40 years have witnessed a steady decline of rainfall. There has also been a decreasing ratio of land to man due to increasing population and a reduction of fertile land [*ibid.*]. One consequence has been the dramatic loss of forest coverage; people talk about the existence of forests 30 years ago in places where you can hardly find a shrub today.

A *Mossi* kingdom was founded in the area in the mid-sixteenth century [*Isard, 1985*], and its strong hierarchical structures still influence daily life in a substantial manner. Thus, villages are not isolated entities. They are subject to outside authorities, especially those located in the former capital of the kingdom, Ouahigouya. Apart from a few stockbreeding *Peulhs*, the *Mossis* are the only ethnic group in the province. They cultivate the land, and some have a few animals which are generally taken to less densely populated areas during the rainy season. Families are relatively independent of each other with regard to production and exchange. Yet, codes of conduct for mutual assistance are widespread, and quite elaborate traditions for collective working groups exist [*Ouédraogo, 1990*]. Within families, some of which number over a hundred people, there are complex and detailed relations between households. The social structure is hierarchical with a family chief at the top. The area is strongly dominated by Islam.

*Ninigui* is a large village with 3,800 inhabitants. The village dates back 200 years or more, and some neighbouring villages have been founded by people from Ninigui. It is an ethnically homogeneous village consisting of the *Mossis* and, at the time of the fieldwork, a single *Peulh* family. Among the *Mossis*, there are different lineages with varying levels of influence in village affairs. The social status of a lineage corresponds to a significant degree with the number of years it has existed in the village. Severe conflicts as to who should rightfully occupy the positions of respect, such as village chief and land chief, have dominated village politics for many years. Agriculture is the main activity, stockbreeding being of marginal importance. People are to a large extent organised in working groups that cultivate fields, dig wells and undertake other similar activities in common.

*Pogoro-Silmi-Mossi* was established 100 years ago. A chief in a neighbouring village granted the newcomers the right to settle on his lands. Approximately ten families arrived during the following 30 years, and today these families constitute their own village with some 400 inhabitants. Ethnically a homogeneous village, it is nevertheless divided into two groups. The group comprising the village chief and his associates are accused of monopolising the social infrastructure provided by the project. Cattle breeding takes place, and people regard themselves primarily as rearers of animals and secondly as agriculturalists. Yet the income of most families comes mainly from agriculture. A number of working groups exist, but most do not work very well.

In Bougouriba Province, the annual rainfall averages 1000 mm. Environmental problems are not felt to be very important, although it is repeatedly claimed that the rainfall is not what it used to be. Until the beginning of the 1980s, parts of the province were sparsely populated. Since then, there has been high immigration into these areas both from more populated areas of the province and from the northern parts of the country. The two villages studied are situated in one such area experiencing substantial inward migration.

At the turn of the century, wars among different ethnic groups took place in the borderlands of what are now Ghana and Burkina Faso. Many *Pougoulis* were forced to flee, and some settled in the uninhabited lands west of the river Poh. They formed six or seven villages with strong links to each other. In the early 1980s, many *Dagaris* started to come to the area, and in 1986, the Burkinian state organised the creation of six additional villages. Today, schools, health clinics, roads and agricultural support have been established. Accordingly, much has been changed in an area which was until recently very isolated. Rivers surround it on three sides, and during the five months of the rainy season it was practically inaccessible. Now, the *Pougoulis* talk about the shortage of land and the need to stop further immigration.

*Tankiédougou* is a village with approximately 400 inhabitants and five different ethnic groups, each with their own language. The chief is a most respected person, but is growing old and no longer so close to village affairs. Tensions between the *Pougoulis*, who control land and collective decisions completely, and the four other newly-arrived ethnic groups (the *Dagaris*, the *Peulhs*, the *Bobos*, and the *Mossis*) exist and reveal themselves periodically. The *Pougoulis* constitute around one-fifth of the population, while the *Dagaris* form the overwhelming majority. Agriculture is the dominant activity for all but two of the *Peulh* families, who rely exclusively on cattle breeding. Although in a suitable area, little cotton is grown. Working groups have existed in the past but collapsed. A new group has recently been created along religious lines.

*Nahirindon*, like Tankiédougou, was founded at the beginning of the century. It remained a small village for many years, but with the high immigration the last twelve years the population has increased fivefold to perhaps 1,000 persons today. Two ethnic groups, the *Pougoulis* and the *Dagaris*, are found in the village. As in Tankiédougou, the *Pougoulis* constitute one-fifth of the population and control village affairs. Tensions between the two groups exist, but they are not very marked. The two chiefs influence village affairs to some extent; yet, the main forum for decision-making during the last fifteen years has been the men's working group. Stockbreeding is of little importance, whereas the growing of cotton is and has brought a significant amount of money to the village.

TABLE 1
MAJOR CHARACTERISTICS OF THE FOUR VILLAGES

| CHARACTERISTICS | YATENGA PROVINCE | | BOUGOURIBA PROVINCE | |
|---|---|---|---|---|
| Villages | Ninigui | Pogoro--Silmi-Mossi | Tankié dougou | Nahiri ndon |
| Inhabitants | 3800 | 400 | 400 | 1000 |
| Number of ethnic groups | 1 | 1 | 5 | 2 |
| Approximate yearly rainfall | 530mm | | 1000mm | |
| Years since foundation | 200+ | 100 | 100 | 100 |
| No. organised working groups | 8 | 5 | 2 | 1 |
| Production of commercial crops | No | No | A few | A lot |
| Population movements | Some seasonal migration | | Significant immigration | |
| Relations to external authorities | Some | | Few | |
| Existence of a village council | Yes | Yes | No | In part |
| Zoning of village lands | No | No | Yes | Yes |

## EXISTING FORMS OF DECISION-MAKING AND THE CREATION OF COUNCILS

Decision-making at the village level largely relates to three issues in the context of natural resource use: religious issues, conflict resolution and collective action. In the two villages in Bougouriba, religion influences natural resource management to some extent. For instance, it is forbidden to work in fields with basic food crops on Mondays and Fridays, since this upsets the spirits. Accordingly, for the Christian minority, only four days a week remain for working in the fields. Conflict resolution is another important matter, as land disputes, struggles between farmers and herders and so on are common. Finally, collective action is needed to implement some resource conservation measures as well as many socio-economic investments.

Decisions on religious issues and conflict resolution are generally perceived to be the responsibility of land and village chiefs. Although the prefect in the department and his representatives in the villages increasingly intervene in disputes, the chiefs are typically regarded as the legitimate decision-makers, who independently mediate and settle serious conflicts. In the Bougouriba villages, the chiefs and a few notables are the only ones who speak on religious affairs; everyone else listens and follows the dicta. Collective action is normally the responsibility of different working groups who cultivate fields in common, dig wells, build storerooms, etc. In most cases these groups are led by one or two leaders who organise the work independently rather than adhering to a collective decision-making process. Moreover, many groups are organised in response to interventions by NGOs, projects and extension officers. These rarely embark on new activities themselves, but may be quite effective at carrying out initiatives proposed by external organisations.

Customary authorities and leaders of working groups are therefore the most important decision-makers at village level in respect of the use of natural resources. However, this is not a fixed truth, as chiefs are increasingly being challenged as the rightful managers of natural resources. Young men increasingly participate in the working groups, and even women are beginning to articulate ideas at village meetings. Thus existing forms of decision-making are being renegotiated, and it is within this fluid social context that the new councils are being introduced.

Village councils are seen as a major element in the land management programme [*GOB, 1989*]. They are supposed to deal with all questions relating to natural resource management within given territories, typically the area of a village. All social groups relying on the natural resources within an area are expected to be represented on the council. Village councils are not recognised in the legal documents on the administrative division of the country, and they have no statutory power to support their decisions, nor do they control financial resources of any kind. Accordingly, they are not able to enforce their decisions with legal sanctions, and they can easily be overruled by state authorities. Councils are only established by projects or NGOs working within the framework of the land management programme. Overall, they are quite vulnerable and dependent on the support of external organisations.

The councils in Pogoro-Silmi-Mossi and Ninigui were established in late 1991 and early 1992, following significant socio-economic analyses by project members working in this part of Yatenga. The project had a broad agenda, including socio-economic development, and primarily focused on natural resource management. It emphasised the need to respond to villagers and saw the creation of village councils as a way of obtaining local partners. The councils have 24–30 members including the chiefs, religious leaders, and a few women. They are divided into a number of sub-commissions dealing with such issues as agriculture, stock breeding, water, health, education.

In Nahirindon and Tankiédougou, councils were created in 1989, being one of the first activities undertaken there by the project working in that area. This project focused directly on natural resource management and the creation of zones for agriculture, stock breeding, forestry, etc. It was less concerned with the functioning of the councils and did not provide support for non-environmental activities in the two villages. The councils were reorganised in 1991–92 and now consist, in principle, of some 12 members, each with responsibility for a particular task covering a wide range of activities. Despite their numerical superiority, immigrants have very few representatives. Instead, the *Pougoulis* control the councils. Women are supposed to hold two seats in each council.

The council in Ninigui seems to perform best. At the time of the fieldwork, the council or major parts of it met approximately every fortnight. The sub-commissions also met regularly to discuss their fields of responsibility. According to respondents, a very wide range of issues pertaining to production, natural resources, and social infrastructure is debated in the council and its sub-commissions. The council has existed for one and a half years; its major achievements have been building a nutrition centre and constructing lines of stones to reduce soil erosion. The council may have been somewhat slow starting owing to a protracted conflict between a village group organised on the initiative of extension officers and the Naam group created by the NGO, Six S.

Over the past six months, a lively debate about future activities has taken place, not least because the project introduced a system whereby a number of villages in the area could bid for financial support for well-founded initiatives. Villagers who were not members of the council took part in this debate, since meetings were open to all. The council never met 'behind closed doors', while the meetings of the sub-commissions appeared to be a matter for their respective members.

In Pogoro, the council met far less regularly. Meetings were held primarily when extension agents or other external personnel requested them, and they were not restricted to the council members. According to the president of the council, people did not show up at meetings, while an opposition faction argued that it was pointless attending meetings since the president and his side monopolised all the benefits stemming from the project. Some sub-commissions appeared to meet occasionally, but far less frequently than in Ninigui. Two of the seven sub-commissions did not function, and another had in reality merged with one of the peasant groups.[2] Within the project framework, the villagers had contributed to digging a well, constructing a water pump, and building a vaccination pen. However, these activities stemmed from a combination of project initiatives and individual villagers' organisational abilities, rather than from council efforts.

Discussions on future activities in the context of the bidding practice instituted by the project were insignificant. One informed villager claimed that it was the project which decided what villagers should propose, although he believed proposals accorded with villagers' wishes. However, the opposition faction was certainly not satisfied with the proposals, which omitted their major requests. Thus the council, as such, had little to do with either selection or implementation of collective actions, and the issue of conflict resolution was not touched upon at all.

The councils in Tankiédougou and Nahirindon did not function in accordance with the project's intentions. No meetings had been held of the villagers formally elected as council members. Some villagers were not even aware that they were council members and no one could name all the members. In Tankiédougou, a little group of *Pougoulis* met in advance of village meetings to decide controversial issues, and they controlled village meetings as well. Recent discussion and activity included the division of the land into agricultural, pastoral and forest zones, a controversy with a neighbouring village over a piece of land and a modest construction of stone lines in the fields. Village meetings were held at the request of project personnel concerning technical matters and when an issue required it. There had been no discussion among villagers about possible activities to improve general living conditions in the village. With respect to natural resource management, the president of the council did not appear to pay attention to villagers' cultivation of fields outside the agricultural zone unless he was specifically made aware of it.

After a period of inactivity, the president of the council in Nahirindon had gathered together a group of people consisting of notables, *Pougoulis* and a few *Dagaris*. This group had begun discussions on issues pertaining to natural resource management. After people started to complain about impoverished soils, the group allotted new fields according to the zoning of the land. The group had also discussed a conflict concerning a divorce, organised village meetings to disseminate information concerning the division of land into zones for different uses and to draw up rules regarding the supervision of sheep, goats and pigs during the rainy season. As in Tankiédougou, recent discussions and activities included a conflict with a neighbouring village concerning land, the zonal division of land, the construction of stone lines, and the digging of a well. Discussions of future activities were few and restricted to a limited circle of people.

Decision-making in Tankiédougou was controlled by a small *Pougouli* group, and it was primarily reactive, responding to problems as they arose. In Nahirindon, a group, not quite identical with the formally appointed council, was discussing village affairs and natural resource management. The implementation of collective action was carried out almost without friction in both villages, and intra-village conflicts seemed to be resolved, although latent contradictions between the *Pougoulis* and the immigrants were obvious in Tankiédougou. Despite the conflicts, no one disagreed that the chief institution was the appropriate one for conflict resolution in the villages. By contrast, decision-making in regard to the direction of collective action was less developed. Few initiatives were undertaken, even in Nahirindon, where financial resources from the cultivation of cotton existed.

Evidently, the councils in Pogoro and especially Ninigui, worked better than those in Tankiédougou and Nahirindon, when judged by the intention of establishing representative councils dealing with natural resource management and the socio-economic development of the villages. However, the Bougouriba villages, in particular Nahirindon, were not necessarily performing badly in relation to natural resource management and conflict resolution. Decisions were being made even though the councils as such did not function. On the other hand, collective initiatives to improve general living conditions were very tentative in all four villages. Decision-making in that respect appeared to be new and difficult to initiate.

## INSTITUTIONAL CONTRADICTIONS

Many factors influence the functioning of the councils. The following discussion concentrates on institutional contradictions between existing ways of deciding and those of the newly introduced village councils. As mentioned above, institutional contradictions can coexist without giving rise to actions leading to institutional change and resolution. However, it does signify both a potential basis for change and a potential barrier preventing planned interventions from reaching their policy objectives. The five institutional contradictions considered below concern the representativeness of the councils, the division of labour within them, the accountability of members, the councils' role as conflict arbitrators, and the legitimacy of decision-making institutions.

The first issue concerns the representativeness of the councils versus existing exclusionary ways of deciding in which institutions do not embody representatives of different socio-economic groups. Customary authority is limited to a few persons, each of whom is the accepted decision-maker in a specific field. Sometimes, chiefs rely on a group of councillors, but these are always elder, respectable men who do not represent diverse interest groups. Peasant groups, the other crucial decision-making institution in the village, are never considered to embrace all villagers, and they are normally led by persons who feel much less bound than the chiefs by the demands of the public weal. Thus, decision-making is the business of a few people. They do not necessarily take decisions which cause serious dissatisfaction among the majority of villagers, but the decision-making process itself is not characterised by discussions and negotiations between representatives of various groups.

The idea of representative councils is based on the assumption that all social groups can participate in decision-making on an equal footing. Two examples illustrate, however, that not all villagers were regarded as legitimate decision makers. Women in all four villages were clearly marginalised and left out of village level discussions. Undoubtedly, women in the Yatenga villages have become more influential over the past 20 years, but according to female council members (who formed eight out of 30 members in Ninigui) their representation was more a reflection of project hopes and external rhetoric than a recognition of their relative importance. Out of the three interviewed female members of the council in Ninigui, one did not know to which sub-commission she belonged and another could not name the chairman of her sub-commission. Yet, a few women did speak at meetings, and this was significant compared to the other villages. In Pogoro, the female members of the council were not always summoned to the meetings, and they regarded the purpose of their presence in the council as being to distribute information about village affairs to the women. They did not see themselves as active participants in the discussions. In Tankiédougou and Nahirindon, I observed no women at the meetings. As a woman in Nahirindon said: 'Here, women and men do not talk.' This was also clear from the women's lack of knowledge about conflicts with neighbouring villages, the creation of the councils, and the zoning of the land.

The immigrants in the Bougouriba villages were another group which was excluded from collective decision-making. Immigrants frequently voiced statements like the following: 'I'm in their village. Therefore, it is the *Pougoulis* who decide'; 'If the village chief says something, we agree'; 'The *Pougoulis* propose, and the rest of the village follows'. Most immigrants were not willing to express a personal opinion on what they and the village needed, partly because this would be seen as a challenge to the *Pougoulis*, and partly because they had not reflected about this since they did not consider it their business to do so. Typically, immigrants were confused when I asked for their point of view. In Nahirindon, one or two immigrants were beginning to gain influence which was not based on the ability to read and write. All the other important decision-makers referred to by the respondents were *Pougoulis*, and decisions concerning such questions as zoning, where to dig wells, how to handle conflicts with neighbouring villages, and whether to deny land to new immigrants, were all made by the *Pougoulis*.[3]

Thus, important social groups and a significant majority of the adult population as a whole were not considered to be legitimate participants in decision-making processes at village level. Most women and immigrants regard themselves as illegitimate decision-makers. They do not wish to take part in discussions on village affairs, and when they are given an influential position, they view their role as one of disseminating information from the 'real' decision-makers to fellow villagers. Thus, they are not only excluded from influence by those who have been in power for many years; they also distance themselves from village discussions. The shared understanding of decision-making at the village level is that it is the preserve of elder male representatives of those lineages who first settled in the villages. A close ancestral relationship is seen as a necessary condition for reaching thoughtful decisions, partly because experience is highly valued, and partly because such a relationship can appease the spirits of the ancestors. A village council with representatives of different social groups, therefore, reflects a symbolic order which contradicts these prior understandings of proper decision- making.

A second institutional contradiction relates to the elaborate division of labour within the councils versus the existing centralist control of all activities. As mentioned above, the projects had quite high expectations on this matter. Again, the premise underlying a clear division of labour is that each member is an able and legitimate actor to whom specific tasks can be delegated. Accordingly, the president and other essential members of the council should not monopolise information and decision-making. Two incidents show that this expectation is difficult to meet.

The chairman of the sub-commission on agriculture in Ninigui approached the president of the council prior to the sowing season. He wanted to contact the extension agent in order to obtain some products for treating the seed grain. The president refused, arguing that the extension agent did not have time to deal with such minor problems. A further request for a product to treat the harvest was likewise refused, leaving the chairman confused and uneasy about not being able to live up to his obligations. He could not see any good reason for not being able to contact the extension agent, but was not inclined to challenge the president's decision. The chairman of another sub-commission stated that the president tended to do all the work himself. He kept messages received from external authorities to himself, notwithstanding the fact that he cannot read. He also kept the council's money box at his house, although it was supposed to be kept by the treasurer. However, the president's monopolisation of information and responsibility did not provoke public criticism because it corresponded to existing decision-making practices. However, the fact that some council members raised the point shows that the understanding of how to organise decision-making was changing.

In Pogoro, the money box also appeared to be kept at the president's and the secretary's house rather than with the treasurer. Furthermore, a member of the sub-commission dealing with agriculture and natural resource management complained that the secretary had appropriated the sub-commission's task of showing strangers around the village. This task was considered a privilege, and the member concerned was inclined to obstruct the sub-commission's work if this responsibility was not returned to the sub-commission. In the Bougouriba villages, it was difficult to identify any division of labour at all. Apart from one person who was supposed to announce village meetings in Tankiédougou, and another who was expected to show immigrants their fields, the presidents organised everything themselves – a practice which passed without comment.

These incidents indicate that a high degree of division of labour does not fit well with existing practices. Both at family and village level, decision-making is the preserve of one or two persons, even where quite trivial matters are concerned. Furthermore, the limited criticism expressed suggests that most people were comfortable with this way of organising collective issues. The fairly elaborate division of labour in the new councils therefore seemed to conflict with shared understandings of decision-making, although these were changing.

The third institutional contradiction is between an accountability based on the ability to substitute decision-makers and one based on the non-implementation of their decisions. This issue has not received much attention in the programme of natural resource management in Burkina Faso. In the official discourse, accountability is ensured through elections. If the villagers are dissatisfied with a member's performance, they can choose someone else to represent them. However, this is not entirely how things work in the villages, as seen in the unanimous 'election' of all council members in the Bougouriba villages.

The question of accountability has two dimensions. One is the information flowing from the council to the villagers; the other is the villagers' opportunity to influence council discussions and decisions. A flow of information from the council to the villagers is a condition for villagers' participation in discussions. In Ninigui, about two-thirds of the male adult population were not aware of the existence of the council. Almost everyone knew of the existence and location of the nutrition centre initiated by the council, possibly because they had participated in its construction, but a majority showed no knowledge of the council and its members. Most men are members of a peasant group but only one out of the fifteen members interviewed knew anything about the financial situation of his group. However, according to the leaders and villagers outside the council, a system for distribution of information does exist. Representatives of each neighbourhood report back at specific places and times, and one respondent could indeed give a fairly precise and correct account of a meeting that he had not attended. Furthermore, it was held to be easy to influence representatives and have them convey the opinions of the neighbourhood.

In Pogoro and the Bougouriba villages, the women were unaware of most village issues as mentioned earlier. According to the president of the council in

Nahirindon, a meeting was held with the women in order to inform them about the zoning of village lands and the places where the women were supposed to collect wood. A group of twelve women maintained, however, that they knew nothing about the zoning decisions or the wood collecting sites. Men were also sometimes unclear about the location of the different zones, and the form in which people were called to village meetings was not very efficient. In addition the tendency to monopolise decision-making does not contribute to a general dissemination of information.

According to a council member in Ninigui, villagers did influence council decisions. Future activities were discussed at village meetings, and participants' views could easily be gleaned from their cheering or reactions to proposals. The villagers' influence was said to be felt by the leaders in the sense that villagers are not likely to participate in activities they disapprove of. Thus, where decisions need the villagers' active co-operation to be implemented, leaders and council members might feel obliged to make a decision supported by a substantial portion of the villagers. By contrast, decisions regarding the distribution of food received from external organisations in return for collective activities, or the location of a water pump drilled by a project, do not have the same degree of accountability built into them and villagers consequently have no opportunity to influence their implementation.

Accountability in Ninigui may depend to some extent on the sharp confrontation between the village groups and the Naam groups. In Tankiédougou, for instance, the *Mossis* exerted no influence on the location of a well, yet they contributed a major part of the labour force. The same applies to decisions concerning the location of the different zones in both Tankiédougou and Nahirindon. In particular, the *Fulani* herdsman with more than a hundred head of cattle was excluded from the discussion of where to establish the pastoral zones. Hence, the existence of accountable relations between decision-makers and villagers is far from evident. There are instances where decision-makers are influenced by villagers, but accountability is certainly not based on a fear of being replaced at elections. In fact, no council elections have taken place in the four villages and none are likely to take place in the near future. The idea of replacing a decision-maker whom one disagrees with contradicts the widespread understanding that a decision maker should be closely related to the village founders.

The fourth type of institutional contradiction is between conflict resolution based on negotiation and compromise by the parties involved and one based on the judgement of respected individuals. There are no examples of disputes being resolved as a result of the councils adopting a process of negotiation to reach an agreement. Normally, an arbitrator with substantial status was needed when a conflict had escalated beyond the control of the parties concerned.

Village chiefs or other leaders considered to be particularly knowledgable could settle such conflicts. The leaders' decisions were generally respected because of the positions they enjoyed and not because the solutions were the result of a negotiated compromise. Accordingly, conflicts were generally taken to the chiefs rather than to the councils.

A number of leading council members in Ninigui were fully aware of the project's proposal that the council should resolve conflicts, but they all agreed that this was impossible for the time being. They consented to the idea in principle, but saw a number of problems with it. One was the conflict inside the council, a second was the village chief's unwillingness to abandon his mediating role, and a third concerned the council's lack of 'force' to settle disputes. This last reservation is of particular interest since it points to the question of whom people recognise as a proper arbitrator. Arbitration requires status, and status is associated with experience and relationship to important individuals in village history; qualities possessed by the chiefs and not by the councils.

An attempt to give the resource-managing bodies some punitive authority was undertaken in Nahirindon and Ninigui. Violations of the rules concerning the survey of domestic animals during the rainy season and the cutting of fresh wood were to be taken to the president and his group in Nahirindon, and to the council in Ninigui. Thus, procedures for conflict resolution in the villages could gradually change, and the councils or some other body for managing natural resources could play an important role. However, at the time of the fieldwork, conflict resolution by representative councils was clearly at odds with existing village institutions.

The fifth institutional contradiction is between legitimacy entrusted in the organisational structure of a decision-making body and one invested in the members of the body. From the point of view of the natural resource management programme and the projects, the legitimacy of the councils is based on two elements. The first is the councils' ability to manage natural resources effectively; the second is the representativeness of the councils, which should guarantee that all voices are heard and that council decisions are respected.

Does the project view of legitimacy accord with local views? Undoubtedly, an effectively functioning decision-making institution is recognised and appreciated by the villagers. This is reflected by the weight which villagers assign to peasant groups who perform well. On the other hand, open discussions between equal representatives of different social groups do not contribute to the legitimacy of an institution. This is quite clear from the discussion on representativeness above. Instead, the legitimacy of a decision-making body depends very much on the particular persons who compose it. Whilst according to a project perspective, replacing representatives does not affect the legitimacy of the council, for the villagers a change of decision-makers may very well undermine the legitimacy of the whole institution. However, it is not easy to determine which of the personal qualifications of decision-makers gives the institution legitimacy. Family, gender, age, and religion are important but so are experience, enthusiasm, intelligence, honesty, and diplomatic skills. Having connections to the first inhabitants of the village guarantees wisdom and knowledge about the land and possibly the spirits, but it is not enough. Personal skills are also needed to become a respected leader.

With respect to council presidents in the four villages, affinity with customary authorities and the first families to have settled in the villages are very clear. If the president is not the village chief himself (Pogoro), he is the son of the land chief (Tankiédougou) or of the chief of the bush (Nahirindon), or he belongs to one of the very first families in the village (Ninigui). In addition, the president in Nahirindon is also the prefect's representative in the village, and the one in Ninigui heads the village groups and knows how to read and write Arabic, a prestigious ability in an Islamic community. Moreover, the presidents are, to various degrees, enthusiastic and experienced persons, who were important, respected decision-makers prior to the creation of the councils. Thus, the fact that they are presidents gives credit to the resource management issue in all four villages. In addition, it would probably be quite difficult to find alternative and equally well-qualified candidates. Thus in Ninigui, the current council president was proposed even by his opponents.

The presence of the two imams in the council in Ninigui indicates that legitimacy is linked to members rather than to the organisation, since they rarely attend council meetings and appear to be unconcerned about non-religious matters. Nevertheless, their formal membership lends lustre to the council. Another example relates to the president of the council in Pogoro. An enthusiastic old man, he nonetheless regards himself as a kind of honourary member who advises and encourages the young. In his formal role as president, he is supposed to ensure that the council reaches conclusions and initiates action. In practice, his role is to provide legitimacy to the council through his presence as village chief.

The question of legitimacy is closely related to the contradictions concerning representativeness and accountability. It epitomises the substantially different ways of ordering reality and different understandings of what is important in a decision-making process. In the eyes of the villagers, legitimacy in decision-making is related more to persons than to organisations, more to relations with ancestors than to fellow villagers, and more to evaluation by superiors than to discussion and negotiation between equals. This contrasts strongly with the view on legitimacy which underlies the representative councils.

## CONCLUSION

This study raises two major considerations. First, institutions, in the shape of rules and shared meanings, are more than external constraints or opportunities that actors confront, assess and exploit as far as possible. They are also ways of understanding the world, of giving meaning to actions, social relations and the natural environment. Accordingly, institutions provide some stability in situations that might otherwise be very unpredictable and insecure. Changing institutions therefore gives rise to uncertainty. It is a demanding and comprehensive process in which people modify their understanding of reality and of important elements of a particular activity like decision-making.

The significance of the symbolic order upheld by institutions was clear on several occasions in relation to the introduction of representative village councils. Women and migrants regarded themselves as inappropriate decision-makers and were confused when asked for their opinion on village affairs. They could not suddenly take part in collective decision-making, since this task was seen to be preserve of elder male members of those families which founded the village. Collective decision-making should not be analysed exclusively as an activity where different individuals come together to develop common ideas. It is also an integrated part of a social system in which existing ways of addressing similar issues carry much weight.

Second, rural development interventions often give rise to institutional contradictions, since they are carried out by actors with substantially different concerns, experiences, and values than those characterising most rural dwellers. In addition to conflicts of interest between extension officers and project employees on the one hand and villagers on the other, interventions may challenge existing rules and well-established practices which villagers are unwilling to change for both material and symbolic reasons. Interventions giving rise to institutional contradictions are likely to have unintended consequences because changes are not wholeheartedly adopted, and because it is very difficult to determine which parts of an intervention are likely to find fertile ground.

The present study found that decision-making was organised very differently in the four villages studied, although they were all subject to fairly similar interventions. The principle of a council with several sub-commissions was adopted in Ninigui in part because it takes into account and integrates the interests of the two major factions. In Pogoro, it was not possible to unify the whole village with the result that an important faction felt bypassed, and decision-making was not greatly affected by the creation of the council. This is also the case in Tankiédougou, where the council with its principle of representation has had no impact. In Nahirindon, the council has not worked, but a few elements have been incorporated into an informal group which was recently set up to manage some of the same tasks. This conclusion supports the idea that rural dwellers tend to 'unpack' interventions [*Olivier de Sardan, 1988; Berry, 1993*], although the process seems to have a dynamic of its own and the consequent organisation of decision-making does not fully meet the interests of any particular local actor.

Although institutional contradictions need to be understood, they should not be regarded as stable and irrefutable. Symbolic orders can be challenged and changed, if gradually and slowly. For instance, young men are increasingly handling relations with state authorities in the two Bougouriba villages, as the chiefs seem to feel uncomfortable with official development discourse. The process is lengthy, however, and difficult to accelerate. Accordingly, representative village councils are not necessarily inappropriate in the long term, because social relations and institutions change and villages in Burkina Faso are subject to significant transformations, not least because of the large number of interventions throughout the country.

From a strategic perspective, the present study suggests that interventions need to be much more aware of the local institutions they seek to change. If no influential local groups support the change, the intervention is not likely to succeed. For instance, a representative decision-making process is out of the question in Tankiédougou, because the immigrants are politically unable to support it. One would probably advance more by directly strengthening those groups who are likely to profit from an institutional change. For example, an intervention favouring vegetable production may stimulate a process whereby women acquire experience and economic resources which enhances their political influence in the villages. The subsequent introduction of a representative decision-making body is then much more likely to be successful.

The aim of the land management programme in Burkina Faso to promote representative local-decision making is worthy, but it does not seem to support the primary objective of ensuring natural resource management. None of the councils in the four villages makes a significant contribution to conservation activities or to resolving conflicts such as those between herders and farmers. Natural resource management does take place, but not as a consequence of the creation of village councils. It would seem, therefore, that supporting existing organisations and forms of decision-making is more promising than the creation of a rather empty organisational shell.

NOTES

1. This sketch of the four villages does not do justice to the complexity and richness of social life in the villages. The intention here is to provide a basis for understanding processes and interactions relating to the introduction of village councils.

2. Peasant groups are slightly more formalised than working groups and they are generally established on the initiative of external actors, such as NGOs and extension officers.
3. Although they often acted as a homogeneous group, the *Pougoulis* were very hierarchically organised. An elder *Pougouli* said that he dared not propose ideas for collective activities because he was not supposed to and would be criticised for interfering.

## REFERENCES


Berry, Sara, 1993, *No Condition is Permanent: The Social Dynamics of Agrarian Change in Sub-Saharan Africa*, Madison, WI: University of Wisconsin Press.

Bromley, Daniel W. (ed.), 1992, *Making The Commons Work: Theory, Practice, and Policy*, San Francisco, CA: ICS Press.

Dugue, P. 1990, 'Les Stratégies des Paysans du Yatenga (Burkina Faso) Face aux Propositions d'Aménagement des Terroirs Villageois', *Cahiers de la Recherche Développement*, No.26, pp.1–14.

Friedland, Roger and Robert R. Alford, 1991, 'Bringing Society Back In: Symbols, Practices, and Institutional Contradictions', in Walter W. Powell and Paul J. DiMaggio (eds.), *The New Institutionalism in Organisational Analysis*, Chicago, IL: University of Chicago Press, pp.232–63.

GOB, (Government of Burkina Faso), 1989, *Rapport de Synthèse et d'Analyse des Expériences Pilotes de Gestion des Terroirs Villageois*, Ministère du Plan et de la Coopération, Programme National de Gestion des Terroirs Villageois.

Isard, Michel, 1985, *Gens du Pouvoir, Gens de la Terre: Les Institutions Politiques de l'Ancien Royaume du Yatenga (Bassin de la Volta Blanche)*, Cambridge: Cambridge University Press.

Long, Norman, 1989, 'Conclusion: Theoretical Reflections on Actor, Structure and Interface', in Norman Long (ed.), *Encounters at the Interface: A Perspective on Social Discontinuities in Rural Development*, Wageningen: Agricultural University, pp.221–43.

Long, Norman and Jan Douwe van der Ploeg, 1989, 'Demythologising Planned Intervention: An Actor Perspective', *Sociologia Ruralis*. Vol.29, Nos.3/4, pp.226–49.

Long, Norman and Jan Douwe van der Ploeg, 1994, 'Heterogeneity, Actor and Structure: Towards a Reconstitution of the Concept of Structure', in David Booth (ed.), *Rethinking Social Development: Theory, Research and Practice*, Harlow: Longman Scientific & Technical, pp.62–89.

Long, Norman and Magdalena Villarreal, 1993, 'Exploring Development Interfaces: From the Transfer of Knowledge to the Transformation of Meaning', in Frans J. Schuurman (ed.), *Beyond the Impasse: New Directions in Development Theory*, London: Zed Books, pp.140–68.

Mosse, David, 1995, 'Local Institutions and Power: The History and Practice of Community Management of Tank Irrigation Systems in South India', in Nici Nelson and Susan Wright (eds.), *Power and Participatory Development: Theory and Practice*, London: Intermediate Technology Publications, pp. 144–56.

North, Douglass C., 1990, *Institutions, Institutional Change, and Economic Development*, Cambridge: Cambridge University Press.

Olivier de Sardan, Jean-Pierre, 1988, 'Peasant Logics and Development Project Logics', *Sociologia Ruralis*. Vol.28, Nos.2/3, pp.216–26.

Ostrom, Elinor, 1990, *Governing The Commons: The Evolution of Institutions for Collective Action*, New York: Cambridge University Press.

Ostrom, Elinor, Larry Schroeder and Susan Wynne, 1993, *Institutional Incentives and Sustainable Development: Infrastructure Policies in Perspective*, Boulder, CO: Westview Press.

Ouédraogo, Bernard Lédéa, 1990, *Entraide Villageoise et Développement. Groupements Paysans au Burkina Faso*, Paris: L'Harmattan.

Spencer, J., 1990, *A Sinhala Village in a Time of Trouble: Politics and Change in Rural Sri Lanka*, New Delhi: Oxford University Press.

Thomas-Slayter, Barbara P., 1994, 'Structural Change, Power Politics, and Community Organisations in Africa: Challenging the Patterns, Puzzles and Paradoxes', *World Development*,

Vol.22, No.10, pp.1479–90.

Thomson, James T., 1992, *A Framework for Analyzing Institutional Incentives in Community Forestry*, Rome: FAO.

Wade, Robert, 1988, *Village Republics: Economic Conditions for Collective Action in South India*, Cambridge: Cambridge University Press.

White, T. Anderson and C. Ford Runge, 1994, 'Common Property and Collective Action: Lessons from Cooperative Watershed Management in Haiti', *Economic Development and Cultural Change*, Vol.43, No.1, pp.1–42.

White, T. Anderson and C. Ford Runge, 1995, 'The Emergence and Evolution of Collective Action: Lessons from Watershed Management in Haiti', *World Development*. Vol.23, No.10, pp.1683–98.

Williamson, Oliver E., 1993, 'Transaction Cost Economics and Organisation Theory', *Industrial and Corporate Change*, Vol.2, No.2, pp.107–57.

# Against all Odds: Coping with Regress in Kinshasa, Zaïre

TOM DE HERDT and STEFAAN MARYSSE

*Drawing on a field-survey carried out in the city of Kinshasa, the authors aimed to gain more insight into the (re)-activation of solidarity networks in times of economic crisis. Solidarity networks, it is argued, have a differential impact on socio-professional groups and hence one should be very cautious about making 'general' statements on their (dys)functional character. Hence, it remains unclear whether the overall informalisation of Kinshasa's economic structure can explain the fact that in the midst of overall regress in Zaïre, the inhabitants of its capital city seem to have been able to consolidate their position.*

## INTRODUCTION

Some years ago the World Bank conference on development economics devoted a session to the economics of regress. This was not without good reason. The stylised facts of an increasing number of developing countries indicate that the category 'developing country' itself should be renamed. Moreover, the word 'coping' in the title of this text refers both to the Zairians and to those development economists writing on the subject.

Zaïre is a well-known example of regress. Statistically speaking, it no longer exists. GDP per head has fallen back to $100, which is around $200 below the survival minimum [*World Bank, 1990*]. Only five per cent of the potentially active population is officially employed. Zaïre is rather a-typical, however. Unlike other countries of Sub-Sahara Africa (SSA) which have experienced similar regress, it has not – at least not until the end of last year – been affected by sudden upheavals like natural disasters or civil wars. In the case of Zaïre, regress has set in gradually. Worse still, regress seems to have become irreversible; even the most optimistic forecasts do not provide much hope for a restoration of the Zairian state in the short and medium term [*Maton, 1992; De Herdt and Marysse, 1996a*].

---

Tom De Herdt, Researcher and Ph.D. student at the Centre for Development Studies, Antwerp University, Ufsia. Stefaan Marysse, Professor of Development Economics and Director of the Centre for Development Studies, Antwerp University, Ufsia. Earlier versions were commented on by L. de St.-Moulin, some representatives of the Belgian Development Administration and two anonymous referees. Any remaining errors are theirs.

In this study, we shall not dwell on the causes of this process. The general hypothesis we want to examine is that the gradual character of regress enabled some social groups at least to adapt themselves to the changing circumstances. Some authors refer to this phenomenon as the 'Zairian miracle' [*Braeckman, 1991; MacGaffey, 1996*] or, more appropriately as we will see, as the 'miracle of Kinshasa' [*Houyoux et al., 1986; Maton, 1992*].

Our study shows that there is indeed a significant gap between official indicators and alternative measures of well-being in Zaïre's capital city, Kinshasa. Moreover, by means of a field survey of some 125 urban families in Kinshasa, we gained more detailed insights into some of the ways in which the *kinois* have managed to cope with regress. The results of this exercise must be interpreted with care, however, since the survey was mainly set up to test the instrument itself, rather than some theoretical hypotheses.

The first section of this article presents some evidence of the 'gap' between (estimates of) economic measures and social indicators of well-being in Kinshasa. The second section provides a short overview of the relevant literature on regress. By considering only the case of Zaïre, our approach deviates from contributions which employ international comparisons [*Sen, 1994; Barro and Lee, 1994*]. International comparisons have the merit of being able to identify some general causes of regress (for example, low endowment in human capital, low capital investment ratio, large public expenditure, political instability). An insight into the consequences of regress requires much more country-specific knowledge, as has been demonstrated convincingly by Sen's analyses of famines [*Sen, 1981; 1984; Drèze and Sen, 1989*]. Our design of a tentative theoretical framework for analysing the phenomenon at a more disaggregated level is based on his work. In the third and the fourth sections, this framework is used to guide us through the results of a small budget survey in Kinshasa. The final conclusions are summarised in the last section.

## I. DECLINE IN ZAÏRE SINCE THE END OF THE COLD WAR

Table 1 provides some summary indicators of social and economic development for the early 1990s. The table shows that Sub-Saharan Africa as a whole attained some moderate economic growth, but that social development stagnated during the same period.[1] If social indicators are regarded as relatively insensitive to short-term changes, this appears not to hold for Zaïre: this country has experienced a period of severe economic and social regress, whatever the measure. In terms of social development, Zaïre has regressed from above average to below average in Sub-Saharan Africa. In terms of its economy, Zaïre came last throughout the 1989–93 period.[2]

The figures on change in GNP per capita during the 1980s show that the end of the cold war was not negative for SSA as a whole. Indeed, on average,

TABLE 1
SOME SUMMARY INDICATORS OF SOCIAL AND ECONOMIC DEVELOPMENT FOR SUB-SAHARAN AFRICA AND ZAÏRE
(1989–95)

| | Zaïre | Subsahara Africa |
|---|---|---|
| % underweight children (1980–1990) | 28 | 33 |
| % underweight children (1990–1996) | 34 | 30 |
| % change | 21,4% | –9,1% |
| infant mortality rate 1990 | 79 | 106 |
| 1995 | 119 | 106 |
| % Average annual change 90–95 | 8,5% | 0,0% |
| Under five mortality rate 1990 | 130 | 175 |
| 1995 | 185 | 175 |
| % Average annual change 90–95 | 7,3% | 0,0% |
| GDP/cap (PPP$°) 1989 | 380 | 1187 |
| 1993 | 300 | 1288 |
| % Average annual change 89–93 | –5,7% | 2,1% |
| GNP/cap ($US) | | |
| % Average annual change 80–90 | –1,5% | –1,1% |

° PPP$ = USD purchasing power parity
*Sources:* UNDP, *Human Development Report* 1992, 1993,1995, 1996; UNICEF, *State of the World's Children,* 1997; UNCTAD, *Handbook of International Trade and Development Statistics,* 1994.

SSA did better in the early 1990s than during the 'lost decade' of the 1980s. In Zaïre, however, the negative growth of the 1980s (which had already set in the early 1970s) became even more pronounced. Before 'democracy arrived' (when President Mobutu announced the end of the One Party State on 24 April 1990) negative growth was explained by the unproductive use of the economic surplus by the country's elite and its donor countries' trading partners [*Peemans, 1982; 1989; Lemarchand, 1988*]. By the end of the 1980s, however, several important gold and copper mines had collapsed and the aid industry's investments in white elephants ended abruptly [*Willame, 1986*]. Hence, the politico-commercial elite lost its classical state-related sources of enrichment. In order to counteract falling revenue, monetary authorities simply printed more money, and the inflationary mechanism was (re)activated. In terms of political economy, inflation is a tax on cash balances, paid by those who cannot escape the use of national currency for daily transactions. As such, the old elite found a new and devastating way of diverting economic surplus from more productive use. Moreover, in 1994, hyperinflation was fuelled by the outright printing of false-legal money by the private but official money printing company of the Central Bank [*De Herdt and Marysse, 1996a*]. However, all these attempts were of no avail, as Figure 1 demonstrates.

FIGURE 1
GOVERNMENT REVENUES, ZAIRE 1980–95

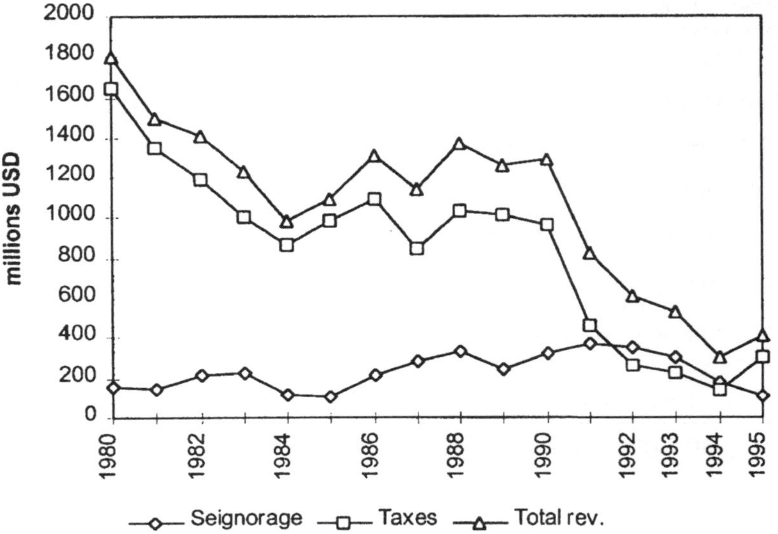


Seignorage revenue in year t is calculated as $M1_t - M1_{t-1})/M1_t \times (M1_t + M1_{t-1})/2$

*Source:* own calculations, based on BNZ, *Rapport Annuel 1982–1995.*

The graph depicts ordinary revenues ('Taxes') and revenues derived from the inflationary mechanism ('seignorage'). The latter were calculated by multiplying the tax rate $(M1_t - M1_{t-1})/ M1_t$ by the tax base $(M1_t + M1_{t-1})/2$ [*Sachs and Larraín, 1993: Ch.12*]. Total revenues ('Total rev.') were calculated by simply adding ordinary revenues and seignorage. Figure 1 clearly shows that, while state revenues provided by the so-called inflation-tax became even more important than ordinary revenues from 1992, the increasing use of this mechanism could not counteract the implosion of ordinary state revenues since 1991. Hyperinflation contributed in fact to the further withering away of the state and of the Zaïrian economy as a whole. The gradual erosion of M1 (the tax base!) reflects both this over-all regress and the self-defeating character of this type of surplus extraction [*De Herdt, 1995*].

*Decline in Kinshasa?*

Unfortunately, there are no economic data which allow us to measure the evolution of urban incomes in a *direct* way. This has everything to do with the difficult situation in which Zaïrians are currently living. The organisation of a scientifically valid survey in the city has become a miracle in itself. The latest income survey in the capital Kinshasa was effected in 1986 [*Houyoux, 1986*], but even its results were later seriously questioned [*Maton, 1992*]. The most interesting *indirect* way of estimating economic evolution is based on macro-economic figures. Using a macro-economic model that incorporates the crisis in copper production (the main provider of state revenue in Zaïre), Maton estimated commercialised GDP and consumption, considering that 'those macro-economic indicators give a rough idea of the development of incomes in the urban areas: for 1993 and 1994 one may expect a further fall of income and consumption in those urban areas of more than 20% a year' [*Maton, 1993: 15*]. Moreover, while these were estimates of an average of decline in all Zaïrian cities, Maton expected the decline to be somewhat less in the cities of the provinces of Kasaï and Kivu (where illegal diamond and gold mining might make a difference), but more pronounced in Shaba (the copper province) and Kinshasa (the centre of the state apparatus). The implicit assumption was that the fall in copper production would cause a serious fall in state revenue, and hence also in state expenses, traditionally biased in favour of the urban population of Kinshasa.

TABLE 2
ECONOMIC DECLINE IN ZAÏRE, 1990–95

| | Commercialised GDP (estim. Maton) | Commercialised Consumption (estim. Maton) | Commercialised GDP (BNZ figures) |
|---|---|---|---|
| | (Index 1988=100) | | |
| 1990 | 92.5 | 94.0 | 91.4 |
| 1991 | 82.4 | 83.2 | 83.8 |
| 1992 | 73.5 | 76.4 | 75.0 |
| 1993 | 55.8 | 60.4 | *64.0* |
| 1994 | 41.2 | 47.0 | *59.4* |
| 1995 | n.d. | n.d. | *59.1* |

*italics:* estimates

*Source:* own calculations, based on J. Maton, *Zaire: Balance of Payments Problems 1992–3*, 1993, p.14; BNZ, *Rapport Annuel 1991*; BNZ, *Condensé Mensuel Janvier 1996*.

Table 2 presents Maton's estimates, together with the 'real' figures and estimates, as published by the Zaïrian National Bank. Apparently, the estimates were more or less 'confirmed' by reality for the 1990–92 period. From 1993 onwards, however, Maton's estimates seem to have been too pessimistic. Nevertheless, it seems safe to state that, according to official figures, the economy has been halved over the last seven to eight years.

The findings on country-wide overall regress, and the prediction of economic regress in the capital contrast sharply with some indicators of social development in Kinshasa during the early 1990s. Table 3 presents some measures of malnutrition. While there are some considerable variations over the years, it seems impossible to detect a consistent trend between 1991 and 1996. In order to interpret this result, it should be noted that malnutrition is very sensitive to short-term changes. It varies significantly, for example between different seasons of the same year [*Arbyn et al., 1995; De Herdt and Marysse, 1996a: 167-71*].

To conclude, the available data on Zaïre and on Kinshasa for the early 1990s suggest that there is indeed a 'gap' between Zaïrian over-all decline and the status-quo in Kinshasa. To call this gap a miracle is probably an exaggeration. It would be more realistic to speak in terms of an airplane crash with only a few injured. It is reasonable to conclude from these figures that

TABLE 3
CHILDREN SUFFERING FROM MALNUTRITION* IN KINSHASA
(1991–1996, END-OF-YEAR SURVEYS)

| | wasting moderate & severe | wasting severe | underweight | stunting |
|---|---|---|---|---|
| 1991 | 6,3 | 1,9 | 22,4 | 26,8 |
| 1992 | 5,1 | 0,9 | 23,2 | 30 |
| 1993 | 4,6 | 0,8 | n.d. | n.d. |
| 1994 | 7,5 | 1,8 | n.d. | n.d. |
| 1995 | 7,7 | 0,7 | n.d. | n.d. |
| 1996 | 6,4 | 1,6 | 22,6 | 28 |

* Moderate and severe wasting: proportion of children (6–59 months) below -2 standard deviations from the median weight for height reference population and/or presence of oedemes; Severe: below -3 s.d. from median w/h reference population and/or presence of oedemes. Underweight: below -2 s.d. from median weight for age for reference population. Stunting: below -2 s.d. from median height for age for reference population.

*Sources:* MSF, *Enquête anthropométrique rapide;* Nov. 1991; MSF, *Enquête nutritionnelle rapide* Sept. 1992; UNICEF/CEPLANUT, *Enquête sur la localisation des poches de pauvreté dans la ville de Kinshasa*, Sept. 1996.

commercialised GDP per head is a poor indicator of social development in Kinshasa.

Further insights into the relation between economic and social development/regress may be gained by comparing different social groups and their coping strategies *within* Kinshasa. First, however, we shall set out our theoretical framework more explicitly.

## II. GRADUAL ECONOMIC REGRESS: SOME THEORETICAL ELEMENTS

The concept of a 'miracle of Kinshasa' is an invention of the students of the Zaïrian informal sector. If there is divergence between economic and social development, this must be because 'official' figures underestimate the 'real' economy. One important problem with the informal sector concept is that part of the economy is defined by reference to what it is not: formal. By considering informality as another part (involving different activities, a different logic, different persons, even different geographical areas [*Leclerq, 1992*]), reality is artificially divided into a 'normal' and an 'abnormal' part. In a country where only five per cent of the potentially active population is officially employed (and where the average salary in the public sector, if paid,[3] does not exceed the price of a one-way bus ticket) such an approach is more illusory than illuminating.

Instead, we chose to link our approach to Sen's theory of entitlements and capabilities [*Sen, 1984; 1985; Drèze and Sen, 1989*]. In the next section we will briefly review Sen's approach – at least a simplified version of it. This will enable us to point to some shortcomings, when his theory is used to gain insight into *gradual* regress.

According to Sen, the central concern of development economics should be located in between (the growth of) GDP per capita (or some other, related variable) on the one hand and (an increase in) individual utility on the other.

> … ultimately, the process of economic development has to be concerned with what people can or cannot do, e g. whether they can live long, escape avoidable morbidity, *be well nourished*, be able to read and write and communicate, take part in literary and scientific pursuits, and so forth [*Sen, 1984: 497*] (our emphasis).

This is the concept of capability. The problem with GDP is that it measures only goods available in a given economy, without inferring whether these goods are indeed (efficiently) used in order to expand people's capabilities. The metric of utility, on the other hand, 'can take a deeply biased form due to the fact that the mental reactions often reflect defeatist compromises with harsh reality induced by hopelessness' [*Sen, 1984: 512*]. Hence, capabilities are seen as a much more 'objective' measure.

In order to clarify the link between availability of goods (approximately measured by GDP) and effective use of them to enhance individuals' capabilities, Sen invokes the concept of entitlements: 'the set of alternative commodity bundles that a person can command in a society using the totality of rights and opportunities that he or she faces' [*Sen, 1984: 497*]. A wage earner's totality of entitlements will for instance be determined by (1) (initial endowments) his capacities in terms of human capital, and (2) (exchange entitlements) the relative buying power of his salary.

In most cases, however, factor income is an insufficient measure of a person's entitlements set. To begin with, most people belong to a household. It makes more sense to speak of entitlements accruing to households than to speak of entitlements accruing directly to individuals. Further, some incomes are independent of the mobilisation of some production factor in the economy. In European welfare-states, for instance, your family can 'earn' an income precisely because you are unable to work, because of illness, unemployment, being too old or being too young. In Third World countries, the 'aid industry' produces similar entitlements, be it that these are much more irregular and erratic than their European counterparts [*Sen, 1984: 500–501*]. Third, the measure of income cannot account for quantity variations in the availability of some goods. The entitlement to health care will not only depend on your income and the cost of treatment, but also on the availability of a hospital, a doctor, and drugs. Fourth, a family's entitlement set can be extended by its (members') insertion in the so-called economy of affection [*Hyden, 1983*]. In times of 'ordinary' distress, one's involvement in networks of family, neighbourhood or friendship can be very functional in terms of one's capabilities.

Sen initially developed his approach to analyse a specific case of economic regress: famines. Natural disasters – and, more generally, sudden external shocks – only lead to famines and, more generally, to economic regress when they induce a (sudden) collapse in the entitlements accruing to some occupational groups. The Bangladeshi famine of 1974, for instance, was not directly caused by a shortage of food. On the contrary, food production peaked in that year. Most victims were rural labourers who lost their (exchange) entitlement to food because the flood made them (technically) unemployed. Furthermore, they were not able to substitute their wage incomes for other incomes.

Note that, according to Sen, in most famines, prevailing rules of entitlement are not changed or even questioned; 'the millions that die in a famine typically die in an astonishingly "legal" and "orderly" way' [*Drèze and Sen, 1989: 22*]. One exception to this rule is, however, the breakdown of the 'informal social security network': in most cases, the collapse in exchange entitlements affects the economy of affection to the point of collapse. This is because, while the 'informal security network' proves effective in managing uncorrelated risks among several households, in the case of famines all households within the network are equally affected. As a result, in most famines one can observe that 'each man has become a thief to his neighbour' [*Drèze and Sen, 1989: 74*]. Sudden regress unleashes the Hobbesian war of all against all.[4]

Drèze and Sen's relative neglect of the role of informal security networks in times of economic regress may be tolerated when analysing processes of sudden economic regress. However, in the case of Zaïre, we propose two arguments which suggest that a breakdown of basic social structures will not occur. First, most authors agree that economic regress is not so much caused by sudden external factors, as by an internal factor, called 'le mal Zaïrois'. For historical, political and country-specific reasons, it is difficult to use the terms 'legal' and 'order' as Drèze and Sen did in the quote above, since these words confer a status of stability and predictability on the 'over-all rules of entitlement' which cannot be taken for granted in Zaïre. According to Drèze and Sen, 'entitlement focuses on a person's legal rights of ownership ... enforceable in a court', while extended entitlements draw on accepted legitimacy. Using these terms, the essence of 'le mal Zairois' is that extended entitlements have always been far more effective than legal entitlements.[5] Second, as regress has been a gradual process, the war of all against all is a far less probable end-result as the informal networks, in which extended entitlements are rooted, will have time to adapt. This reasoning can be found in Maton [*1992*]. Maton suggests that, in the current Zaïrian situation, 'the rich have to pay a price for maintaining a relative safety in the network they are dominating'. The 'price' is passed 'through the intricate network of relations that exist between a *pater familias* at the top of a hierarchically structured group and the subordinate members or clients down the ladder of a complex system, that from the outside looks as a paternalist system' [*Maton, 1992: 3*].

Maton's suggestion of a causal link between political instability (or, in Sen's terms, disorder in the rules of entitlement) and the (re)activation of informal networks can be illustrated by the example of the inflation tax. Standard analysis of hyperinflation suggests that the people will react to the government's policies by diminishing monetary balances [*Sachs and Larraín, 1993; Cukierman, 1992*]. This strategy has been shortcut, however, by the fact that the whole formal financial system collapsed together with the rise in consumer prices (1991). While black foreign currency markets emerged to take over its role, the public's access to foreign currency depends, among other things, on their ability to create a trust-relationship with one of the foreign currency exchangers, who were predominantly seen as immoral criminals rather than as merchants [*De Herdt and Marysse, 1996b*]. Other coping strategies were coupled much more to pre-existing social networks: monetary balances can be minimised if money received by A will be spent immediately on 'urgent needs' of B, who is involved in one of the networks A is also involved in. Indeed, within a network where individuals can give 'credit' to each other – albeit that the term 'credit' is perhaps not appropriate in this context[6] – velocity can be increased, and the burden of the inflation tax can be circumvented. More spectacular coping strategies also involve the collective refusal of new banknotes. Indeed, the 1993 looting was the immediate consequence of the merchants' refusal to accept the Z 5 million banknote, with which the soldiers were paid in January of that year. In the international press, it was said that the refusal of the bill was politically inspired by 'opposition leader' Tshisekedi, but it seems that the refusal was initiated by the women merchants at the *Grand Marché* in Kinshasa. Another example is the refusal of the 'Nouveau Zaïre' by two Zaïrian provinces. As the nominal value of Z 1 million had fallen below its printing cost (and since the Z 5 million banknote was refused), the levying of an inflation tax became more and more difficult, which is why the New Zaïre was introduced in October 1993. By refusing the new currency, however, the Kasaï provinces managed to circumvent the inflation (tax) [*Yav Karl Yav, 1995*].

The above example supports Maton's suggestion that informal networks can, to some extent, compensate for changes in a society's rules of entitlement. It also reveals that these informal networks do not necessarily correspond to hierarchically structured paternalist systems. Moreover, it is suggested that informal networks partly overlap, operate at various levels, with a different intensity, and that some change in the overall structure of the social tissue in which Zaïrians are embedded is possible. We like the comparison of the social tissue of Kinshasa with what has been called 'organised anarchy' in the literature on organisations [*Cohen, March and Olsen, 1988*]: much as occurs in organisations (like universities) which are characterised by inconsistent and/or ill-defined preferences, unclear technologies and fluid participation, the structure of the social tissue of Kinshasa seems to be constantly redesigned in function of the most urgent problems, the most readily available solutions and the capability of 'political entrepreneurs' to re-allocate problems and solutions to 'their' garbage can.[7]

These issues are beyond the scope of this article, however. Here, suffice it to say that social networks can indeed partly compensate for the withering away of legal entitlements. Undoubtedly, the Zaïrians' strategies of coping with gradual economic regress are not limited to a reconstitution of the 'economy of affection'. At least two other levels can be distinguished. First, one may expect changes at the household level, in addition to changes in informal networks. Indeed, African (urban) households typically comprise more than only the nuclear family. The boundaries between the nuclear family and the extended family are relatively vague, and constantly changing. It may be assumed (and it will be tested) that the composition of the household, as well as the household budget, will also be adapted to 'economic regress'. Second, one can also expect to observe strategies for coping with economic regress at the individual level. Individuals can (and are sometimes obliged to) change activities, or combine their 'official' jobs with other, less orthodox means to preserve their 'normal' means of livelihood. However, as we have discussed individual-level and household-level coping strategies elsewhere [*De Herdt and Marysse, 1996a*], we will focus on coping strategies which go beyond the household level.

Finally, our critique of Drèze and Sen's (relative) neglect of the role of informal networks and coping strategies, should not lead us to forget that, while in the aggregate, these strategies can compensate for a collapse of the overall rules of entitlement, this is not necessarily true at a more disaggregated level. This is implied by the image of the social tissue of Zaïre, and of Kinshasa in particular, as organised anarchy. Hence, coping strategies at the three above-mentioned levels are likely to vary significantly between different classes of people.

## III. SAMPLE SPECIFICATION AND MEASURES OF WELL-BEING

In order to test our amendments of Sen's framework of analysis, we drew up a small budget survey. Interviews were carried out by 25 students of a postgraduate course in development economics (five interviews per person). The questionnaire was discussed with them before and after the first interview, in order to adapt it to local circumstances and to improve standardisation of questions and answers. Since there were no secondary sources available on the total population (the last population survey was carried out in 1984), we had to start from a 'probable' typology of socio-professional groups, derived from earlier work on the 'real economy' in Zaïre [*Cour, 1989; MacGaffey, 1991; De Herdt and Marysse, 1996a*]. The following socio-professional groups were distinguished *ex-ante*:

(1) Households headed by *artisans* (petty commodity producers), whose incomes derived predominantly from activities carried on in small (micro-)enterprises: carpenters, tailors, shoe-repairers, taxi-drivers.

(2) Households headed by *intellectuals*, that is those who derive their incomes mainly from white-collar work: administrators, university personnel, architects, doctors.

(3) Households headed by *merchants* ('commerçants')

(4) *Elite* households, headed by persons who occupy high positions in private and/or public institutions, or in the army

(5) Households whose incomes are derived from *survival activities*: shoe-polishers, *pousse-pousseurs* (transporters hiring push-carts) street-vendors. These activities are not *artisanal* since they require no education. They are distinguished from *merchant* activities in that they do not require an initial capital.

In order to facilitate reliability, we opted to let the interviewers select the interviewees themselves from people whom they knew personally on the grounds that truthful answers depend to a considerable extent on a minimum of trust between interviewer and interviewee.[8] Another problematic element is our implicit assumption that the 'household' is a unity. In reality, different members control different resources and are responsible for different kinds of outlays [*Houyoux, 1986*]. Accuracy could be increased by interviewing several members of the same household, but budget constraints did not allow this.[9] Despite the above caveats, the survey results enabled us to formulate some interesting working hypotheses about the 'miracle of Kinshasa', which can be tested in some future and more representative survey.

*Current Well-being*

Table 4 presents the socio-professional groups defined above in terms of their income, measured by totality of outlays. According to these figures, the yearly income of a member of the poorest household type (survival) is estimated at $260, which is less than $1 per day,[10] one of the 'poverty lines' considered by the World Bank [*1990*]. Does this mean that our survey has failed to capture the poorest layers of Kinshasa? While we cannot exclude this possibility, the limit of $1 per day may be too low for Zaïre, where the cost of living has increased markedly because of the absent state. To begin with, general (transport) infrastructure has collapsed. Further, since public services like schools and health care are almost de facto totally privatised in Zaïre at this moment [*De Herdt and Marysse, 1996a*], the cost of education and health care accrue to the family budgets.

Taken together, the typology of households is apparently capable of explaining 30 per cent of total variation in our sample. One discordant fact which can be noted is that intellectuals earn less (or rather can spend less) than the artisan households! A measure of 'historical' well-being suggests that this is a rather recent phenomenon. Another interesting observation can be made when dividing household revenue by the number of household members. Whilst average survival households' revenue is approximately 1/30 of the elite's, this ratio drops to 1/13 when average revenue is measured per household member. We will come back to this phenomenon later.

TABLE 4
TOTAL OUTLAYS PER HOUSEHOLD* AND PERSON (USD)
PER TYPE OF HOUSEHOLD

| Type of household | Cases | Household budget | Outlays per person | Approximate weight of type in total population° |
|---|---|---|---|---|
| survival | 13 | 953 | 260 | 20% – 30% |
| intellectual | 29 | 3029 | 462 | 10% |
| artisan | 35 | 3435 | 580 | 30% – 40% |
| merchant | 25 | 8008 | 1380 | 25% – 35% |
| élite | 16 | 27611 | 3554 | 1% |
| $Eta^2$ | | 0.30 | 0.27 | |

* a household is defined as 'the socio-economic union of persons living under the same roof and sharing the same cooking pot'

° estimation of weights in 1986, based on Cour [*1989*].

Finally, the last column of Table 4 presents an estimate of the weight of each household type in the total population of Kinshasa. The figures were derived from a study by J.-M. Cour [*1989*], who constructed a Social Accounting Matrix for Zaïre in 1986. Kinshasa has evidently changed dramatically since then. Cour himself estimated the intellectuals' revenues at $853, and the revenue of elite households at $8333. The divergence from our estimates ($462 and $3554 respectively) falls within the limits of the possible, although one should conclude, on the basis of these figures, that elite households have suffered more from recent economic regress than 'intellectual' households. This result was not confirmed by our own estimates (see below).

### *Historical Well-being*

As the survey was carried out at just one point in time (May 1995), we have no direct indicators of the recent evolution in household budgets. However, we attempted to measure 'historical' well-being by means of the variable NIVSOC ('Niveau social'), which is an estimate of the quality of each household's habitat. This indicator of 'historical' well-being was suggested by Katzman [*1989*] and Ghysels and Martinez [*1995*], although the former did not 'summarise' the habitat-variables into one statistical measure.

In order to compare the two indicators of well-being, we transformed them into ordinal measures, assigning a rank to each household, from the poorest (1) to the richest (125). It follows that any discussion of enrichment or decline is always relative. Our data do not allow us to discuss dynamics in an absolute sense.

In Table 5, we compare the evolution in households' ranking per household type. The information is summarised in terms of the median (or second quartile), and the first and the third quartiles. Assuming that NIVSOC is a measure of 'historical' well-being, the table allows us to make the following observations.

First, the level of well-being of median survival households, intellectual-headed households and merchant households has declined. More detailed analysis of the causes of these dynamics will be provided later, but it can already be noted that the decline we observed in the intellectual-headed households confirms experiential knowledge, summed up in a popular *Kinois* expression: 'one doesn't have to be able to speak French to eat'. Indeed, it was to be expected that the collapse of the state would be accompanied by the collapse of white-collar professions. The decline of the survival and the merchant households has undoubtedly to do with the recent looting. One of the merchants we interviewed formulated this as follows: 'After the looting of 1991 and 1993, we have suffered very much. The conditions of living of the population are deteriorating, we have many difficulties with selling our products. Everything is stagnating. Impossible to plan for tomorrow'.

TABLE 5
COMPARISON OF HOUSEHOLDS RANKING ON TOTAL OUTLAYS (DEPTOT) AND QUALITY OF HABITAT (NIVSOC), PER HOUSEHOLD TYPE

| Household | 1st quartile | | median | | 3rd quartile | |
|---|---|---|---|---|---|---|
| type | NIVSOC | DEPTOT | NIVSOC | DEPTOT | NIVSOC | DEPTOT |
| Survival | 14 | 7 | 26 | 10 | 46 | 22 |
| Intellectual | 37 | 32 | 61 | 52 | 76 | 75 |
| Artisan | 20 | 30 | 40 | 57 | 76 | 86 |
| Merchant | 55 | 62 | 90 | 78 | 106 | 106 |
| élite | 102 | 83 | 112 | 109 | 119 | 117 |

Second, only the artisans have been able to increase their (relative) well-being. Note that, while there have always been exceptions, the median initial position is fairly comparable to that of the survival-households. One could formulate the tentative hypothesis that the enrichment of artisans is explained by the same phenomenon which caused the decline of the other categories: the looting of 1991–93 not only eliminated the artisans' 'official sector' competitors, it is also probable that some equipment was moved from the enterprises and the technical schools to the artisan workshops.[11]

## IV. MEASURING EXTENDED ENTITLEMENTS

The extent to which households' overall level of entitlements is determined by extended entitlements can, in our opinion, be measured either indirectly, by looking for indicators that measure a household's (members') insertion in an 'economy of affection', or directly, by measuring some of the direct advantages deriving from these extra-household solidarity networks.

A first direct indicator is the degree to which households incurred debts during the year preceding the interview. This measure can be considered as an indicator of extended entitlements because of the characteristics of such a debt. In the majority of cases, families contracted only limited loans (most less than $100) and for a very short duration (not more than one year). Moreover, all loans were contracted without charging any interest, sometimes even without conversion into dollars. The creditor thus loses out, especially in a period of high inflation. Furthermore, loans were not secured from the bank but from friends, employers, merchants, or (in a minority of cases) a member of the extended family. Taken together, we can infer from this that access to loans is a good indicator of 'extended entitlements', as defined in Section II of our study.

TABLE 6
EXTENDED ENTITLEMENTS

| Household type | % of indebted households | % of households where health outlays are financed by | | |
|---|---|---|---|---|
| | | members | employer | gifts |
| Survival | 29 | 83 | 8 | 8 |
| Intellectual | 62 | 61 | 18 | 21 |
| Artisan | 19 | 87 | 6 | 6 |
| Merchant | 20 | 91 | 9 | 0 |
| Elite | 11 | 71 | 29 | 0 |

In Table 6, we differentiate the proportion of indebted households per household type. One can clearly observe that the majority of intellectual households are indebted. While artisan households' revenues are only slightly higher, the proportion of indebted artisan-headed households is comparable to that of the merchant and the elite households. Hence, income level is a poor predictor of the degree of indebtedness. Note also that the majority of 'survival' households is virtually excluded from loans, despite the fact that they might be the ones most in need.

The rather exceptional position of the 'intellectual' households with respect to their social network is further confirmed by information on financing health care. Note the contrast with the artisan households who, like the survival households, are virtually on their own.[12] However, a more detailed analysis shows that the crucial difference between the upwardly mobile and the downwardly mobile artisan households could be explained by their differential insertion in a wider solidarity network. Whereas the upwardly mobile artisans enjoy considerable 'extended entitlements', the downwardly mobile artisans do not.

Taking indebtedness and health care financing as indicators of a household's extended entitlements,[13] we can conclude that it is precisely those artisan-headed households who are embedded in a solidarity network which have managed to enrich themselves.[14]

### *Measuring Embeddedness in an Economy of Affection*

A first measure of a household's insertion in wider solidarity networks – the infrastructure which produces extended entitlements – is the percentage of the household budget devoted to 'social gifts'. On the basis of this measure, one can claim that by far the most 'solidary' households are the ones headed by intellectuals, or persons belonging to the elite. These groups spend on average 7.4 per cent and 13.8 per cent of their incomes respectively on 'social outlays'. By contrast, these percentages are fairly negligible for the other groups. The elite's bent for 'benevolent behaviour' can probably be understood by referring again to Maton's concept of the 'paternalist system'. The high percentage for intellectuals seems more difficult to explain, unless as a remnant of their past status. 'Intellectuals' are still considered to be 'representatives' of the extended family in modern life and, once they have completed their studies (financed by the wider family) it is natural to ask them for a contribution in cases of birth, marriage or bereavement.

Household composition can be a second indirect measure of extended entitlements. To begin with, there is nothing unusual about some members of the nuclear family living in other households or for some members of the household not to belong to the nuclear family (parents and children). The interesting point is that this partial non-correspondence between the household and the nuclear family allows African households to adapt their composition according to economic circumstances.

According to Table 7, household composition varies widely between socio-professional groups. At one extreme, more than 70 per cent of households headed by intellectuals are extended families. In the case of merchant and elite

TABLE 7
SOCIAL INSERTION

| Household type | gifts as % of outlays | Family composition (% of households per type) | | |
|---|---|---|---|---|
| | | incomplete | nuclear | extended |
| Survival | 1 | 50 | 14 | 36 |
| Intellectual | 9 | 10 | 18 | 72 |
| Artisan | 3 | 19 | 45 | 36 |
| Merchant | 4 | 16 | 24 | 60 |
| Elite | 16 | 6 | 33 | 61 |

households, the high proportion of extended families may also be seen as an indicator of the family-based character of their income-earning strategies. In fact, the only cases where one can indeed speak of a 'family enterprise' can be found among merchant and elite households. The richest case in our sample, for instance, defines himself as a high-ranking public functionary. Officially, he works in an administrative office in the interior of the country. This job accounts for 12 per cent of his household's total income, whilst 55 per cent is derived from the diamond trade, an activity in which three household members (including the head himself) are involved.

At the other extreme, households headed by artisans are predominantly of the 'nuclear family' type. Incomplete families (where one of the parents is absent) comprise a minority, except in the 'survival'-type of households, where they predominate. Moreover, a closer look reveals that almost half of these 'incomplete families' are in fact not families at all but associations of friends or brothers. One respondent can serve as an example. In this case, the 'head' of the household (aged 27), lives with his younger brother and a friend. Their parents live elsewhere in Kinshasa. The two friends are both shoe-polishers, while the 'little brother' combines his studies (secondary school) with selling cigarettes (per unit) and sweets. They decided to live together in 1990, when the household head earned an income as a worker in a shoe-producing enterprise. His friend had a house, but could not survive on his own, as a shoe-shiner.

Taking direct and indirect measures of extended entitlements together, we interpret the data as follows.

First, the position of the intellectual-headed households is interesting in two respects. To begin with, the measure of indebtedness is an indicator of insertion in non-family networks; intellectuals seem to occupy an enviable position in such networks – a position which probably allows them to counteract the negative consequences of the implosion of the formal economy in which they are employed. Studying seems to have the interesting side effect of creating new solidarity networks, and/or the individual capability to create social networks. Further, the intellectual-headed households' position in more traditional networks seems much less enviable. Although they have severely suffered from the recent period of economic regress, they still assign a considerable percentage of their outlays to social gifts. Moreover, 90 per cent of intellectual-headed households are of the 'extended household' type. It seems that intellectuals have to 'pay' today for the extended-family solidarity they enjoyed at the time of their studies.

Second, Matthew's saying that 'he who gives shall be given' is not inappropriate to describe the logic of solidarity networks operating in the richer layers of society. We saw that the merchant and elite households' active involvement in the extended family (as measured by the proportion of extended families in their categories) corresponds well with the family-based character of their income-earning activities.

Third, it is also interesting to observe the position of artisan households: even if they could not count on their 'brothers', they were still able to withstand the current crisis, and even to better themselves *vis-à-vis* the intellectual-headed households. We attribute this process of enrichment to better economic opportunities for the artisans, given the elimination of their formal-sector competitors after the looting of 1991–93. This does not mean, however, that solidarity networks are of no significance for them; on the contrary, more detailed analysis shows that it is precisely the upwardly mobile group who are relatively more inserted in 'modern' as well as 'traditional' solidarity networks.

Finally, our data indicate that the poorer layers of Kinshasa, concentrated in the so-called 'survival'-group, are largely excluded from extra-household solidarity networks. The only strategy which keeps them alive is to restructure the household itself, even to the point where the founding family disintegrates altogether, and where households may be characterised as 'non-family associations'. Drèze and Sen's thesis that solidarity networks breakdown under severe strain is still relevant for this type of household.

More generally, it can be concluded that family restructuring, and social solidarity networks are not an automatic 'means' of coping with economic regress. Our analysis suggests that the way in which solidarity networks are activated varies between socio-professional classes (our 'household types'). In the case of survival households, the lack of access to wider solidarity networks obliges them to cope with regress by restructuring household composition. In extreme cases, households are simply falling apart. Though the artisans' access to wider solidarity networks is equally limited, they seem to have benefited from economic opportunities to better themselves. However, a more detailed analysis suggests that greater insertion in wider solidarity networks enables them more easily to 'realise' the opportunities offered by the economic opportunity structure. Intellectuals are 'by nature' more inserted in social solidarity networks but, as solidarity is a process of giving and taking, the final outcome is not straightforwardly positive.

Finally, the thesis that 'African solidarity' limits development would seem to be misplaced. First, our evidence shows that precisely the most 'modern' *Kinois* (the intellectuals) do in fact make use of 'traditional' solidarity – even reproducing it beyond the boundaries of the extended family. Second, there seems to be a positive correlation between the economic mobility of the artisan households (the only group to experience a relatively positive evolution during recent years) and their insertion in solidarity networks. Third, more detailed analysis shows that the actors' ability to reconstitute social structure in function of their economic needs varies with socio-professional position; in this sense, the above thesis neglects the heterogeneous character of African society.

## V. CONCLUSION

Our study aims to contribute to a better understanding of the phenomenon in which the citisens of Kinshasa seem to escape their fate as Zairians. Although a full explanation of this phenomenon is still wanting, our evidence illustrates a wider regularity, often noted by students of regress: namely, that regress, like progress, affects different occupational groups in different ways.

This thesis applies at a more detailed level as well. The findings of a field survey carried out in Kinshasa demonstrate that patterns of immiserisation and enrichment diverge widely between socio-professional groups. Our data suggest that, in the city, economic regress has above all been a process of implosion of the 'modern' sector. Households headed by 'intellectuals' were by and large the group most affected by recent regress. At the higher levels of modern society, however, the 'elite' groups have managed to maintain their position, mainly by using their visible activities as a cover for less 'legal' but highly lucrative activities. Another group that seems to have benefited relatively from the recent crisis is the group of artisan-headed households. We explain this by the fact that they benefited from the elimination of their formal sector competitors after the looting of 1991–93. Moreover, they were not heavily affected by the definitive collapse of the state and the plundering of state facilities because they had already been excluded from the formal economy before democracy arrived.

The central focus of this study is on the relation between well-being and access to solidarity networks. 'African solidarity' is often discussed in two ways. On the one hand, it allows – or helps – people to survive. On the other hand, it facilitates 'parasitism': if one member becomes rich, this has to be shared with others. A radical version of this is the thesis that African countries will never achieve economic development, since accumulation and investment are held back by pressures to share, in the name of African solidarity. A radical version of the former viewpoint would argue that it is African solidarity which explains the 'miracle of Kinshasa', the gap between overall regress in Zaïre and the relative stagnation of the capital.

Our data suggest a more differentiated view. Not only are different socio-professional groups embedded in extra-household networks to varying degrees, but these networks sometimes act as constraints and sometimes as opportunities. In the case of artisans and survival groups, solidarity networks can clearly be seen as opportunity structures. Likewise, merchant and elite households draw on solidarity networks to build family enterprises. The intellectuals are located in-between. As representatives of their family in a modern world, they carry the burden of traditional solidarity, whilst also receiving something in return.

Finally, it must be emphasised that these findings are only preliminary, being based on a pilot survey. We hope, however, that our conclusions will serve as interesting working hypotheses for further testing by more representative budget surveys and other types of research as well.

## NOTES

1. Note that the indicator of underweight children diverges somewhat from the general pattern, in the sense that it seems relatively more optimistic than the other two indicators. Our interpretation is that this has more to do with imprecision arising from the time-period covered, than with the insensitivity of the indicator itself (see below).
2. It should be mentioned that GDP calculations were revised in 1990 in order to include so-called 'informal activities' [*Banque Nationale du Zaïre, 1990*].
3. In the public sector (which accounts for one third of total employment), payment is very irregular. This can be explained by real budget problems but also by the fact that the persons, charged with paying the salaries, withhold them temporarily in order to speculate on the black dollar market.
4. Although Drèze and Sen [*1989: 74*] do suggest that 'the breakdown of social ties is a common feature of the advanced stages of famines, and ... in the early stages greater sociality may well be observed'.
5. This issue requires further discussion. According to North [*1990*], legality is meaningless if it is not perceived as legitimate. One could also make a further distinction between legitimate extended entitlements and illegitimate but informally enforced extended entitlements.
6. For example, the custom of collecting funds on the occasion of a funeral, birth or marriage. Another, less traditional example is the system of *tontines* (*likelemba* in Zaïre), which seems to be very popular in Sub Sahara Africa.
7. To understand processes within organisational hierarchies, 'one can view a choice opportunity as a garbage can into which various kinds of problems and solutions are dumped by participants as they are generated. The mix of garbage in a single can depends on the mix of cans available, on the labels attached to the alternative cans, on what garbage is currently being produced, and on the speed with which garbage is collected and removed from the scene' [*Cohen, March and Olsen, 1988: 296–7*].

8. This argument is based on the observation that there is an often neglected trade-off between a degree of confidence between interviewer and interviewee, a necessary condition to obtain trustworthy answers, and the requirement to maintain confidentiality, which implies that the interviewer does not know the respondent. We opted to ignore (partly) the latter in favour of the former requirement.
9. Some cases were not taken into account precisely because interviewees did not distinguish between their personal outlays and the outlays of their household.
10. The poverty-line was calculated by the World Bank [*1990*] as $1, the dollar being valued at its 1985 purchasing power. Assuming an average annual inflation rate in the United states of 3 per cent during the period 1985-1995, $260 (current dollars) is roughly equivalent to $340 (1985 dollars).
11. This was neither confirmed nor contested by our interviews. There are, however, some 'known' cases. The question remains whether this (latent) redistributive function of the looting had a significant impact, measurable at the aggregate level.
12. Another surprising fact is that approximately 30 per cent of elite health care expenses is financed by the employer; the famous 'Matthew effect' [*Deleeck, 1979*] is apparently also at work in this type of social security!
13. Social networks are evidently (re)activated for other reasons. One of the interviewees, a white-collar employee in an oil-company, gives an example: 'I have a friend who is relatively well placed, who is the author [*sic*] of at least 85 per cent of the gifts [I spent on health care, clothing and even social outlays]. From time to time, I help him with one of his activities.'
14. Another, secondary, observation from Table 6 is that a proportion of the downwardly mobile artisan households were only part-time artisans, as some of them can turn to their (family member's) employers for health care.

## REFERENCES


Arbyn, M., Dedeurwaerder, M., Miakala, M., Bikangi, M. and M. Boelaert, 1995, 'Surveillance de l'état nutritionnel de la population de Kinshasa, Zaïre (1991–1994)', in *Ann. Soc. Belge Med. Trop.*, No.75, pp.115–24.

Barro, R.J. and J.-W. Lee, 1994, 'Losers and Winners in Economic Growth', in World Bank, *Proceedings of the World Bank Conference on Development Economics*, Washington, DC: IBRD, pp.267–98.

Banque Nationale du Zaïre, 1990, *Rapport Annuel 1990*, Kinshasa.

Braeckman, C., 1991, 'Le Zaïre au-delà des statistiques', in G. De Villers (ed.), *Zaïre 1990–1991: faits et dits de la société d'après le regard de la presse*, Brusells: CEDAF, pp.50–52.

Cohen, M.D., March, J.G. and J.P. Olsen, 1988, 'A Garbage Can Model of Organisational Choice', in James G. March, *Decisions and Organisations*, Oxford: Basil Blackwell, pp.294–334.

Cour, J.-M., 1989, 'The Unrecorded Economy of Zaïre and its Contribution to the Real Economy (Second Draft Report).

Cukierman, A., 1992, *Central Bank Strategy, Credibility and Independence: Theory and Evidence*, Cambridge, MA and London: MIT Press.

De Herdt, T., 1995, 'Politique Monétaire et Informalisation de l'Economie Zaïroise', paper presented to the colloquium, *le Secteur Informel*, Kinshasa, 24–26 May 1995.

De Herdt, T. and S. Marysse, 1996a, *L'économie informelle au Zaïre, survie et pauvreté dans la période de transition*, Brussels and Paris: CEDAF/ L'Harmattan.

De Herdt, T. and S. Marysse, 1996b, 'La réinvention du marché par le bas et la fin du monopole féminin dans le cambisme à Kinshasa', paper presented to the international colloquium on *L'Argent, feuille morte?*, Louvain, 21–22 June.

Deleeck, H., 1979, 'L'Effet Mathieu', in *Droit Social*, No.11, Nov., pp.375–84.

Drèze, J. and A. Sen, 1989, *Hunger and Public Action*. Oxford: Clarendon Press.

Ghysels, J. and T. Martinez, 1995, 'El combate contra la pobreza: un factor determinante para el desarrollo', draft, Nicaragua: UCA-Nitlapan.

Houyoux, J., Kinavwuidi Niwembo and Okito Onya, 1986, *Budgets des ménages, Kinshasa 1986* Kinshasa-Brussels: BEAU/ICHEC.

Hyden, G., 1983, *No Shortcuts to Progress: African Development Management in Perspective*, London: James Currey.

Katzman, R., 1989, 'La heterogeneidad de la pobreza. El caso de Montevideo', *Revista CEPAL*, No.37.

Leclerq, H., 1992, 'L'économie populaire informelle de Kinshasa: approche macro-économique', in G. De Villers (ed.), *Economie populaire et phénomènes informels au Zaïre et en Afrique*, Cahiers du CEDAF Nos.3/4, pp.139–60.

Lemarchand, R., 1988, 'The State, the Parallel Economy and the Changing Structure of Patronage Systems', in N. Chazan and D. Rotschild (eds.), *The Precarious Balance: State and Society in Africa*, Boulder, CO and London: Westview Press.

MacGaffey, J., 1996, '"On se débrouille": The International Trade of Zaïre's Second Economy', paper presented at the seminar *L'argent: feuille morte?*, Leuven, 21–22 June.

MacGaffey, J. (ed.), 1991, *The Real Economy of Zaïre: The Contribution of Smuggling and other Unofficial Activities to National Wealth*, London: James Currey.

Maton, J., 1993, 'Zaïre: Balance of Payments Problems 1992–3, Forthcoming Import Problems, Impact of Falling Exports on the Level of Commercialised GDP and Consumption', unpublished mimeo, University of Ghent.

Maton, J., 1992, 'How do the Poor in Kinshasa Survive: Miracle, Enigma or Black Box?', unpublished mimeo, University of Ghent.

North, D.C., 1990, *Institutions, Institutional Change and Economic Performance*, Cambridge: Cambridge University Press.

Peemans, J.-P., 1982, 'Les nouvelles formes de la dépendance économique', paper presented at the Russell Tribunal, Rotterdam.

Peemans, J.-P., 1989, 'Le Zaïre sous le régime Mobutu', in CNCD, *Pile et face; bilan de la coopération belgo-zaïroise*, Brussels: La revue Nouvelle/CNCD, pp.22–58.

Sachs, J.D. and F. Larraín, 1993, *Macro-economics in the Global Economy*, New York: Harvester Wheatsheaf.

Sen, A.K., 1981, *Poverty and Famines: An Essay on Entitlement and Deprivation*, Oxford: Clarendon Press.

Sen, A.K., 1984, *Resources, Values and Development*, Oxford: Basil Blackwell.

Sen, A.K., 1985, *Commodities and Capabilities*, Oxford: Oxford University Press.

Sen, A.K., 1994, 'Economic Regress: Concepts and Features', in World Bank, *Proceedings of the World Bank Annual Conference on Development Economics*, Oxford: Oxford University Press for World Bank, pp.315–33.

UNDP, 1996, *Human Development Report*, New York: Oxford University Press.

Willame, J.-C., 1986, *L'épopée d'Inga; chronique d'une prédation industrielle*, Paris: L'Harmattan.

World Bank, 1990, *World Development Report, Poverty Study*, Oxford: Oxford University Press for World Bank.

Yav Karl Yav, 1995, 'L'espace monétaire kasaïen', in *Zaïre-Afrique*, April, Kinshasa: CEPAS.

# Recuperation in the Peruvian Andes

FIONA WILSON

*Violent conflict is highly damaging for human security and the entire fabric of regional society. Individuals and groups confront situations that are unpredictable, threatening and impoverishing in material and cultural terms, and many communities are dislocated and de-territorialised. But conflict and instability do not in themselves constitute useful points of departure for the analysis of post-conflict situations. In this contribution I seek to highlight which actors, social relations and constellations of power come to prominence in the aftermath of violent conflict; examine the tensions arising from the different meanings given to 'recuperation'; and investigate the spatial practice of social actors taking part in processes of recuperation. This contribution builds on an ongoing fieldwork study in a province of the Peruvian Central Andes.*

## INTRODUCTION

Re-conciliation, re-cuperation and re-construction are terms commonly used to describe processes taking place after violent conflict. The prefix in each case stresses the idea that social life goes back roughly to what it was before. The terms further suggest a number of positive characteristics: state intervention, participation by the people, a sharing of values, resumption of normality and re-appearance of institutions guaranteeing peace, law and order, democracy and a measure of prosperity. The terms are value-laden and highly politicised, for the roots, practices and after-effects of conflict are brushed aside and assumed to leave little discernible trace on social relations or the social imagination. Although we can continue to use such terms as a kind of short-hand, they need to be explored in much greater detail. It is important to understand more about the different kinds of 'peacetime' conflicts that affect social organisation in regions which have suffered violent conflict, and acknowledge that new constellations of power come to the fore and govern who sets the agenda and who can be pressed into following the new rules of the game.

---

Fiona Wilson, Centre for Development Research, Copenhagen, Denmark.

This article focuses on the situation in the Central Andes of Peru in the aftermath of the war waged by *Sendero Luminoso* (the Shining Path), a violent Maoist political movement that took up armed struggle against the state in 1980. Its point of departure is the analysis of a particular event, an 'act of recuperation', which took place on the borders of a region that had been totally abandoned during the later years of violence. Brought together by the 'act of recuperation' were several groups of social actors: representatives of the peasant communities that had been displaced and de-territorialised; members of adjacent settlements and communities that had been harassed but not abandoned; and a number of officials, local leaders, most of whom held posts in local government. On the sidelines were the two earlier protagonists, *Sendero Luminoso* and the army; and a foreign researcher.

When participating in the event, I had accepted that it largely concerned a practical matter: how to organise and implement the construction of a short stretch of road that might eventually link the abandoned region to the nearest transitable road. But on becoming more familiar with the social context of the recuperation, the encounter took on a different character. It had been given a performative character; important messages were being given, received and acted upon by different individuals and groups. In retrospect, the event appeared to encapsulate and partially reveal certain aspects of the social relations and struggles occurring at the borders of the state; relations and struggles which in everyday life were more fragmented and submerged.

The article begins with a reconstructed situational analysis of the 'act of recuperation'. Then concepts of social interface, everyday forms of state formation, and production of space will be introduced in order to reflect on the ambivalent position of the officials; the different meanings attached to recuperation; and the fraught situation and choices facing displaced people.

## RECUPERATING A REGION

Cayash was a sparsely populated region of some 30,000 square hectares in the Central Andes. It is a highland zone of around 3,300 metres which borders the steep drop down to the tropical lowlands to the east. The region lies on the northern perimeter of the province of Tarma. Before the war some 4,000 people lived in the region's six land-holding communities, all of which had been legally recognised as peasant communities. Cayash was invaded by two battalions of *Sendero* troops in 1990 and subsequently made one of their support bases (*bases de apoyo*). From then on, Cayashinos were forbidden to leave. The region was 'liberated' by the military in 1993, and the people fled from the destruction and retribution exacted by the army. Displaced Cayashinos lived in poverty either with kinsmen in one rural community near Tarma town, or in the squalid *barrios* surrounding the towns of Tarma, La

Oroya, Huancayo and Lima.

One Sunday in October 1994, a mini-bus left the provincial capital, Tarma town, before dawn transporting a group of local government and community representatives to Pullao Tingo, a village to the north of the Cayash region and some 4 hours' drive from Tarma. Pullao Tingo was the road point nearest to Cayash; the village lay at the highland end of an ancient route way that led down the Ulcumayo river to the tropical lowlands. At Pullao Tingo various mule-tracks converged and a small trading post had grown up. Before the war, however, most Cayashinos had more frequently travelled on foot a much longer route, of more than 50 kms, south to the regional market and provincial capital of Tarma.

Pullao Tingo, abandoned in 1992, was being re-populated in late 1994. A couple of shops now sold beer, soft drinks, cigarettes, candles, matches, salt and tins of tuna fish. The truck traders had returned bringing in industrially-made clothing and plastic goods to exchange for potatoes, especially the prized *papas de color*, grown in the surrounding communities. Families of *campesinos* with richly caparisoned mules came and left. Most houses were still empty and bore signs of *Sendero*'s recent occupation: crude red graffiti threatened 'death to informers' and warned that 'a thousand eyes and ears' watched and listened.

An hour away up the road was a military post where soldiers controlled movement in and out of the zone. All vehicles were stopped and travellers questioned. The officer in charge had warned the occupants of the mini-bus that we travelled at our own risk, and suggested dryly that we should report on any subversive activity – if we came back.

For the officials and representatives of the abandoned communities, this was closest they had come to Cayash since the military take-over. The ostensible purpose of the visit was to organise the surveying of a stretch of road and the provision of communal labour to extend the track by four kilometres to an abandoned hamlet, Anturchay. This, the officials claimed, was the first stage in the construction of a motor road to serve the Cayash communities. Widening the section of mule-track that ran alongside the Ulcumayo river posed no great engineering problem, but constructing the remaining 21 kilometres over a massive range of mountains was a much more daunting prospect.

The officials making the journey included a *Regidor* (elected office-bearer) of the Tarma Provincial Council; the Mayor of San Pedro de Cajas, the district within whose jurisdiction the Cayash communities lay; the Mayor of Cayash; a young Peruvian agronomist from a Catholic NGO; and a transport economist from Tarma's municipal authority. These men were all young, had a background as school teachers and distinguished themselves from the *campesinos* by wearing spotless white shirts and sun-glasses. They were joined by a number of older men, representatives of three Cayash communities who were living in exile in Tarma town; and myself, the only woman in the group. I had been invited by the Mayor of Cayash at the last minute. A foreign researcher had symbolic as well as potentially practical value in that she represented the world outside, the possibility of global links, and the chance of attracting a foreign NGO. However, I do not believe my presence altered the event to any extent and I was not asked to take an active part in the formal proceedings. The main expectation was that I might pay for the beer – which I did.

After arriving at Pullao Tingo, the group of officials and representatives paced and chain surveyed the route to Anturchay and the transport economist took note of the places where dynamite would be needed to blast rock outcrops. Anturchay's ruined school was inspected and commented upon at length. By the time the group returned, some 30 *campesinos* from the neighbouring communities (which had not been abandoned) waited to attend a meeting called by the officials to organise the road work. The atmosphere was tense and formal; we learnt later that a few thought *Sendero* had called the meeting. Three ill-clad youths observed the gathering from a distance, everybody knew they were *Sendero* informers. People remained silent and uncertain; nobody asked questions nor volunteered information. Nobody appeared enthusiastic about the idea of contributing voluntary labour to construct a road to Cayash.

Declamatory speeches were delivered by the *Regidor* and Mayors. Each spoke emotionally of the damage done during the subversion and pledged his support for reconstruction, though there were variations in tone and content. They agreed that the provision of a road had to be given top priority so that people could return to live in Cayash. The whole region would progress once there were roads. But when mention was made of the state, local leaders revealed their different political positions. According to the most radical, people must lend a hand as the government would not take action unless pressed to do so. These were communities neglected and forgotten by all governments; worse, they had been despised by Peru's aristocratic state. But the state had a moral obligation to assist people so they could go home joyfully. The state should be compelled to provide the communities with *obras* (public works) and services. The people should not continue to suffer, and live in misery and poverty. They should demand support from the authorities, it was their right, but they should never go down on bended knee to beg for help. The presence of a foreigner was noted with satisfaction as indicating a possibility of future foreign aid.

The *Regidor* from Tarma promised to send road-levelling equipment from Tarma town. He cajoled the Mayor of San Pedro into agreeing to provide drums of fuel and promised to seek food rations from PRONAA, the

Government's food-for-work programme. Then with great difficulty, representatives were elected from each community. These men were asked to organise the contributions to the *faena* (voluntary labour project). Their names were carefully written down in the *Libro de Actas* (official minute book) of Cayash. A road committee was inaugurated with the *Regidor* as its President and members, standing to military attention, were formally sworn in.

Later over beers and a meal, the embarrassed NGO agronomist told the *campesinos* that he had been unable to bring the sacks of seed potatoes they had expected but gave them a new delivery date. This was part of a rotating credit scheme organised by the NGO. The Mayor of Cayash informed the assembled *campesinos* in more conversational tones of the progress made in the re-organisation of the Cayash communities and their plans for re-settling their lands. But the atmosphere darkened when the *Sendero* youths edged closer and I was escorted away to the safety of a shop.

In early November 1994, the heavy road-levelling equipment made the long, expensive journey from Tarma to Pullao Tingo; its deployment to a place so far from home ruptured relations between the *Regidor* and the Tarma Mayor. Some 350 *comuneros* with picks and shovels gathered for the 3-day *faena*. The bulk of the labour was supplied by Cayashinos who had financed their own transport or walked from Tarma town. Families registered as members of Cayash's de-territorialised communities had to pay a cash sum if they did not participate in the *faena*; this money went towards paying for food and fuel. Women came with food and cooking pots, which was just as well as the food rations promised by PRONAA's regional director in Huancayo never materialised. Nor did the fuel drums arrive from San Pedro. The military, however, did insist on participating. The *Regidor* was provided with an escort of 6 armed soldiers who accompanied his every move. Tarma's television station sent a reporter to film the work and interview participants; but the half serious plans of sending a helicopter to video the *faena* from the air never got off the ground.

The road was duly extended, but Pullao Tingo remains the local trading point and truck destination. The new stretch of road is of no practical use, but that perhaps was never the main point of the exercise.

## CONTESTS OF POWER AT THE BORDERS OF THE STATE

Thinking about the encounter raises questions of how one might analyse the differences in power/knowledge, cultural interpretation and forms of organisation distinguishing the different groups. While some of the social actors represented rival local interests (as seen in the underlying competition between neighbouring peasant groups), others belonged to different social fields and authority levels within regional society (as seen in the officials' desire to take command over peasant labour). This suggests that one might begin by discussing the extent and ways in which local officials were acting as representatives of local government or the state during this encounter.

In this context, the concept of social interface can be usefully employed to distinguish social actors. According to Long [*1989: 2*], a social interface has a dynamic, emergent character and can be defined as 'a critical point of intersection or linkage between different social systems, fields or levels of social order where structural discontinuities, based upon differences of normative value and social interest, are most likely to be found'. The concept helps highlight what takes place in face-to-face encounters between individuals or units, differentiated in terms of power and resources, and demonstrates 'the interplay and mutual determinations of so-called "external" and "local-level" processes' [*Long, 1989: 5*]. The idea of social interface has helped analysis of developmentalist interventions by bureaucrats in peasant societies, not least in showing what goes wrong and why each side fails to appreciate or understand the other.

When describing the 'act of recuperation', the officials visiting Pullao Tingo have been given various labels, being also called local leaders and local government representatives. This reflects the underlying ambiguity as to their appropriate categorisation. Though holding office, they were not bureaucrats, nor did they clearly espouse the interests and views of the state. One cannot therefore make an a priori assumption that they in some abstract sense represented a different structural level, let alone the state. As Drinkwater [*1992: 370–71*] has commented in his critique of the social interface concept, problems arise when interfaces are considered both 'junctions where "different levels of social order" (the local and the larger-scale) intersect' as well as face-to-face encounters where '"the broader structural context" has been brought down to representative individuals or units; it has become local and tangible'.

The concept of social interface is insufficient. One needs to look more closely at the 'internal' interfaces of the officials as social actors. A relevant theoretical debate here concerns the exploration of everyday forms of state formation, a line of approach that has been developed recently in relation to the history of Mexico [*Gilbert and Nugent, 1994*]. This owes much to E.P. Thompson's analysis of the contested nature of power in British history and Foucault's understandings of power and governance. The approach seeks to unearth what a state looks like and claims to be when seen from the vantage point of those who are remote, socially and/or geographically, from the seat of state power. Underlying this view of the complexity of the relations between ruling and subaltern classes, between state and popular culture, is a re-reading of the concept of hegemony. As Roseberry has proposed, we can

> use the concept not to understand consent but to understand struggle; the ways in which the words, images, symbols, forms, organisations,

> institutions, and movements used by subordinate populations to talk about, understand, confront, accommodate themselves to, or resist their domination are shaped by the process of domination itself. What hegemony constructs, then, is not a shared ideology but a common material and meaningful framework for living through, talking about, and acting upon social orders characterised by domination [*Roseberry, 1994: 360–61*].

Enquiry into hegemony and how the state makes its presence felt in everyday life leads to two sets of questions. First, one can ask who can be seen as representing the state in particular historical conjunctures; why and how do people act for or take a position broadly in line with the state? In the distant provinces, to what extent can a state come into being through representatives (governors, military, police, ministry officials), employees (teachers, health workers) and surrogates or substitutes (from oligarch to decentralised governing bodies)? Second, what kind of regime of ruling, state-people relations, comes into play? To what extent do people's actions confirm and legitimise the state, or to what extent do they undermine state power and authority? How are the various forms and expressions of state presence linked with popular concepts of culture, progress and modernity?

Concepts of social interface and everyday state formation lead us directly to the pivotal position of the officials in the Cayash borderlands. As shown by the 'act of recuperation', the power of the officials lay in their capacity to provide support and patronage, and this rested on their personal abilities to plot themselves into the action often in a mixture of roles: as representatives of the state, as spokesmen for the people, and as mediators between the two.

Although officials in their speeches at Pullao Tingo emphasised their wish to serve and represent the people, they clearly sought to take command over the community leaders and deploy community labour. In the road project, the abilities of officials to summon up resources – to be seen as useful patrons – had met with some success. Machinery, labour and a foreign witness had been delivered; but the failure of PRONAA, the state's food-for-work organisation, to send supplies revealed a point of weakness in leaders' relations with the state. Local government officials could not count on badgering resources out of state entities.

The ambiguity and possible duplicity of local government officials was not lost on the military. The *Regidor*'s armed escort during the *faena* was a visible reminder of state presence and power of surveillance and control under the guise of protection. However, the awkward young soldiers provided a ludicrous spectacle. Their uniforms and arms could not protect them from undercurrents of ribaldry and ridicule, played upon to great effect by the quick-witted *Regidor*. The 'act of recuperation' served partly to undermine the power of the military so that memories of military brutality could be buried through the weapon of laughter.

Local officials slipped between representing and acting on behalf of local government and being popular leaders. Formality, declamatory speech, respect for procedure, strict attention to bureaucratic detail signalled their occupation of official roles. But the content of some of the speeches and their way of being outside the formal proceedings indicated how these men also prided themselves on being popular leaders. One speech in particular could be interpreted as being in opposition to the Fujimori government, even anti-state in its sentiments. Its discourse betrayed signs of the confrontational Marxism characteristic of university milieux in the 1970s and 1980s and was clearly linked to *Sendero* thinking. In post conflict situations, positions in local government could be filled by those with a revolutionary past.

According to local terminology, the officials/leaders gathered at Pullao Tingo were *cholos*, which as Mayer [*1991*] notes is a descriptive term, insulting or endearing, ascribed to people of Andean cultural background who are rapidly trying to acculturate. They were school teachers, men of humble background, *paisanos* (fellow countrymen) whose families had originated in these same communities. They were on home ground, sons of the soil. This came through in persons known, experiences shared and stories told during the long journey to and from Tarma. Though leaders belonged to rival political parties, conviviality underscored verbal jousting. These men represented a new type of leader, one who broke with previous tradition and stereotypes.

The writings of earlier historians and anthropologists, and the much-cited novels of José María Arguedas, emphasise how Andean society had long been dominated by mestizos, known as *mistis*. According to Arguedas

> Between 'mistis' and Indians there is no communication. The former speak Spanish, the latter Quechua. Their customs are different: they despise each other. The only contact which exists is through the violence exercised by the 'misti': private, daily violence which can count on support from the police and authorities (cited in Flores [*1986: 290*]).

Carlos Iván Degregori [*1991: 240*] makes a similar point: after independence from Spain, 'the category of "Indian" was fused with that of "poor campesino" and the "mistis" took over the role of intermediaries who controlled and often blocked communication between the world of the Indians and that of modernity'.

In the Andean region, agrarian reform (in the 1970s) followed by war led to an exodus of white and mestizo property-owning families from towns like Tarma; and what is commonly referred to as a 'power vacuum' was created. That is one side of the picture. The other is that a new class of local leaders was emerging; men of peasant background who had won a higher education in the expanding universities, technical and teacher training colleges. They had differentiated histories in political and religious movements and each had managed somehow to survive the dangers of the *Sendero* years. They are now the predominant group in local politics, seeking to control the interstices of power. An overriding aim is to bring modernity to the people and actively intervene in the communication between Andean and outside worlds. Unlike previous generations of mestizo leaders, the power of the new *cholo* leaders lies in facilitating this contact, not in blocking it.

The quest for modernity on the part of local leaders is reflected in the importance they attached to *obras* (public works). Indeed, the Independence party to which the *Regidor* belonged, adopted as its slogan for Tarma's municipal elections in November 1995: *obras y más obras* (works and more works). Much had been made of the preparation and execution of the road works at Pullao Tingo; it had indeed been a complicated organisational feat. But extending the road was not necessarily considered by the *campesinos* as their most pressing need. A more important resource for daily survival had been the seed potatoes which had been promised but not delivered by the NGO. Arguably, this was the prime reason why non-Cayashinos had come to Pullao Tingo; it had not been to offer voluntary labour. But the NGO agronomist was not in a position of power and had been out-manoeuvred by the others.

An important symbol of the road project was its interim destination, the abandoned school at Anturchay. The leaders thought that a road would bring the school to life again. The striving for modernity has been discussed most perceptively in recent years in Peru in relation to the rural school. Ansion [*1989: 41*] has argued: 'in the actual process of the peasantry's integration in national society the school is seen as a weapon which must be conquered'. Degregori notes how

> schools in the Andean communities are somewhat like a 'black box', a technological package-deal imported from outside and the contents of which are unknown with any precision ... it is a kind of capsule of modernity that is placed in the main square where the children may learn the secret mechanisms that will allow them to get on in today's world, especially the urban world [*Degregori, 1991: 240–41*].

In the provision of roads and schools, the aspirations of local leaders appear to coincide with the poverty alleviation policies now sponsored by the Fujimori government. The central government donates materials for school buildings (often later inaugurated personally by Fujimori) and channels funds for rural roads and *obras* (including bridges, small irrigation works, drinking water, sewage) through FONCODES, the well-funded body run from the Ministry of the Presidency. Peru is a highly centralist state, and local government budgets are small. Access to government funds is largely a political question; they are channelled to provinces, districts and communities that support the government. Hence, although they may be politically in opposition, it is important for local leaders to manoeuvre themselves into a position where they can get access to and manage funds emanating from central government.

## SPACE, TERRITORY AND HUMAN SECURITY

The territoriality of conflict and recuperation suggests that an analysis of space in particular can lead to a better understanding of processes of social organisation and the unfolding of power relations. Though done without great pomp or ceremony, pacing, measuring and making the road was a performance in which officials and community representatives signified that they took possession and exerted dominion once again over a territory previously lost. The performative nature was underlined by the presence of a TV reporter and camera during the *faena*.

On the face of it, both officials and *campesinos* appeared to be engaged in the same 'act of recuperation'. But concepts of social interface, and everyday forms of state formation suggest that this could not be the case. The social relations and social imagination, experiences and aspirations of displaced *campesinos* were neither felt nor shared by the officials. One way to depict the contrasting worlds to which the two groups belonged is to focus on their differential representations and practices with respect to the production of space.

Lefebvre has argued that every society produces space, its own space, and this finds expression in a conceptual triad. There is spatial practice 'which embraces production and reproduction, and the particular locations and spatial sets characteristic of each social formation' [*Lefebvre, 1991: 33*]. There are representations of space or 'conceptualised space, the space of scientists, planners, urbanists, technocratic subdividers and social engineers ... all of whom identify what is lived and what is perceived with what is conceived' [*ibid.: 38*]. And there are representational spaces 'embodying complex symbolisms, sometimes coded, sometimes not, linked to the clandestine or underground side of life' [*ibid.: 33*].

One can argue that the 'act of recuperation' was a fusion of two separate symbolic acts with respect to space that were rooted in the contrasting spatial practices, representations of space and understandings as to the way space embodied complex symbols held on the one hand by the leading officials and on the other by displaced Cayashinos. These two views will be explored in turn.

In terms of spatial practice, the local leaders are constantly on the move; they travel frequently within the province and also to the regional capital,

Huancayo and to Lima. Much attention is paid to keeping their spatially diffuse social networks functioning. They had come to Pullao Tingo in their capacity as representatives of local government. The visit by so large a number of officials was a declaration that the abandoned region was now being brought within the sphere of government. The information gathered on the borderlands would not remain in the locality but be lodged with the provincial government in distant Tarma. According to the leaders' vision, territory was conceived as abstract, technical space, space over which they might take control. This was space that could be re-absorbed into the province and governed by its institutions.

The leaders were not alone in holding an abstract conception of space. So too had *Sendero* and the military. Though whether it was *Sendero*, the military or the state which considered it dominated the region carried profound implications and consequences for the population in terms of their security.

Under *Sendero*, Cayash had been made a space of 'total domination'. As a 'support base', the party had tried to control all productive, social and political activities. *Sendero* troops had constantly pressed for food and recruits; people's movements were constantly watched and restricted; school teachers had been directed as to what they could teach; and *comités populares* (people's committees) had replaced the communal organisation. Though apparently self sufficient and with plentiful land, the Cayashinos' way of life (as in so many parts of the Andes) had depended on exchange relations with people living in other ecological zones. After *Sendero*'s occupation, trading circuits broke down: there were potatoes but no maize.

Under *Sendero*, Cayash community leaders and owners of the largest numbers of animals, as well as suspected rustlers, crooked traders and adulterers, had most to fear from the *Sendero* cadres who in their guise of exterminating angels imposed morality through punishment and execution. More than 20 people, including a Mayor of Cayash, had been executed, most on the pretext of being informers and of trying to alert the military to *Sendero*'s presence.

When the military came in, those who had not managed to escape before took the chance to do so. The military did not only flush out the *Sendero* troops, but together with the *ronda campesina* (peasant militia) from the neighbouring district of Huasahuasi to the south, they removed livestock and ransacked houses. Huasahuasi district then declared Cayash an empty land which could be appropriated legally by the district authorities. Many, especially the young, were imprisoned and tortured by the military on the grounds of being subversives; some were 'disappeared'. The threats spurred the de-territorialised, de-moralised Cayashinos to organise, though people were very frightened and many continued to live in hiding. Since the Cayashinos had been branded collectively as subversives, and many had their identity papers (the precious *libreta electoral*) confiscated by *Sendero*, their first struggle was to clear their name and have their rights as citizens restored.

The threat to the Cayashinos' rights to land had been serious. There was a general feeling in Tarma that the population should be punished for collaborating with the enemy. Furthermore, the communities did not actually possess their land titles, the legal proof of their existence. These had been retained by the old district capital of Yanec (now a shadow of its former self) and decades of petitioning had failed to secure their release. The lack of documentation weakened their position in the fight against the densely populated, influential district of Huasahuasi. Thus people were pressed into recovering their land rights through taking action.

The Cayashinos who came to Pullao Tingo, both to walk the road and work in the *faena*, were participating in a different 'act of recuperation'. It was both a home-coming and a signal to the communities on the northern perimeter as well as to the district of Huasahausi, now a greater threat than the delinquent remnants of *Sendero*, that despite temporary abandonment, the lands were not unoccupied. Furthermore, they showed that they could count on the support of officials and authorities in the defence of their rights.

This vision of recuperation had nothing to do with abstract or technical space. It rested on the symbolic act of processing, an ancient practice whereby territorial conflicts between rival communities are brought to a close through a peace-bringing procession at the boundaries of the disputed land in the presence of an authority, usually the *Juez de Tierras* (land judge) from Tarma. Processing is a spatial practice which seeks to inscribe in local social memory a new state of play with respect to rights, meanings and boundaries. It rests on an understanding of place as a lived environment in which history is recorded and remembered through the geographical features of a landscape. As Fentress and Wickham [*1992: 113*] comment, this is one of the very few cross-cultural markers of peasant memory: 'the constantly recurring importance of local geography as a structure for remembrance: hills, caves, farmhouses, and fields all carry their memories for peasants to talk about'.

In terms of the identity and emotional security of the displaced Cayashinos, their 'act of recuperation' was clearly important. But not all have – or will – return. Up to May 1996, only some 50 families have gone back to live in the region; they were neither the most impoverished nor the most prosperous. Yet in the case of the largest of the six communities, more than 400 families have registered as members. For those living in exile, displacement has altered profoundly their spatial practice and way of perceiving space.

In Tarma town, poor *desplazados* manage just about to survive when the whole family earns a little cash in precarious (so-called informal) urban jobs. Most of the men find work as porters in the market (with the ubiquitous *tricicletas*); others work in restaurants and bakeries, as night watchmen and as agricultural and building labourers. Women work in domestic service and as washer-women; in restaurants; and some sell a few potatoes or vegetables in the market. Children try to sell minute quantities of sweets, ice lollies and bread in the streets; work as shoe-shine boys or, according to their own parents, are delinquents.

In contrast, a small group of better off exiles have opened small businesses, restaurants in particular, and may provide work for indigent kinsmen. These are wealthier families, who had often held posts in the communal organisations and who earlier had sent their children to study at secondary school in Tarma. The image of the remote, isolated peasant community, of *Peru olvidado* ('forgotten Peru') was a myth long before the *Sendero* years. Sending sons and daughters to be educated and find work in the towns had been an important way to colonise new resource niches and migrants maintained enduring contacts with home [*Golte and Adams, 1987; Smith, 1989*].

Several reasons can be put forward to explain why the majority of families have opted not to return to Cayash. Their choice often reflects their assessment of security, both present and future. The most frequently stated reason for not returning is the family's aspiration to give children a better education. This expresses both concern with quality of schooling and their experiences during the *Sendero* years when teachers proselytised and recruited their children. To have educated children, who will not be reduced to the life of *campesinos*, is a strategy by which families hope to gain a greater measure of economic security in future.

A second reason for remaining in Tarma, though not usually stated directly, is the continued tension and fear of feuds and reprisals. This is a question of physical security. While most had resisted *Sendero*, some are thought to have collaborated. Amongst the imprisoned, those who managed to get away from the anti-terrorist branch of the military, were often suspected of having named names in order to win their freedom. Some now refuse to acknowledge their Cayashino origins and seek the greater anonymity only possible in the town; that too is an important aspect of human security in the aftermath of violence.

Then, there is the weighing up of feelings: a distaste of the concrete, noise, dirt and crime of the town as against the gripping fear and pain of going back to ruined homes and to the hard, relentless work and discomfort of living in the countryside. Yet over time, memories of the harshness of life in Cayash is receding; it is fast becoming a representational space: a place of memory, nostalgia and utopia.

## BY WAY OF CONCLUSION

One can suggest that in post conflict situations at the borders of the state, power relations may be revealed in striking ways. The discussion has suggested that the new class of local leaders that has emerged during and after the war are keenly interested in providing the links between the indigenous peasantry and the outside world. It was they who took the initiative and mediated the recuperation of Cayash. Their actions are shaped both by the need to intercept and manage the funds and resources emanating from the central state and by the need to present themselves as popular leaders. In this latter capacity they may be voted into local government office, and may directly confront or oppose the state.

But despite the ambivalent relations between local leaders and representatives of the central state, they share a belief in public works, and see *obras* as things of importance in themselves. One can say that regions in the highlands are being opened up and subjected to government by *obra*. This was an important aspect of the recuperation of Cayash, from the leaders' point of view.

From the perspective of the Cayashinos, the aim of the recuperation was supposedly to open up possibilities for the displaced families to return home. Yet this is not happening to any great extent. Instead, the violent years have served to speed up tendencies already apparent in Andean peasant society for many years: the movement or drift away especially by the young, some for reasons of education, others to find income-earning work. But although the recuperation is not transforming the daily life of many, it has been of overwhelming symbolic importance. Cayashinos know they have a place to which they might return, should they wish; and perhaps more importantly, they have Cayash as a place in the mind's eye on which to anchor their memories and hopes.

## REFERENCES


Ansion, Juan, 1989, *La Escuela en la Comunidad Campesina*, Lima: FAO Proyecto Escuela, Ecología y Comunidad Campesina.

Degregori, Carlos Iván, 1991, 'How Difficult it is to be God', *Critique of Anthropology*, Vol.11, No.3, pp.233–50.

Drinkwater, Michael, 1992, 'Visible Actors and Visible Researchers: Critical Hermeneutics in an Actor-oriented Perspective', *Sociologia Ruralis*, Vol XXXII, No.4, pp.367–88.

Fentress, James and Chris Wickham, 1992, *Social Memory: New Perspectives on the Past*, Oxford: Blackwell.

Flores Galindo, Alberto, 1986, *Buscando un Inca: Identidad y Utopía en los Andes*, Havana: Casa de las Américas.

Gilbert, Joseph and Daniel Nugent (eds.), 1994, *Everyday Forms of State Formation*, Durham: Duke University.

Golte, Jürgen and Norma Adams, 1987, *Los Caballos de Troya de los Invasores: Estrategias Campesinas en la Conquista de la Gran Lima*, Lima: Instituto de Estudios Peruanos.

Lefebvre, Henri, 1991, *The Production of Space*, Oxford: Blackwell.

Long, Norman, 1989, 'Introduction: The Raison d'Etre for Studying Rural Development Interface', in N. Long (ed.), *Encounters at the Interface: A Perspective on Social Discontinuities in Rural Development*, Wageningen: Agricultural University.